EX AUDITU

An International Journal for the Theological Interpretation of Scripture

VOL. 25   **2009**

Ex Auditu is published annually by Pickwick Publications, an imprint of
Wipf and Stock Publishers, 199 West 8th Avenue, Suite 3, Eugene, Oregon 97401, USA

SUBSCRIPTIONS

Individuals:
U.S.A. and all other countries (in U.S. funds): $20.00
Students: $12.00

Institutions:
U.S.A. and all other countries (in U.S. funds): $30.00

This periodical is indexed in the ATLA Religion Database, published by the American Theological Library Association, 300 S. Wacker Dr., Suite 2100, Chicago, IL 60606, Email: atla@atla.com, WWW: http://www.atla.com/; *Internationale Zeitschriftenshau für Bibelwissenschaft; Religious and Theological Abstracts; and Old Testament Abstracts.*

Please address all subscription correspondence
and change of address information to Wipf and Stock Publishers.

©2010 by Wipf and Stock Publishers
ISSN: 0883-0053
ISBN: 978-1-60899-748-0

EX AUDITU

An International Journal for the Theological Interpretation of Scripture

Klyne R. Snodgrass, Editor
Stephen J. Chester, Associate Editor
D. Christopher Spinks, Associate Editor

North Park Theological Seminary
3225 West Foster Avenue
Chicago, Illinois 60625-4987
USA

Tel: (773) 244-6243
Fax: (773) 244-6244
email: ksnodgrass@northpark.edu
Web site: http://wipfandstock.com/journals/ex_auditu

EDITORIAL BOARD

Terence E. Fretheim, Luther Seminary, St. Paul, MN
Richard B. Hays, The Divinity School, Duke University, Durham, NC
John E. Phelan, Jr., President of North Park Theological Seminary, Chicago, IL
Jon R. Stock, Wipf & Stock Publishers, Eugene, OR
Miroslav Volf, Yale Divinity School, New Haven, CT
John Wipf, Wipf & Stock Publishers, Eugene, OR

THE EDITORIAL BOARD MEMBERS AND CONSULTANTS represent various disciplines and denominations. Theological Interpretation of Scripture is a task to be taken seriously by scholars who are committed to the Christian faith and tradition. However, as one editorial consultant stated: "let people gradually get used to the idea that a sane hermeneutics is both oriented in advance toward agreement/consent and is simultaneously exigent, discriminating, critical."

EDITORIAL CONSULTANTS

Richard Bauckham
University of St. Andrews, Emeritus
St. Andrews, Scotland

M. Daniel Carroll R.
Denver Seminary
Denver, Colorado

Jan Du Rand
Rand Afrikaans University
Johannesburg, South Africa

Willie Jennings
The Divinity School
Duke University
Durham, N. Carolina

Robert Johnston
Fuller Theological Seminary
Pasadena, California

R. Walter L. Moberly
University of Durham
Durham, England

Kathleen M. O'Connor
Columbia Theological Seminary
Decatur, Georgia

Iain Provan
Regent College
Vancouver, B.C.

Anthony Thiselton
University of Nottingham
Nottingham, England

Augustine Thompson
University of Virginia
Charlottesville, Virginia

Marianne Meye Thompson
Fuller Theological Seminary
Pasadena, California

Kevin J. Vanhoozer
Wheaton College
Wheaton, Illinois

Geoffrey Wainwright
The Divinity School
Duke University
Durham, N. Carolina

Sondra Wheeler
Wesley Theological Seminary
Washington, D.C.

William H. Willimon
Bishop of the North Alabama Conference
The United Methodist Church
Birmingham, Alabama

N. T. Wright
Bishop of Durham
Durham, England

We were saddened this year to learn of the death of one of our editorial consultants, Professor Graham Stanton. He will be sorely missed for his scholarship, his deep Christian commitment, and his kind and generous character. This edition of the journal is dedicated to his memory.

EX AUDITU

VOL. 25   2009

CONTENTS

Announcement of the 2010 Symposium	vii
Abbreviations	viii
Introduction *Stephen J. Chester*	ix
Conversion Studies, Pastoral Counseling, and Cultural Studies: Engaging and Embracing a New Paradigm *Lewis R. Rambo*	1
Response to Rambo *Phillis Isabella Sheppard*	17
Observations on "Conversion" and the Old Testament *J. Andrew Dearman*	22
Response to Dearman *Rajkumar Boaz Johnson*	37
The Conversion of Simon Peter *Markus Bockmuehl*	42
Response to Bockmuehl *Michael J. Gorman*	61
Zacchaeus's Conversion: To Be or Not To Be a Tax Collector (Luke 19:1–10) *Wyndy Corbin Reuschling*	67
Response to Corbin Reuschling *Elizabeth Musselman Palmer*	89
Towards Individual and Communal Renewal: Reflections on Luke's Theology of Conversion *Frank D. Macchia*	92

Response to Macchia *D. Christopher Spinks*	106
Was Paul a Convert? *Scot McKnight*	110
Response to McKnight *Eric James Gréaux Sr.*	133
Romans 7 and Conversion in the Protestant Tradition *Stephen J. Chester*	135
Response to Chester *Mary Veeneman*	172
Ambrose, Paul, and the Conversion of the Jews *J. Warren Smith*	175
Response to Smith *George Kalantzis*	199
I Thank Christ Jesus our Lord: 1 Timothy 1:12–17 *Eric James Gréaux Sr.*	203
Annotated Bibliography on Conversion	211
Presenters and Respondents	223
Ex Auditu – Volumes Available	225

ANNOUNCEMENT OF THE 2010 SYMPOSIUM

North Park Seminary in Chicago, Illinois, is pleased to announce that the twenty-sixth Symposium on the Theological Interpretation of Scripture will take place September 23–25, 2010. The symposium will start at 7:00 p.m. on September 23 in Nyvall Hall and will extend through a Saturday afternoon worship service on September 25. The theme in 2010 will be the Atonement. The following persons have agreed to make presentations:

> Brian Bantum, Seattle Pacific University, Theology
> Viktor Ber, Evangelical Theological Seminary, Prague, Old Testament
> Hans Boersma, Regent College, Vancouver, Theology
> William Brown, Columbia Theological Seminary, Decatur, Old Testament
> Michelle Clifton-Soderstrom, North Park Theological Seminary, Theology
> Michael Gorman, St. Mary's Seminary & University, Baltimore, New Testament
> Peter Martens, St Louis University, Church History
> Carol Norén, North Park Theological Seminary, Preaching
> Linda D. Peacore, Independent Scholar, Theology

Persons interested in attending sessions should contact before September 1, 2010:

> Ms. Guylla Brown
> North Park Theological Seminary
> 3225 W. Foster Avenue
> Chicago, Illinois 60625
> Phone: (773) 244-6214
> Email: gbrown@northpark.edu

Meals may be taken at North Park and assistance can be provided in finding nearby lodging.

ABBREVIATIONS

Unless included in the list below, all abbreviations are as specified in Patrick H. Alexander et al., editors, *The SBL Handbook of Style: For Ancient Near Eastern, Biblical, and Early Christian Studies* (Peabody, Mass.: Hendrickson, 1999).

CR	*Corpus Reformatorum*, ed. K.G. Bretschneider et al
ESV	English Standard Version
DOI	Digital Object Identifier
LW	*Luther's Works,* ed. Jaroslav Pelikan
NLT	New Living Translation
PLS	Patrologiae cursus completus, Series latina, Supplementum, ed. J.-P. Migne
WA	Weimarer Ausgabe, *D. Martin Luthers Werke: kritische Gesammtausgabe*

INTRODUCTION

The New Testament writers are not wary of making large claims for what has been accomplished through the death and resurrection of Jesus. Motivated by God's unlimited love for the world (John 3:16), Christ's death for our sins is instrumental in breaking the power of the present evil age (Gal 1:4). The ultimate consequence is that creation itself will be liberated from decay and enjoy the freedom of the glory of the children of God (Rom 8:21). There will be a new heaven and a new earth where God, having made all things new, will dwell with men and women (Rev 21:1–5). Through Christ, God is reclaiming God's creation, bringing it out of the shadows of sin and death into fullness of life. It is in this context that the Church proclaims the necessity of conversion for each and every individual. If human beings are to participate in God's reclamation of the marred and damaged creation of which they are a part, they too must be made new. If human beings are to enter into life that is eternal, they too must be liberated from death. If human beings are to become dwelling places for God (John 14:23, Rom 8:9), they must be forgiven their sins and set free from their sins. It is only from such radical new beginnings that a common life as God's people can flow, marked by the presence and the power of the Holy Spirit, which demonstrates the wider hope for the whole world (Rom 8:20, Jas 1:18).

Conversion is therefore a topic of perennial relevance in biblical interpretation, and the awe-inspiring ways in which it is described—new creation (2 Cor 5:17, Gal 6:15), new birth (John 3:3, 1 Pet 1:3) turning from darkness to light (1 Pet 2:10), leaving behind everything to follow Jesus (Mark 10:28), to name but a few—are a perpetual inspiration and rebuke. Yet there are also reasons why the early years of the twenty-first century are ones in which the topic of conversion demands particular attention. We live in the aftermath of the missionary movement of the nineteenth and twentieth centuries, which resulted in an unprecedented globalization of Christianity but which also saw considerable confusion of biblical categories of conversion with western cultural values. Even when conversion is now discussed in relation to western cultural contexts, the questions raised by that confusion remain with us. What are the authentic contours of conversion, and how are they to be distinguished from more ephemeral concerns? Further, we also live in a period of broad reaction against the understanding of conversion espoused within revivalism, a reaction shared even within many evangelical circles. Any earlier consensus has evaporated that conversion is an experience or sequence of experiences leading to a conscious and dateable moment of decision to accept Christ as savior.

We thus find ourselves in a historical moment when fresh engagement with biblical texts concerning conversion is necessary for the mission and ministry of the church. The papers given at the symposium and contained in this issue of the journal are a contribution to that task. Each of them engages with biblical texts exploring different aspects of Christian conversion, and the bibliography provided is one concerning Christian conversion. Nevertheless, Christian conversion does not exist in isolation from religious change in other traditions, and its study does not take place in isolation from the study of conversion more generally. Several recent studies of conversion in the Bible draw inspiration and theoretical resources from new developments in the discipline of conversion studies. We are delighted to include in this issue a paper by Lewis Rambo, one of the most distinguished figures in the field, whose reflections help us to understand these developments and their significance for the study of Christian conversion.

As always we are deeply appreciative of the commitment of all the presenters and respondents who invested the time and effort necessary for the symposium to be a fruitful time of reflection and learning. The common commitment to dialogue and to hearing all of the voices of those present was apparent throughout. As in every year special thanks is due to Guylla Brown from North Park's staff without whose hard work, dedication, and good humor the symposium would be impossible. Thanks this year is also due to Erin McDermott and Nathanael Putnam, who assisted in preparing the journal for publication.

Stephen J. Chester
Associate Editor

CONVERSION STUDIES, PASTORAL COUNSELING, AND CULTURAL STUDIES
Engaging and Embracing a New Paradigm[1]

Lewis R. Rambo

The formative role of religion in both public and private life in many locations around the globe is no longer in doubt. With the resurgence of Islam in many parts of the world, the revitalization of Christianity in Africa, Latin America, and Asia, and the rise of a plethora of new religious movements, the rebirth of once moribund or static religions, and the awareness of these phenomena through almost instant communications media, scholars of religion are undertaking new approaches to the study of religion. How people change (indeed, how people are transformed) has become a topic of extensive debate and research.

The new approach embodies several characteristics. First, the study of religion has become globalized.[2] Parochial approaches to religion are no longer viable. Second, interdisciplinary approaches are crucial in order to explore the complexity and diversity of religious phenomena. Interdisciplinary and comparative studies of conversion do not, of course, obviate the importance of continuing to study carefully the particular, the local, and the distinctive phenomena of various religions in particular areas of the world. Third, what was once assumed to be true in various assumptions, methods, and theories is no longer taken for granted. Critique of virtually all approaches is the order of the day. Fourth, the definition of conversion is undergoing serious reconsideration as new methods, new religions, and new paradigms are examined. Indeed, some are asking if the word "conversion" may be correctly applied to Islam, Christianity, Buddhism, Judaism, and new religious movements. The study of conversion (or perhaps better conversions or converting)

---

1. This paper was first published in *Pastoral Psychology*: accessed 1 April 2010, published 17 March 2009. DOI 10.1007/s11089-009-0202-1. Online: http://www.springerlink.com/content/lgq7t 29v7048441x/. It is reproduced here with kind permission of Springer Science and Business Media.

2. See M. Juergensmyer, *The Oxford Handbook of Global Religions* (New York: Oxford University Press, 2006); and F. Wijsen and R. Schreiter, eds., *Global Christianity: Contested Claims* (Amsterdam: Rodopi, 2007).

provides us with a fascinating window through which to more fully understand the dynamics of religion, spirituality, and culture in the 21st century.

Globalization of Conversion Studies

In order for the field of conversion studies to move forward, several foundations must be established. The first major requirement for the enrichment of the field of conversion studies is to broaden the data base. With few exceptions, especially in psychology and sociology, past study of conversion has generally focused on conversion to Christianity, Judaism, and, more recently, New Religious Movements. It should also be mentioned that even within the study of conversion to Christianity, the focus has tended to be evangelical and conservative forms of Christianity, with the neglect of Roman Catholics (with more than one billion adherents worldwide), Orthodox Christianity (about 220 million members worldwide), and the wide range of "mainline" Protestants, such as the Anglican Communion (an estimated 80 million worldwide) and the Reformed Tradition (about 75 million members worldwide).[3]

One of the most urgent requirements for competent conversion studies is to include Islam and Buddhism. With more than 1.3 billion adherents, Islam has been virtually ignored in conversion studies (there is, fortunately, a growing literature). In psychology and sociology, however, very few studies have been done.[4] Even anthropologists have devoted little time to the so-called major religious traditions of the world, and have, rather, focused on indigenous religions or so called primal religions.[5] These studies are extremely helpful to the overall study of conversion, but attention must be given to religions with global impact that thus require sustained attention.

---

3. D. B. Barrett, *World Christian Encyclopedia: A Comparative Study of Churches and Religions in the Modern World, AD 1900–2000* (Nairobi: Oxford University Press, 1982) and D. B. Barrett, G. T. Kurian, and T. M. Johnson, eds., *World Christian Encyclopedia: A Comparative Survey of Churches and Religions in the Modern World* (2nd ed.; New York: Oxford University Press, 2001).

4. A. Kose, *Conversion to Islam: A Study of Native British Converts* (London: Kegan Paul, 1996); A. Kose and K. M. Loewenthal, "Conversion Motifs Among British Converts to Islam," *International Journal for the Psychology of Religion* 10 (2000): 101–10; A. M. McGinty. *Becoming Muslim: Western Women's Conversion to Islam* (New York: Palgrave Macmillan, 2006); and C. M. Rouse, *Engaged Surrender: African American Women and Islam* (Berkeley: University of California Press, 2004).

5. Exceptions include A. Buckser and S. D. Glazier, eds., *The Anthropology of Religious Conversion* (Lanham, Md.: Rowman & Littlefield, 2003); A. M. McGinty, *Becoming Muslim: Western Women's Conversion to Islam* (New York: Palgrave Macmillan, 2006); and R. W. Hefner, ed., *Conversion to Christianity: Historical and Anthropological Perspectives on a Great Transformation* (Berkeley: University of California Press, 1993).

The inclusion of Islam, Buddhism, and a host of other religions raises the vexing issue of how to define conversion. Many scholars rightfully express their concern that the language of conversion is largely derived from Judaism and Christianity.

Closely related to the need to be more inclusive of various religions, the study of conversion must be more geographically inclusive.[6] Religious change in various parts of the world must be included in the field of vision for conversion scholars. In this regard anthropologists and mission studies scholars have already led the way. For their entire history, anthropologists have been in virtually every part of the world. Ethnographic research has required them to spend extended periods of time in many locations requiring them to learn new languages, customs, life styles, etc. While many in social science circles do not want to be associated with mission studies scholars, a few—if they are knowledgeable and totally honest—would admit that missionaries and mission studies people have the most in-depth knowledge of particular locations because they have devoted substantial amounts of time and energy to serving the needs of people in many parts of the world.

While recognizing their ideological orientations (the advocates of conversion to a particular religion—in most cases, Christianity), many missionaries are, in fact, themselves transformed through their encounter with people and cultures radically different from their own. Some missionaries have become anthropologists and have made enormous contributions to the study of conversion.

Interdisciplinary Perspectives

Interdisciplinary resources must be deployed in order to improve the field of conversion studies. The phenomenon of religious change is so complex and multifaceted that researchers must work with colleagues from many different disciplines, including anthropology, psychology, and sociology. Doing so will correct an error in thinking, since in the history of these disciplines there have been few who genuinely bridge these disciplines in creative ways.

Interdisciplinary work is, of course, excruciatingly difficult. Scholars in any of these three disciplines have worked hard to develop skills in respective fields of interest. Many are thus not interested in the work of colleagues in closely related disciplines. The research traditions, assumptions, methods, and, even, I would say, ideologies prevent genuine consultation, much less collaboration, but conversion

---

6. L. R. Rambo and C. E. Farhadian, eds., *The Oxford Handbook of Religious Conversion* (New York: Oxford University Press, forthcoming).

studies may not move forward unless experts in various fields authentically respect the alternative perspectives each discipline may provide.

This statement should not be read as advocating a form of interdisciplinary interaction requiring that each discipline jettison its distinctive contributions to the study of conversion. But scholars must be encouraged to open their minds and hearts to perspectives that, while very different, may offer valuable insights into the phenomenon of religious change.

Religious and Theological Perspectives on Conversion

It is imperative that conversion scholars devote time and energy to studying the religious content, including beliefs and practices, of the group into which and out of which a person is converting. Such research is crucial since the conversion scholar may learn about the expectations, metaphors of change, patterns of relationships within the group, and the group's norms for who is considered a "real" convert. Without learning about the group's theology and practices, the conversion scholar may be misled to think the convert's description of his or her conversion is idiosyncratic. While each conversion has unique qualities, most conversions into various religious organizations are shaped, to some degree at least, by the norms, practices, expectations, beliefs, and patterns of the group.

It may be argued that the group's norms and theology (or ideology, if one prefers) shape consciousness and form the basis of the experience of conversion. In certain cases, people have conversion experiences radically different form the norms of the group. With few exceptions, these differences cause major problems for the convert. In some situations, the differences are so great that converts are expelled from the group.[7]

The study of religion in the exploration of conversion processes is also valuable since, with very few exceptions, the language converts use is theological or religious. Virtually no convert discuss his or her conversion as a process in which they resolved emotional issues, enhanced their upward social mobility, or other language that is common to the social sciences. Some skeptical scholars reject the convert's language as merely a form of self-deception (which, of course, it may be), but this is a point of view radically different from the convert's. The point is that converts convert because they believe the new religion is true, that it was ordained by God,

---

7. E. L. Cleary, "Shopping Around: Questions about Latin American Conversions," *International Bulletin of Missionary Research* 28 (2004): 50–54; and P. L. Glazner, "Christian Conversion and Culture in Russia: A Clash of Missionary Expectations and Cultural Pressures," *Missiology* 29 (2001): 319–30.

or that it was a gift from God (or equivalent language used in various religions). The interesting questions for the scholar of conversion are, *How do people acquire a new definition of the nature of truth, and how do they align themselves with that new understanding?*

Phenomenology of Conversion

Scholars need to explore the nature of the conversion experience of particular individuals. Each person has distinctive issues that he or she must address during their journey of religious change. In turn, each person, even those who meticulously strive to follow the rules and rituals of the group into which they are converting, has aspects of experience distinctive to him or her. The careful scholar may find new and often unexpected paths of interpretation when the authentic, complex reality of a person's experience of conversion is taken fully into account. In the past, phenomenology sought to find universal structures or themes of various phenomena. The use of phenomenology here, in contrast, is to seek out the unique and distinctive aspect of a particular person's experience of conversion.[8] Pastoral counselors could provide invaluable insights into the intricacies and depths of converting processes.[9]

Historical Perspectives on Conversion

It is important that particular conversions be placed within a historical context. While conversions are rooted in various theological traditions and have, at the same time, distinctive, personal qualities, it is crucial to understand that conversion, even within the same theological tradition, is not the same over time. New themes, issues, rituals, and beliefs develop within traditions. One cannot assume that a conversion to the Roman Catholic Church in the 19th century is the same as in the 21st century. There are, of course, certain theological beliefs that are asserted over many years, but the careful historian recognizes that variations take place as the tradition confronts new challenges and constructs new insights. It may be argued that dif-

---

8. L. R. Rambo and L. A. Reh, "The Phenomenology of Conversion," in *Handbook of Religious Conversion* (ed. H. N. Malony and S. Southard; Birmingham, Ala.: Religious Education Press, 1992), 229–58; and C. Smith, "Why Christianity Works: An Emotions-Focused Phenomenological Account," *Sociology of Religion* 68 (2007): 165–78.

9. I am currently working on a paper (Rambo, forthcoming) about the study of conversion through the lens of more than 50 years of articles in *Pastoral Psychology*. It is interesting to note that, with few exceptions, conversion studies and pastoral psychology/theology rarely overlap in the last two decades.

ferent configurations of motivations play a different role at different times in the history of a particular religion at different stages of its history. Becoming a Baptist in 18th century Pennsylvania is different from becoming a Baptist in the 21st century. Regarding the former, this would mean a rejection of the religious status quo dominated by the Puritans in the early colonial period of the United States. Converting to the Baptist Church in the 21st century is, more than likely, a rather neutral political act with virtually no significant consequences *vis à vis* the larger society. Historical studies also alert the scholar of conversion to the reasons behind the contours of the rhetoric of conversion at a particular time in history.[10]

Cognitive and Neuropsychology of Conversion

One of the most recent and exciting developments in the study of human beings is the study of the human brain. With sophisticated new technologies (MRI or Magnetic Resonance Imaging, for example) experts are now able to examine in great detail the working of the brain. Many, if not most, neuroscientists see this field as conclusively ruling out any supernatural explanations for various religious beliefs and practices. For some, this field is the ultimate reduction of virtually everything to the hard science of the brain and its capacities. There are, however, numerous scientists who advocate the view that the human brain is, in a sense, "wired" for God or the transcendent. Whatever the ultimate findings of this new field will be, it is imperative that conversion scholars pay attention to the field for potential clues on the nature of conversion.[11]

The work of Davis and Rambo, for instance, is a preliminary investigation of this field of study.[12] While certainly too early to be conclusive, Davis and Rambo find that cognitive and neurological issues are foundational to the ways in which human beings process information, form concepts, and how human beings change.

---

10. For an excellent example see J. A. Sandos, *Converting California: Indians and Franciscans in the Missions* (New Haven, Conn.: Yale University Press, 2004).

11. See especially the work of K. Bulkeley, ed., *Soul, Psyche, Brain: New Directions in the Study of Brain-Mind Science* (New York: Palgrave Macmillan, 2005) and *The Wondering Brain: Thinking about Religion with and beyond Cognitive Neuroscience* (New York: Routledge, 2004).

12. P. M. Davis and L. R. Rambo, "Converting: Toward a Cognitive Theory of Religious Change," in *Soul, Psyche, Brain: New Directions in the Study of Brain-Mind Science* (ed. K. Bulkeley; New York: Palgrave Macmillan, 2005), 159–73.

Indigenous and Cultural Psychology

One of the most recent and important developments in the field of psychology is the emergence of what scholars are calling "indigenous and cultural psychology." Many psychologists around the world, many in locations other than Europe and the United States, are seeing the impact of western culture on the very foundations of psychology as a science. The questions researched, the methods deployed in this research, and, most important, the assumptions guiding the enterprise of scientific psychology have been formed within the matrix of European, British, and American institutions and culture.[13]

While not rejecting the goals of developing a sophisticated science, indigenous and cultural psychologists advocate locating psychology within the context of culture. Culture, rather than being a distraction to the goals of psychology, thus becomes the center of concern in order to develop a psychology that is intimately connected to the human experience of living in various cultural communities, with their world views, assumptions, beliefs, religions, rituals, philosophies, and modes of family relationships, life cycle formation, etc.

Archie Smith, Jr., in his excellent essay review of Kim, Yang, and Hwang's *Indigenous and Cultural Psychology: Understanding People in Context*, reminds us that religion itself is a cultural force that plays a crucial role in the lives of millions of people.[14]

Critique of Conversion Models, Paradigms, and Methods

By reviewing a number of recent studies of conversion and especially articles that seek to discover themes and patterns in conversion studies and also provide critique of the various methods, assumptions, and goals of those who study conversion, much may be learned.[15] One of the impressions gained is the vivid awareness that

---

13. A. Roland, *In Search of Self in India and Japan: Toward a Cross-Cultural Psychology* (Princeton, N.J.: Princeton University Press, 1988); U. Kim, K. Yang, and K. Hwang, eds., *Indigenous and Cultural Psychology: Understanding People in Context* (New York: Springer, 2006); and S. Kitayama and D. Cohen, eds., *Handbook of Cultural Psychology* (New York: Guilford, 2007).

14. A. Smith, "Indigenous and Cultural Psychology: Where does Faith Come in?" *Pastoral Psychology* 56 (2008): 95–104 and R. J. Barro and J. Hwang "Religious Conversion in 40 Countries," National Bureau of Economic Research Working Paper Number W13689 (2007): Cited 1 September 2008. Online: http://www.papers.ssrn.com/sol3/papers.cfm?abstract_id=1077815.

15. See especially the work of Cleary, "Shopping Around." Also, McGinty, *Becoming Muslim*. Also F. Yang, "Between Secularist Ideology and Desecularizing Reality: The Birth and Growth of Religious

human change in general, and conversion in particular, are dynamic processes that do not allow us to view conversion as a static, onetime event, or to view conversions or, for that matter, any human change processes as total, complete, or irreversible. Human beings are always on the move. We are always negotiating our identity. We are always exploring new options and we often desire novelty and stimulation.[16]

Forty years ago Scoggs and Douglas published "Issues in the Psychology of Religious Conversion."[17] That the seven issues they raised are still with us today is both fascinating and disconcerting. The first issue discussed was the problem of definition. As we will see below, the very nature of conversion itself is contested. Second, they explored whether conversion is a healthy, normal or a pathological process. While this issue is not debated in precisely those terms today, there are many who want to know if conversion emerges out of person's psychopathology or some vulnerability rendering them susceptible to proselytizers or to psychological experiences leading to conversion. The third issue regards the notion of some people being "convertible types." One rarely finds this issue in the current literature of conversion. The fourth issue is what Scoggs and Douglas call the "ripe age" for conversion. In today's language, the focus would be specifically related to the human life cycle. In the early days of the psychology of religion, this focus was on adolescence as the time for conversion. Current scholars tend to look at various crises or turning points in the developmental stages as being prime times for the acquisition of new beliefs and the creation of new religious allegiance.

The fifth issue has become a crucial point of debate in conversion studies: to what extent is a convert an active agent and to what extent a person who is subject to forces beyond him or herself? In other words, is the person active or passive?

Research in Communist China," *Sociology of Religion* 65 (2004): 101–20; *Chinese Christians in America: Conversion, Assimilation, and Adhesive Identity* (University Park: Pennsylvania State University Press, 1999); "Chinese Conversion to Evangelical Christianity: The Importance of Social and Cultural Contexts," *Sociology of Religion* 59 (1998): 237–57; "Lost in the Market, Saved at McDonald's: Conversion to Christianity in Urban China," *Journal for the Scientific Study of Religion* 44 (2005): 423–41; and "The Red, Black, and Gray Markets of Religion in China," *The Sociological Quarterly* 47 (2006): 93–122. Also F. Yang and H. R. Ebaugh, "Religion and Ethnicity among New Immigrants: The Impact of Majority/Minority Status in Home and Host Countries," *Journal for the Scientific Study of Religion* 40 (2001): 367–92; and "Transformations in New Immigrant Religions and Their Global Implications," *American Sociological Review* 66 (2001): 269–88. Also F. Yang and J. B. Tamney, "Exploring Mass Conversion to Christianity among the Chinese: An Introduction," *Sociology of Religion* 67 (2006): 125–29.

16. E. L. Cleary, "Shopping Around."

17. J. R. Scroggs and W. G. T. Douglas, "Issues in the Psychology of Religious Conversion," *Journal of Religion and Health* 6 (1967): 204–16.

The sixth issue points to the conflicts between those with a religious orientation to conversion and those who are working from a scientific point of view. That issue still stirs conflict. In our context in the social scientific study of religion, even those with profound religious convictions tend, while they are operating as scientists, to be "methodological atheists." As discussed above, this spit often causes theologians and religious studies scholars to not communicate with social scientists, and vice versa.

The seventh issue raises a persistent and very current issue: what is the most adequate framework in which to study conversion? Many assumptions, methods, and goals are possible. How does one adjudicate between the many options? In most cases, the problem is resolved by the kind of socialization we receive in our graduate programs in our respective disciplines.

These issues deserve far more time than may be devoted to them in this brief paper. Exploring the options in consultation with one another is important especially with regard to a critical issue in conversion studies: definition.

Converting: Personal and Cultural/Social/Historical Transformations

One of the most vexing, but important, issues in conversion studies is defining the term "conversion." Perhaps a better term to define is the verb converting instead of the noun conversion. Whatever else converting is, it is dynamic and malleable. While some scholars seek a precise definition of conversion, it is clear that the word covers a range of phenomena that are defined in alternative ways by different scholars. To make things even more complicated, even if one focuses on the meaning of converting within one religious tradition, there are variations of meanings.[18]

What follows is a preliminary, heuristic proposal about expanding the canvas on which scholars seek to define conversion and also link the more narrowly defined field of conversion studies and the larger contextual issues serving as the matrix in which conversion takes place. What are the interconnections, forces of cause and effect, and dialectical interrelationships between the conversion processes of an individual and the larger forces of what may be characterized by terms such as Confucianization, Christianization, and Islamization?

It is important first to look at the microcosmic issue of definition as it regards individuals and then outline the contours of issues of the various factors involved in processes we are characterizing as Islamization, etc. This paper will then seek to

---

18. Those interested in the importance of defining and theorizing within conversion studies, pastoral counseling, and cultural studies should read the stunning book by Thomas A. Tweed, *Crossing and Dwelling: A Theory of Religion* (Cambridge, Mass.: Harvard University Press, 2006).

propose interconnections between the two. The goal is to work toward a research agenda that does not separate psychological processes experienced by the individual from the broader social, cultural, and historical forces involved in religious change.

Converting: Personal Dynamics

Several important issues should be explored when discussing definitions of conversion/converting. They are:

1. Who defines? What is the person's disciplinary point of view, theological assumption, or research tradition?

2. What is the specific focus of a definition: Person, group, beliefs, practices, experiences?

3. What is the data base? What group of people, religion, or group is the scholar studying and/or is his/her religion of origin?

4. Regarding political/ theological implications of the definition: Who is included and who is excluded? What are the consequences of a particular definition?

5. What is the relationship of the definition to particular persons concerned: converts, members, and scholars?

6. What is the relationship between the normative and descriptive issues of a particular definition?

7. What has to change? How much does it have to change to constitute conversion?

More than 40 years ago, Earl H. Furgeson stated the problem clearly:

> Religious conversion, like any other human behavior, may be studied from many points of view—theological, philosophical, sociological, ethical, or psychological—and the definition of the subject will reflect the purpose of the study and the orientation of the investigator. The bewildering variety in definitions of religious conversion reflects such relativities, so much so that a fresh study of the matter seems needed and may perhaps be welcomed.[19]

---

19. Earl H. Furgeson, "The Definition of Religious Conversion," *Pastoral Psychology* 16 (1965): 8–16 (8).

His 1965 article on defining conversion, however, called for a complete rejection of any notion that conversion could be gradual or a part of a developmental process. Furgeson argues "If we are to be redeemed from terminological anarchy, the gradualists will need to accept the heuristic dogma that the event of conversion is not gradual. The alternative is conceptual confusion."[20]

Furgeson then proposes his own definition:

> Religious conversion, from the psychological point of view, is an abrupt, involuntary change in personality in which the subject, under the pressure of resolving internal conflict or tension, surrenders the control of his [her] life to beliefs and sentiments previously peripheral or repressed; the change occurs suddenly at a time of crisis and is not psychologically identical with gradual growth or development; the results of the change may be regenerative and progressive, partly regenerative and progressive, and regressive and degenerative.[21]

Another conversion scholar, Richard Travasino, joined the fray and wrote:

> Alternations are transitions to identities which are prescribed or at least permitted with the person's established universe of discourse. Conversions are transitions to identities which are proscribed within the person's established universes of discourse, and which exist in universes of discourse that negate these formerly established ones. The ideal typical conversion can be thought of as the embracing of a negative identity. The person becomes something which was specifically prohibited.[22]

Even today, many students of conversion argue for a narrow, strict definition of the term. These definitions, however, are rooted in either theological or disciplinary norms (as in the case of Furgeson's theological and psychoanalytic proclivities) or so limited to a particular data base they tend to ignore phenomena that do not fit their own group's theology and experience. Travasino's definition was based on his research of Messianic Jews. Given the tragic history of relationships between Jews and Christians, it is no wonder that conversion to Christianity by a person of Jewish origin would be considered a betrayal and rejection of one's Jewish family, culture, and religion. Few other types of conversion are located so firmly in a history of such

---

20. Ibid., 11.

21. Ibid., 16.

22. Richard Travasino. "Alternation and Conversion as Qualitatively Different Transformations," in *Social Psychology through Symbolic Interaction* (ed. G. P. Stone and H. A. Faberman; Waltham, Mass.: Ginn-Blaisdell, 1970), 594–606 (601).

animosity. Should this data base provide a definition that is to be applied universally? Absolutely not.

Other definitions are very specifically located within a particular tradition. Gordon Smith, an evangelical theologian, defines conversion in the following manner:

> The work of Christ makes conversion possible; even more, the actual focus and dynamic of conversion is that an individual comes to faith in Christ Jesus. Conversion is the act of believing in Jesus, choosing to follow Jesus and being united with Jesus as Lord and Savior. To be converted is to become a Christian. And the purpose of conversion is that we may ultimately be transformed into the image of Christ Jesus. Although all three members of the Trinity are actively involved in the conversion experience, the focus is on Christ. In fact, conversion is the fruit of an encounter with the risen Christ himself, as witnessed to and experienced within a Christian community. Conversion is not the result of an encounter with truth or principles or spiritual laws; rather, it comes from meeting Jesus.[23]

This definition is legitimate, but only from a particular theological point of view. Needless to say, it cannot be used as the basis for a general definition of conversion for the social scientist of religion.

In my book, *Understanding Religious Conversion*, I made the assertion that "conversion is what a group says it is."[24] Defining conversion—at least if we mean one, precise, and universal definition—is not only impossible, but is a distortion of the scientific study of religious change. Based on this belief, I am now proposing that we reframe conversion studies into a broad framework. While particular definitions may be appropriate to a certain religion at a certain time and place, there is no universal definition.

William L. Merrill articulates the most viable approach to the issue of defining conversion when he concludes that:

> No single, universally applicable definition of conversion is possible or even desirable. Instead, conversion is better conceived more relativistically. A relativistic notion of conversion acknowledges that different religions define and evaluate conversion differently. It also recognizes at least two perspectives in any conversion situation—that of existing ad-

---

23. Gordon Smith. *Beginning Well: Christian Conversion and Authentic Transformation* (Downers Grove, Ill.: InterVarsity, 2001), 16.

24. L. R. Rambo, *Understanding Religious Conversion* (New Haven, Conn.: Yale University Press, 1993), 7.

herents of the new religion and that of the supposed converts—and that these perspectives can differ. By allowing for multiple perspectives this view accommodates the complexities and political dimensions of conversion. It recognizes, for example that the status of 'convert' can be withheld, refused, or contested as well as bestowed and accepted and that people can appropriate the beliefs and practices of a religion at the same time that they reject formal affiliation with it.[25]

In 1989 I proposed the following definition of conversion:

> A process of religious change that takes place in a dynamic force field of people, events, ideologies, institutions, expectations, and experiences. It is assumed that (a) conversion is a process, rather than a single event; (b) conversion is contextual and cannot be extricated from the fabric of relationships, processes, and ideologies which provide the matrix of religious change; and (c) factors involved in the conversion process are multiple, interactive, and cumulative. While there are unique aspects of particular conversions, it is also assumed that there can be broad descriptions of conversion that are useful in the comparison and assessment of conversion theories. There is no one cause of conversion and no one simple consequence of the process.[26]

For a completely different approach to the issue of definition, see the interesting work of Paul Hiebert.[27]

Converting: Social, Cultural, Political, and Religious Transformations

If one chooses to define the literature of conversion studies in an inclusive manner, there is a body of work falling under the broad headings of Christianization and Islamization models and theories. These studies explore the religious, historical, cultural, social, political, economic, and ideological factors and forces that create and

---

25. William L. Merrill, "Conversion and Colonialism in Northern Mexico: The Tarahumara Response to the Jesuit Mission Program, 1601–1767," in *Conversion to Christianity* (ed. R. W. Hefner; Berkeley: University of California Press, 1993), 129–63 (154).

26. L. R. Rambo, "Conversion: Toward a Holistic Model of Religious Change," *Pastoral Psychology* 38 (1989): 47–63 (48).

27. Paul G Hiebert, "The Category "Christian" in the Mission Task," *International Review of Mission* 72 (1983): 421–7; "Conversion, Culture, and Cognitive Categories," *Gospel in Context* 1 (1978): 24–9; "Conversion in Hinduism and Buddhism," in *Handbook of Religious Conversion* (ed. H. N. Malony and S. Southard; Birmingham, Ala.: Religious Education Press, 1992), 9–21; *Transforming Worldviews: An Anthropological Understanding of How People Change* (Grand Rapids: Baker, 2008).

sustain comprehensive processes by which religions, in these cases Christianity and Islam, are disseminated, cultivated, consolidated, and sustained by a wide range of forces that create an environment in which individual religious change takes place. These processes have parallels in discussions of other inclusive processes called Sankritization, Sinicization, Confucianization, Hellenization, Westernization, modernization, secularization, etc. Some conversion scholars reject the application of the term conversion to this all-embracing process. However, both in some studies of conversion and in the ordinary use of the term, it is not unusual to speak of the conversion of Armenia, the Roman Empire, the Philippines, Syria, and so forth. Conversion must be seen as more than merely individual religious change because it usually entails the transformation of political, social, and cultural environments that create what might be described as ecologies of conversion that make individual conversions possible. Christianization and Islamization create infrastructures and superstructures that cultivate and consolidate processes of religious change and make them institutionally viable over time.[28]

All-inclusive studies often focus on geographical areas in which Christianity or Islam gain ascendancy. In the case of Christianity, these include explorations of the Christianizations of the Roman Empire, British Isles, Europe, Russia, Latin America, and the Philippines.[29] A recent book, edited by Armstrong and Wood, has a title that captures the essence of this discussion: *Christianizing Peoples and Converting Individuals*.[30] Studies of conversion to Islam include such geographical areas as Arabia, Iran, Egypt, Africa, South East Asia, India, the Malay Archipelago, Britain, Europe, and so forth.[31] Few of these studies emphasize individual experience, but rather the roles persons might play as missionaries, emissaries, leaders (charismatic or otherwise), or traders. Most focus on Christianization or Islamization, in other words, on the creation of social, cultural, religious, and political environments in which individuals, families, communities, and societies flourish as part of Christian or Muslim zones of influence and power. Many such studies are, of course, histori-

---

28. L. R. Rambo and C. E. Farhadian, "Conversion," in *Encyclopedia of Religion*. (vol. 3; ed. L. Jones; 2nd ed.; Detroit: Thompson & Gale, 2005), 1969–74.

29. R. MacMullen, *Christianizing the Roman Empire A.D. 100–400* (New Haven, Conn.: Yale University Press, 1984).

30. G. Armstrong and I. Wood, eds., *Christianizing Peoples and Converting Individuals* (Turnhout: Brepols, 2000).

31. R. W. Bulliet, *Conversion to Islam in the Medieval Period: An Essay in Quantitative History* (Cambridge, Mass.: Harvard University Press, 1979). N. Levtzion, ed., *Conversion to Islam* (New York: Holmes & Meier, 1979).

cal, but there are also examinations of the processes of Christian or Islamic conversion using various interpretative models such as the diffusion of innovation theory by Bulliet.

In the study of Islamization other theoretical explanations for Islamic conversion include the use of force, the attractiveness of Islam as a movement for the liberation of slaves and soldiers, compliance with new political regimes, the desire for the privileges of Islamic political power (e.g., tax relief), the influence of traders (through intermarriage and patronage relationships), and the attractiveness of monotheism (especially for those from "pagan" and "primal" religions), and the provision of mystical and transcendent experiences through such things as Sufi modes of spirituality. In the case of Christianization, explanations for conversion include experiences of healing, the attraction of communities of grace and fellowship, the appeal to women of new understandings of the role of women, and the deployment of various forms of persuasion, coercion, and force.

Throughout the history of conversion worldwide there have been times when conversions were imposed by force or, at least, strongly encouraged in order for people to prosper in a newly established social order. The use of military force, social pressure, and economic incentives has been employed by followers of world religions at least at some points in their histories to bring people into the fold. These external forces of conversion can be potent motivators for religious change, and sometimes the fundamentalist interpretation of a religion may in part provide legitimation for such aggression. The history of colonialism is replete with instances of forcible conversions, where external forces played a significant role in conversion patterns.

Kapstein states these issues well in his book *The Tibetan Assimilation of Buddhism: Conversion, Contestation, and Memory*:

> Customarily, when we think of conversion, it is individual conversion that we have in mind. Following James, we sometimes think of this as a sudden and dramatic reorientation of consciousness, marked by profound changes of sentiment and of faith. By contrast, what I have attempted to illustrate here is that when it is conversion of a nation that is at issue, the gradual transformation of cosmological frameworks, of ritual, intellectual and bureaucratic practices, and of historic and mythic narratives through which the national identity is constituted are among the themes to which we must attend.[32]

---

32. M. T. Kapstein, *The Tibetan Assimilation of Buddhism: Conversion, Contestation, and Memory* (New York: Oxford University Press, 2000), 65.

Another example of the transformation of the infrastructures and superstructures of a nation, culture, or region is meticulously examined by Martina Deuchler's *The Confucian Transformation of Korea*.[33] Robert Montgomery's work is also valuable in the study of the macrocosmic religious changes.[34] The writings of James Duke and Barry Johnson, and more recently, the work of Robert J. Barro and Jason Hwang, and Washburn and Reinhart are noteworthy.[35] The task ahead is to find ways of creatively linking microcosmic and macrocosmic studies of converting. Robert L. Montgomery provides a compelling model for such an enterprise.[36] A new and promising approach is provided by the impressive work of Washburn and Reinhart in their edited volume *Converting Cultures: Religion, Ideology, and Transformations of Modernity*.[37]

This paper is an invitation to those of us who are engaged in pastoral counseling and psychotherapy to see conversion studies as an important resource to expand the horizons of pastoral theology. By viewing conversion studies as a field that is becoming more global, interdisciplinary, multi-religious, and multicultural, and inclusive of the personal, social, cultural, and political dimensions of the human predicament, it can be a valuable resource for pastoral counseling in the 21st century.

---

33. Martina Deuchler, *The Confucian Transformation of Korea* (Cambridge, Mass.: Harvard University Press, 1992). See also J. Haboush, H. Kim, and M. Deuchler, eds., *Culture and State in Late Choson Korea* (Cambridge, Mass.: Harvard University Press 1999).

34. Robert Montgomery, *The Diffusion of Religions* (Lanham, Md.: University Press of America, 1996); *Introduction to the Sociology of Missions* (Westport, Conn.: Praeger, 1999); *The Lopsided Spread of Christianity: Toward an Understanding of the Diffusion of Religions* (Westport, Conn.: Praeger Publishers, 2001); "The Spread of Religions and Macrosocial Relations," *Sociological Analysis* 52 (1991): 37–53; and *The Spread of Religions: A Social Scientific Theory Based on the Spread of Buddhism, Christianity, and Islam* (Hackensack, N.J.: Long Dash, 2007).

35. James T. Duke and Barry L. Johnson, "Rates of Religious Conversion: A Macrosociological Study," in *Research in the Social Scientific Study of Religion* (ed. M. L. Lynn and D. O. Moberg; Greenwich, Conn.: JAI, 1993), 89–122; "Religious Transformation and Social Conditions: A Macrosociological Analysis," in *Religious Politics in Global and Comparative Perspective* (ed. W. H. Swatos; New York: Greenwood, 1989), 75–109; "The Stages of Religious Transformation: A Study of 200 Nations," *Review of Religious Research* 30 (1989): 209–24; Robert J. Barro and Jason Hwang, "Religious Conversion in 40 Countries." Also D. Washburn and A. K. Reinhart, eds., *Converting Cultures: Religion, Ideology, and Transformations of Modernity* (Leiden: Brill, 2007).

36. Robert Montgomery, "Conversion and the Spread of Religions," in *Oxford Handbook of Religious Conversion* (ed. L. R. Rambo and C. Farhadian; New York: Oxford University Press, forthcoming). See also his other works detailed above in note 34, especially his 1991 article that focuses on Korea.

37. Washburn and Reinhart, *Converting Cultures*.

RESPONSE TO RAMBO

Phillis Isabella Sheppard

I would like to thank Dr. Rambo for his paper and the opportunity to reflect on it and to respond to it. His paper challenges pastoral theologians and pastoral counselors to "re-engage" both the phenomenon and study of conversion, and it has, as promised, explored many of the developments in the field. I hope that my comments, which are offered from a Womanist perspective, allow us to engage the task that he has set before us.

When I think of conversion studies, and conversion stories, I wonder what theological anthropology is embedded in the discourse. Does the field of conversion studies speak meaningfully to us about *imago Dei*? Can it cross-examine those subtle and blatant assumptions that humanity's embodiment of being created in God's image is most fully realized in those who have converted (are converting) to Christianity? What convictions about revelation, salvation, and hope frame the questions considered? Womanist practical theologians assert that theological concerns such as these need to be contextualized in terms of social location, power, efficacy, and, certainly, the pastoral practices that contribute to experiences of conversion.

My approach to engaging the concerns raised by this paper come out of my interdisciplinary training and vocational identity. I am a practicing psychoanalyst and a Womanist practical theologian. At the heart of my questions concerning conversion is a concern for a theological anthropology that takes the psychological seriously while not dismissing the religious and faith dimensions. I would venture to say that a theological anthropology without attention to the psychological is one in which the human capacity for change, transformation, hope, and despair is short-changed. Taking these dimensions seriously means that what one experiences as "conversion" is complex, highly motivated by multiple needs—both known and unconscious, and profoundly social and individual, and shaped not only by the religious setting but by broader social realities as well.

Rambo has suggested that conversion studies can be a valuable resource for pastoral counseling in the 21st century, and I am inclined to think that he is right. This is especially so since my own training in pastoral psychotherapy barely prepared me for the hip-looking but anxiety ridden fifty-something Jewish man who entered treatment with me partly because he still had questions about his "religious identity." He had been raised in Alabama in a rural town of about 7,000 people. His family was one of the few Jewish families in a very Protestant community, a community he referred to as the bible-belt of the coastline. These people, he said, knew Jesus and were proud of it, and anybody who did not *know* Jesus was going straight to hell. As a teenager his family decided, for a variety of reasons, to send him to a Christian residential school for high school. Yes, he stood out, and was isolated and lonely for most of his first and second year. He could seldom arrange for a ride to a synagogue some six or seven miles away, and all students were mandated to attend chapel. During the second semester of his sophomore year, he had a religious experience through which he decided to be baptized and thereafter joined the choir and began receiving communion. These many years later, and after consultations with rabbis, he still wondered if he could really be a Jew or if he had done something irrevocable. His anxiety was somewhat abated when one rabbi informed him that once a Jew, always a Jew. He brought great hope to his decision to be baptized and yet, though he continued to wrestle with meaning of his experience, he no longer identifies himself as Christian.

My question is, was this a conversion? Was he in the process of converting—and then, soon after graduation from high school, his converting process terminated or was even impeded by the experiences of college? The Christian community at his school said his conversion was *real* and claimed him as a part of the fold. He chose to be baptized and to receive communion, and yet later he determines that he is not Christian; he did not *re-convert* to Judaism, he re-identified as a Jew. We could suggest that factors such as social isolation and adolescent angst were implicated in his experience—would this fall under the perspective that there is a "ripe age" for conversion? Or would it be a conversion or converting process that occurs during a time of crisis? Clearly we would want to understand why his conversion did not consolidate around, in the self psychological sense, a cohesive identity. Was his questioning of the conversion a "resistance" in the psychological and political sense to the subtle and blatant imposition of Christianity he experienced at the parochial school? Was his conversion an act or process of differentiating between himself and his family? Or, was it evidence of his internalization of the devalued depiction of Jews to which he was subjected? One thing is clear, there were broader social, cultural, and psychological forces involved in his meaningful religious "conversion," however short-lived.

However, even if we could determine and sort out all of the social, cultural and psychological forces at play—what is the psychoanalyst and Womanist practical theologian to do with this experience? Is she to help this man understand the forces at play so that he might have a better understanding of himself and gain greater confidence in his Jewish identity? Does one trained in psychoanalysis have and convey a perspective on his converting experience? It is readily apparent to me how conversion studies is situated to broaden the psychotherapeutic lens and the meanings that a pastoral psychotherapist might bring to clinical material related to conversion—especially so for the psychotherapist familiar with the legacy of Freud's ambivalent, and sometimes hostile, response to religion—but not as clear how specifically it might serve as a resource for counseling situations, pastoral or otherwise. Possibly my own blind spot comes from teaching a doctoral course to social workers on diversity in terms of race, gender, sexuality, and, more frequently, religion. These students are trained from a psychodynamic perspective and are to bring this understanding to issues we address in the class. Inevitably, the majority in the class think diversity is important in terms of identity formation but in most of their case studies, the idea that religious experience as well race, nationality, and culture should impact their conceptualization and therapeutic response is seldom apparent. A fair number believe that the *intrapsychic* is the *intrapsychic*—once you get to the defenses, resistances, transferences, and regressions—culture disappears! This attachment to privileging the intrapsyhic/internal/individual over the social/communal is a long standing problem in practical theology and psychoanalytic psychology, and I wonder if it is also deeply entrenched in conversion studies.

On November 18, 1978 the world was confronted with the tragedy of the event called the "white night" in Jonestown, Guyana. Jonestown, you will remember, was founded by James Warren Jones who was born in a small town in Indiana which was, according to the historian of religion, Jonathan Z. Smith, the seat of both Christian fundamentalism and the Ku Klux Klan. Jones ultimately chose to commit to Christianity rather than the KKK, formed an interracial church in Indianapolis in 1953 at a time when his views on civil rights and his vision of a racially integrated society led to his ostracism by other white Christian leaders. Jones eventually moved his integrated congregation—The Peoples' Temple—mostly comprised of African Americans, to the San Francisco Bay Area. Most of us know the story: over a period of years, and by December 1977, Jones had moved most of the 1000 member congregation to Guyana. Periodically Jones had been the subject of exposés for practicing excessive discipline in the church, for poor observance of personal boundaries, and for his exploitative connection to those in high places. I will not pursue more of the details of this tragedy, but I do want to ask, when 900 people meet their death by suicide because they knowingly drink poisoned Kool-Aid—and we know some resisted—how do we understand their conversion? Furthermore, how do we bring a gendered analysis to the fact that 587 of those who died were women (66%)? Of this total, 438 (49%) were black women; 121 (13%) were white women; 4 were American Indian, 12 were Latina; 2 were Asian; 10 were Mexican. Among the 303 (34%) men who died, 200 (22%) were black men; 88 (10%) were white men; 7 (1%) were American Indian; 15 (2%) were Latino; 3 were Asian; 18 (2%) were Mexican.

Shawn Copeland, a Womanist ethicist, defines suffering as "the disturbance of our inner tranquility caused by physical, mental, emotional, and spiritual forces that we grasp as jeopardizing our lives, *our very existence.*"[1] The black feminist poet Pat Parker, who wrote about Jonestown, recalled a message learned early in life: "Black folks do not commit suicide. Black folks do not. Black folks do not commit suicide. On November 18, 1978 more than 900 people, most of them Black died in a man-made town called Jonestown. Newscasters' words slap me in my face. People's tears and grief emanate from my set and I remember lessons . . . Black folks do not commit suicide."[2]

I certainly learned this lesson—black folks do not commit suicide. The numbers from Jonestown say otherwise. I could give more statics, but the question, for us, I believe, is whether or not conversion studies or attending to conversion can help us understand these numbers—especially the greater percentage of *African Americans* who died? Did they not learn that black folks do not commit suicide? And what are we to make of the children: 367 of those who died were children (younger than 11) and young adults (up to 21 years of age). Furthermore, for all Jones' conversion from the racism of his day—of his Planning Commission team, comprised of 37 members, only 6 were black.[3] What are we to make of Jones' *conversion?*

---

1. Shawn M. Copeland, "Wading Through Many Sorrows: Toward a Theology of Suffering in Womanist Perspective," in *A Troubling in My Soul: Womanist Perspectives on Evil and Suffering* (ed. Emilie M. Townes; New York: Orbis, 1993), 111.

2. Pat Parker, "Jonestown," in *Jonestown and Other Madness: Poetry by Pat Parker* (New York: Firebrand, 1985).

3. See Rebecca Moore, "The Demographics of Jonestown," n.p. [accessed September 1, 2009]. Online: http://www.jonestown.sdsu.edu/AboutJonestown/JTResearch/demographics.htm. See also Archie Smith, *The Relational Self: Ethics and Therapy from a Black Church Perspective* (Nashville: Abingdon, 1982).

To speak of imago Dei with both these examples of conversion before us means that we find a way to concretize our theological assumptions—that is, to see what it means to be Jewish in the bible belt, to be Black in a racist society where that social reality informs pastoral leadership contexts, and to be a woman in a sexist religious community—and, having really seen these things, that we counter the reading of conversion that denies that all are fully created in the image of God and we pursue the conversion of those social and religious structures of our societies that enforce a negative theological anthropology. We have to give flesh to conversion, recognizing that salvation is irreducibly social and is mediated through individuals, families and communities. Salvation is a turning away from the cultural ethic of domination to an ethic of, dare I say it, love. Womanist theologian Delores Williams asserted "there can be no holiness, no unity and no catholicity of the Christian church until it identifies itself in active opposition to all forms of violence . . ."[4] An ethic of love does not run from suffering, it challenges its roots.

Clearly the interdisciplinary approach that Rambo has put forward is necessary for understanding both of these vignettes. And if conversion studies can help understand the kinds of issues raised by these cases, does it also posit a social and psychological analysis that leads us to particular kinds of action? In other words, for example, what is the place of the field of conversion studies for responding to the intersection of sexism and racism, as well as of religious and ethnic prejudice? My final questions are:

1. What is the aim of conversion studies?

2. In Professor Rambo's interdisciplinary approach, is there any perspective (Christian, theological, sociological, or psychological) that is always privileged and for what reasons?

3. Professor Rambo's vision of conversion studies is inclusive of various perspectives, theories, and religions. How does he and those of like mind envisage a gendered, or a Feminist or Womanist, reading of religious conversion impacting conversion studies?

4. Finally, what does the field of conversion studies bring to our theological interpretation of scripture?

---

4. Delores Williams, "Straight talk, Plain Talk: Womanist Words about Salvation in a Social Context," in *Embracing the Spirit: Womanist Perspectives on Hope, Salvation, and Transformation* (ed. Emilie M. Townes; New York: Orbis, 1997), 97–121 (esp. 119).

OBSERVATIONS ON "CONVERSION" AND THE OLD TESTAMENT

J. Andrew Dearman

There are various ways in which a concept like conversion can be related to the OT. Broadly defined, conversion has to do with fundamental change and transformation. With respect to the practice of religion or the reconfiguring of identity, it also has to do with change and more particularly with the embrace of new commitments and a new self-understanding on the part of people or communities. From the former perspective one can talk about the transformation of the world in an eschatological future as seen primarily by the OT prophets. Indeed, nothing less than a new heavens and a new earth are portrayed in prophetic portrait (Isa 65–66), and we might think of such a transformation as the conversion of creation. Also in this future environment, there are depictions of changed relationships and roles among the nations of the world, including Israel, the primary focus of the OT writings. Conversion in these broad senses would be one way to describe the realization of God's rule over a previous recalcitrant world and the triumph of his promise to bless all the families of the earth (as will be treated below).

With regard to the conversion of Israel, there are expectations of institutional transformation, in which royal city, holy temple, and Davidic monarchy are changed (Isa 2:2–5; 11:1–10; Jer 33:14–18; and Ezek 40–48). Just as creation itself is renewed and redone, so particularly are the geography and role of the central institutions of city and temple and the administrative rule of the Davidic monarch. Whereas these institutions had previously experienced historical failure, their renewal plays important roles in bringing healing to the nations.

One can speak, furthermore, of Israel's conversion in the sense that the election of the people to be a holy nation, obedient to its covenantal responsibilities and rightly related to the Lord, is finally to be realized. For example, there is prophetic expectation that Israel will receive a new covenant (Jer 31:31–34) and a new heart and new spirit (Ezek 36:22–32) through which to fulfill their election by God.

If one thinks of conversion more specifically as the turning of an individual to God, perhaps in rejecting former commitments or in an initial exercise of faith and trust, or even as acknowledgment of divine power, then the OT is also relevant. Such examples, however, are infrequent compared to the emphases on the transformation of cosmos and communities, and few details regarding their "conversions" are provided.[1] The various writers of the OT think in terms of corporate belonging as a primary way to define personal identity and responsibility. Persons are defined by their membership in an extended family, clan, and/or tribe. In the case of the OT the emphasis is on Israel and its characteristics, which should shape the life of individual Israelites, rather than what might be called tribalism, but the latter is certainly assumed as a factor in the life of the people. Indeed, Israel is metaphorically God's family (Exod 4:22; Hos 11:1). Of course, there is a range of emphasis and understanding of communal identity in the OT, but it is fundamental to the worldview of ancient Israel and much of antiquity. Moreover, its centrality should not be seen from a modern vantage point as a denial of personal identity or capacity for fundamental change; it is best understood in the anthropological sense that personhood is decisively linked to the basic institution of ancient society, namely the extended family or clan. Religious practice, social status, marriage, and other such realities are shaped by this communal identity. Thus Israel (or Judah) is the primary subject of the historical narratives of the OT and the primary entity addressed by the prophets. From a modern Christian assessment we might think of this communal emphasis in ecclesial terms. The OT is primarily the story of the people of God, and their identity before God takes center stage in the OT.

In what follows, the topic of conversion and the OT is discussed under three rubrics. The first contains observations on some of the ways in which the narrative traditions of Israel portray the inhabited world and Israel's place in it. The promise that Israel will be a blessing to the families of the earth is then briefly examined. The second discusses prophetic portraits of a transformed future, using a particular text, Isa 2:2–5/Mic 4:1–5, as a point of evaluation and departure. The third takes up the short story of Ruth, including the ways in which the account of the Moabite ancestress of David has been understood in Jewish and Christian interpretation.

---

1. One thinks, for example, of Rahab (Josh 2:1–24) and Naaman (2 Kgs 5:1–19). On Ruth, see below. The post-biblical document known as Joseph and Aseneth narrates the conversion to Judaism of Aseneth, the Egyptian woman who married Joseph and became the mother of Ephraim and Manasseh (cf. Gen 41:45, 50–52). Her "conversion," which has a number of surprising details, is prompted by her love for Joseph, rather than the proselytizing efforts of Jews.

Israel's Story and Place Among the Nations

Israel's primary history, contained in the Pentateuch and Former Prophets, traces the beginnings of the inhabited world and then concentrates on the formation of a particular community in it, namely Israel. The narratives that supplement the primary history, such as 1 and 2 Chronicles and Esther, are consistent with this approach. All of the earth and inhabitants belong to the Lord, their creator, while Israel is called to be a holy people and a priestly kingdom (Exod 19:4–6) in response to the covenant that the Lord made with them. Individuals play a crucial role in the narratives of the primary history, but as noted above, the angle of vision is essentially on peoples and nations, and on the elect role of Israel among the nations. It is the case that individuals such as Abraham and Sarah or Moses and David are presented to readers as persons on a journey, who have the capacity for change in response to divine activity, yet their lives are interwoven with the larger account of God's work among his people. Conversion, therefore, whether considered more broadly as a form of transformation or more specifically as a turn to the living God who created heaven and earth, should first be seen from the perspective of peoples and nations.

The primeval history (Gen 1–11) sets the stage for a world in which humanity has responsibilities before God and where its fallibility is brought to light. It is a double-sided existence that characterizes both creation and its human inhabitants. On the one hand, viable communal existence is established outside of the garden, and various links establish continuity in it over generations of time (Gen 4–5; 10). From the beginning creation's derivative goodness made communal life possible, and God's blessing offered structures and potential joy (Gen 1:26–31; 2:15–25). On the other hand, outside of the garden creation's other side (e.g. disease and famine) and human fallibility, including violence and the potential of self-destruction, make life precarious and subject to divine restraint and judgment (Gen 3; 4; 6–9; 11:1–9).

Those descended from Noah will have conflict and coalesce in different ethnic communities, plus they will contend against the limits and identity assigned by God (Gen 9–11). From the perspective of the Scriptural narratives, this is the inhabited world in all its glory and fallibility. It is also the context for the Lord's call of Abram and Sarah and his promise of blessing to them and through them to all the families of the earth (Gen 12:1–3). From the perspective of conversion as fundamental change, this projected blessing to all the families of the earth is of great significance. Against the background of the flood and a tower of hubris, Abram and Sarah are called to leave their homeland and go to a land that the Lord will show them. The promises extended to them include making their descendants a great nation, giving to Abram a great name, blessing those who bless them and cursing those who curse them, and their being a catalyst for blessing to come to all the families of the earth.

Genesis 12:1–3 serves as a hinge in the book of Genesis, as the ancestral accounts in chapters 12–50 are shaped in part by the outworking of the promises made to Abram and Sarah. The passage reflects God's intention to bless over against the debilitating powers in the inhabited world. Indeed, a good case can be made that the partial outworking of the promises in this hinge passage also serves as the theme of the Pentateuch as it is now constituted.[2] "Partial" seems a fitting adjective in recognition that Israel's primary history does not stop with Deuteronomy, the last book of the Pentateuch. Deuteronomy contains much about covenantal blessings and curses for Israel (cf. Deut 26–28), as well as indications of the ways in which they may be operative in Israel's subsequent history. In the Pentateuch the promises in Gen 12:1–3 can be linked back to God's intention to bless his creation (Gen 1:26–31) and forward to the increase of Abraham and Sarah's descendants, to the blessings recounted in Gen 49 and Deut 33 about them, and to their formation as a covenant people to provide priestly service (Exod 2:24; 19:4–6). Nevertheless, neither the outworking of the promises nor the history of Abraham and Sarah's descendants concludes with the Pentateuch. The Former Prophets, the historical narratives in Joshua, Judges, Samuel and Kings, continue on in the recounting of nation building and decline, as Israel providentially suffers the vicissitudes of history. It seems fair to say that the outworking, the further "filling out" of the promised blessings enunciated in Gen 12:1–3, remains in the background of the Former Prophets as they rehearse Israel's place among the nations. But such promises are not obsolete. Although 2 Kings ends with the tragic account of Judah's exile from the promised land and the temporary destruction of the institutions of temple and monarchy, Israel's history among the nations does not end at this point and neither does its place in the outworking of the promised blessings. Israel's primary narratives follow the pattern of historical development, national failure and exile, with a partial national restoration after exile.[3] Other writers, in particular the prophets, see in national failure and exile opportunities for the "outworking" of God's intended blessings of the inhabited world (cf. Isa 42:1–4; 49:1–6; 51:4) as they also project a greater transformation to come.

---

2. D. J. A. Clines, *The Theme of the Pentateuch* (2nd edition; JSOTSup 10; Sheffield: Sheffield Academic, 1997).

3. For a discussion of this pattern, along with analysis of the projected eschatological restoration, see Roy E. Ciampa, "The History of Redemption," in *Central Themes in Biblical Theology: Mapping Unity in Diversity* (ed. Scott J. Hafemann and Paul R. House; Downers Grove, Ill.: InterVarsity, 2007), 254–308.

The blessings promised to Abram and Sarah in Gen 12:1–3 are associated specifically with their descendant(s), who will be a channel for world-wide blessing (Gen 22:17–18; cf. Gen 12:3). It is not simply that their descendants will themselves become a fruitful nation; it has also to do with their role as catalysts and vessels on behalf of other peoples. In the first instance their descendants are identified as Israel, and so the role of catalyst and vessel for divine blessings is understood in communal terms. Yet, the seed of promise in 22:17–18 is grammatically a singular noun (*zeraʿ*) and is also reckoned in an individual sense, as applying to Judah and his tribe and to one from that tribe.[4] In this second sense also the promises are taken up by other biblical writers. To fast-forward for the moment, Paul sees the advance of the gospel as an outworking of God's promised blessing to the nations through Jesus the Messiah, the particular "seed" of Abraham and Sarah. In a wonderful turn of phrase, Paul describes the promised blessing of nations through the "seed" of Abraham as "preaching the gospel beforehand" (Gal 3:8). This focal point does not negate the corporate role of Israel but emerges from it. Just as Israel corporately is Abraham's seed and God's "son" (Exod 4:22; Hos 11:1), so also is the Messiah Abraham's seed and God's son, and he is the instrument of God's blessing to the nations.

The narratives of Israel's history are not crafted explicitly with reference to a transformed eschatological future. The prophets provide that horizon and psalmists anticipate its realization. Thus, on the one hand, the promised blessing to the families of the earth, so prominent in Genesis, does not find an ultimate fulfillment in the national narratives themselves. It sits there unrealized, projecting God's promise to bless on an international scale from the beginning of the history. On the other hand, it is in accord with the conviction of prophets and psalmists that God's rule will be made manifest in blessings on a cosmic scale.

The Prophets and a Transformed Future

With few exceptions (e.g., Jonah) the books of the Latter Prophets offer varying vistas of fundamental change to come. These prophecies are not formulated systematically but are visionary projections of God's triumph in the world. In some cases the change to come is the defeat of Israel and God's enemies and/or an era of peace (Isa 34–35; 60:1–16; Ezek 38–39; Joel 3:1–23; Zeph 3:8–13; Zech 12–14). Even

---

4. See the studies by T. Desmond Alexander, "From Adam to Judah: The Significance of the Family Tree in Genesis," *Evangelical Quarterly* 61 (1989): 5–19; and "Further Observations on the Term 'Seed' in Genesis," *TynBul* 48 (1997): 363–367. See also James Hamilton, "The Seed of the Woman and the Blessing of Abraham," *TynBul* 58 (2007): 253–273.

resurrection from the dead, understood by some as a metaphor for release from exile (Ezek 37:1–14), could be a part of the coming transformation (Isa 26:16–21; Dan 12:1–3). In others it is the conversion of nations to the worship and service of the Lord (Isa 2:2–5) and/or the procession of kings and peoples to Jerusalem to offer tribute (Isa 60:1–16). And yet in others it is the transformation of Israel into a fit vessel to serve the Lord and to carry out its elect status among the nations (Ezek 36–37; 40–48). David's greater son would serve as ruler (Isa 9:1–6; 11:1–10; Jer 33:14–26; Ezek 36:24–28). In the prophets' own day the Lord was worshiped in Jerusalem as cosmic king and the ruler of nations. In Jerusalem the psalmists sang of the Lord's exaltation among the nations, that even now they should hold the Lord in reverence, and that his ultimate triumph was assured. Prophet and poet alike projected a world to come based on the conviction that the Lord is judge and redeemer of the world.

Among the prophetic books Isaiah is replete with portrayals of cosmic and international change to come. The book is an anthology, an epitome of prophecy, containing harsh evaluations of peoples and nations, along with stunning portrayals of cosmic renewal and change to come.[5] In all of this there are numerous connections to material in other prophetic books. No one text in Isaiah or any other book captures all the richness and variety of projected change. Having said that, a text like Isa 2:2–5 is a focal point, a crystallized aspect, for much that is projected elsewhere in prophetic texts about the future.

> In the latter days the mountain of the Lord's house shall be established as the head of the mountains, and it shall be lifted above the hills; all the nations shall stream to it. Many peoples shall come and say, "Come, let us go up to the mountain of the Lord, to the house of the God of Jacob; that he may teach us his ways and that we may walk in his paths." For from Zion shall go forth instruction, and the word of the Lord from Jerusalem. He shall judge between the nations, and shall adjudicate for many peoples; they shall beat their swords into plowshares, and their spears into pruning hooks; nation shall not lift up sword against nation, nor shall they train for war any longer. O house of Jacob, come, let us walk in the light of the Lord![6]

The substance of this passage also occurs in Mic 4:1–5. The two passages, however, are framed differently. Isaiah 2:1 provides an introduction to the prophecy and sets its contents in the context of what the prophet "saw" concerning the future

---

5. See the analysis of Brevard Childs, *Isaiah* (Louisville: Westminster John Knox, 2001).
6. Unless otherwise stated, all biblical quotations are the author's own translations.

of Jerusalem. The book of Micah does not offer an introduction to this particular prophecy about the "latter days," a phrase that designates the future, remote or otherwise. Micah's version serves as a counterpoint of historical judgment to come on Zion because its leaders have failed in their responsibilities before the Lord (3:9–12). With respect to their conclusions, Micah offers an expanded depiction of future peace in v. 4 and acknowledges in v. 5 that in the interim nations will continue to walk in the name of their own deities.

Although as books Isaiah and Micah differ considerably in size, they share two traits that assist readers in interpreting them and the significance of this shared vision about the future. The first trait is that they contain prophecies directed against the separate entities of Israel and Judah, as befits their common prophetic origins in the third quarter of the eighth century B.C.E., when the resurgent Neo-Assyrian empire first threatened and then moved through parts of the eastern Mediterranean (cf. Isa 1:1; Mic 1:1). This is a period of time summarized also in 2 Kings 14–20. Both prophetic books assume that the Lord is at work historically to judge and to redeem his people, initially by using the Neo-Assyrian army and then in the future (as in the "latter days") when and how it suits him. Secondly, the two books assume that God's future work, what we might broadly call prophetic eschatology,[7] will include other nations and peoples as well as Israel. Furthermore, Jerusalem will play a pivotal role in the divine plan for other nations. This second trait finds focused expression in the passage under consideration—hence its significance.

Historical exegesis of the books has concluded that both of them reached their present form over a considerable period of time and that they are the result of editorial shaping that transcended the historical setting of Isaiah of Jerusalem and Micah of Moresheth in the eighth century B.C.E. Readers, therefore, will encounter various viewpoints among scholars regarding the dating of the passage held in common: whether, for example, the portrayals of a transformed Jerusalem and reconciled nations are earlier than Isaiah or Micah (i.e. a common tradition upon which each drew); the creation of either Isaiah or Micah and adapted by the other; or the product of later editors involved in the compiling of the prophetic books. A decision on this matter is less important than the recognition that the passage represents *in nuce* a significant segment of prophetic eschatology, and it is this function that deserves attention.

---

7. The term "eschatology" is used here in a basic sense to refer to God's decisive work in the future in which his ultimate purposes for Israel and for the nations are portrayed.

The poetic parallelism of Isa 2:3 has divine revelation coming forth from Zion/Jerusalem. Taken out of context, readers might see in this description an indication that God's word will be carried forth from Jerusalem to permeate creation. That sense, however important in other contexts, is not the primary sense of 2:3 where place indicates origin or source but not necessarily dispersal. The Lord's instruction originates in Jerusalem and is encountered there. More particularly, it comes from the Lord's "house," i.e. the temple located on Mt. Zion where the Lord is worshiped. The passage begins with the exaltation of the Lord's house and continues with a portrayal of nations coming "up" to the temple where they receive divine instruction and adjudication, and as a result the need for war is no more. In context, therefore, the directional language is primarily that of pilgrimage, the act of coming to Jerusalem for worship and instruction so that the life of peoples and nations is then fundamentally transformed. It is the transformed life predicted for Jerusalem's future that is shared with the nations (cf. Isa 11:6–10). To summarize, on an international scale this is a primary way that the OT thinks of what we might call conversion. Nations and peoples present themselves before the Lord where they offer worship and receive instruction as entities included in the cosmic rule of the Lord.

Isaiah's vision about the latter days assumes that Jerusalem is a place of God's own choosing, the location of his "house" where he might be encountered and worshiped, as it was in the prophet's own day. Such an angle of vision is consistent with the data of 1 and 2 Samuel and 1 and 2 Chronicles, whereby Zion/Jerusalem is incorporated into the Israelite polity by David, the Lord's chosen vessel to shepherd Israel. Subsequently a temple for the worship of the Lord is built by Solomon. In both narrative versions the planning, construction, and dedication of the temple occupy a central role (1 Kgs 6–8; 1 Chr 22—2 Chr 7). As the locus of divine revelation, the temple was a place of pilgrimage for the Israelite tribes. Put simply, the temple draws people to it because it is the place where people came to "behold the Lord." Although the pilgrimage aspect of worship is not mentioned explicitly in Solomon's dedicatory prayer for the temple (1 Kgs 8:22–61), it seems presupposed in the repeated reference to those who come and pray "toward this place" (1 Kgs 8:30; 2 Chr 6:21). The directional aspect of praying "toward the place" is the same as pilgrimage; it indicates a turning to the temple and an acknowledgment that the Lord is present there. It is clear, however, from other texts that God's people came to Jerusalem to seek the Lord and to worship in the temple. The Pentateuch contains instruction for Israelite males to present themselves before the Lord three times a year (Exod 23:14–17; cf. Lev 23; Deut 12:8–27; 16:1–17). Although Jerusalem is not named in the Pentateuch, the identification of the place that the Lord "will choose as a dwelling for his name" (Deut 12:11), the place where the people are to go to offer sacrifices, became identified with the temple mount in Jerusalem (cf. 1 Kgs 8:44; 2 Chr 6:20). There is an important pattern to be observed here. What was a constituent practice for God's people during the time of an Isaiah or Jeremiah becomes in prophetic vision the pattern in the future conversion of the nations.

The Psalms are replete with references to people going up to Jerusalem for worship. To take one example, Ps 122:1-4 celebrates in the following fashion:

> I was glad when they said to me, 'Let us go to the Lord's house.'
> Our feet stand within your gates, Jerusalem.
> Jerusalem—like a city built together firmly.
> There the tribes go up, the tribes of the Lord,
> As commanded to Israel, to offer thanks to the Lord's name.

In this psalm one encounters the familiar language of "house" for the Lord's temple, an appreciation for the sanctity of Jerusalem, and recognition that it is the place where Israel goes to praise the Lord's name. The poetry of the psalm is not formulated in the language of Deuteronomy or 1 Kings, but it too joins "house/place" and "name of the Lord" in the context of those assembled to worship. It uses, furthermore, the same language of "coming/walking" (*hālak*) and "ascending" (*ʿālāh*) to meet the Lord (vv. 1, 4) that is used of the nations in Isa 2:3.

In considering the role of Zion/Jerusalem as a place of divine revealing, one should note the poetic resume of Israel's history in Ps 132. According to Israel's historical narratives, God made several choices as means to instruct and to provide for his people. As noted above, two of them were the city of Jerusalem and David and his family; the family to provide shepherds to rule the people and the city as the home of the temple (2 Sam 7). Psalm 132 brings together the traditions of David's desire to provide a place for the Lord to dwell (i.e., a "house" or temple), the king bringing the ark of the covenant into Jerusalem, affirmation of the Lord's choice of David to rule over his people, and confirmation that Zion is indeed the place that the Lord has "chosen" (v. 13) for his own habitation.[8] These central institutions—Jerusalem, temple, Davidic ruler—will all be transformed in prophetic eschatology.

In Solomon's dedicatory prayer for the temple, the king notes that the Lord had called his father David and his descendants to walk in ways that were pleasing to him (1 Kgs 8:25; cf. 1 Kgs 3:14). "To walk in a way" is a metaphor for fidelity to a pathway that has been marked out. It indicates the manner in which persons marshal their

---

8. Cf. Ps 78:67-72. We should note in this regard that Zion/Jerusalem is called both the "City of David" and the "City of God" (2 Sam 5:6-7; 1 Kgs 8:2; Ps 46:4; 48:1).

resources and make their commitments, in recognition that paths lead somewhere and have consequences (cf. Ps 1). The same terminology is used for Israelites, who are to walk in God's "good way," which is tantamount to their obeying his instructions (1 Kings 8:36, 58, 61). The context is important. To worship the Lord at his house is one form of the good way that he wills for his people; a related "way" is that of obedience to his revealed will in other aspects of life.

The terminology used for the latter-day pilgrim nations in Isa 2:3 follows a similar pattern. The instruction that the nations will receive at the Lord's house is according to "his ways," and the result is that they will walk in "his paths." Stated somewhat differently, the fidelity expected from God's chosen people is now extended to the nations in a future time of multinational transformation. In this regard Isaiah's vision of the latter days is related to another aspect of worship already in evidence at the Jerusalem temple of Isaiah's own day, namely, worship offered by a foreigner. In his dedicatory prayer Solomon interceded for the foreigner who may come to the temple from a distant land and who then prays to the Lord (1 Kgs 8:41–43). It is assumed as a practice during the first temple period. His prayer does not envisage the wholesale turning of a foreign nation to the Lord for guidance, nor intimate that such will happen in the latter days, but it does assume the primacy of the temple as the locus for divine hearing and instruction for Israelite and for willing foreigner alike. Non-Israelites can learn to "fear" the Lord and recognize that the Lord is God—"there is no other" (1 Kgs 8:60; cf. Isa 56:1–8).

The latter days of Isaiah's vision are a time of peace, an era portrayed as the absence of war between nations. Like everything else in the prophecy, the transformative international peace is an expansion of the Lord's blessing of his people as celebrated in Jerusalem of the prophet's own day (cf. Ps 72).[9] Micah's rendition of the vision elaborates on the "swords to plowshares" motif with a depiction of familial bliss, where people sit under their vines and fig trees (4:4). The description evokes the scene sought by all agriculturalists in pre-modern societies: productivity, on the one hand, and security on the other. It is recognized as a blessed state of events in the primary history during Solomon's reign (1 Kgs 5:5; cf. 2 Kgs 18:31; Jer 8:13; Joel 2:22; Zech 3:10), where people can enjoy the produce of the land (Deut 8:8). Of course, the scourges of warfare, instability, and disease loom as threats at various

---

9. Psalm 72 celebrates the benevolence and security provided by the Davidic king. Note the conclusion where nations may be blessed in him (v. 17). This expression of hope recalls the blessings promised in Gen 12:1–3 and 22:17–18.

times to agricultural production (Jer 5:17; Joel 1:12; Amos 4:9), so that a future era of international peace and productivity would be quite the change.

In Jerusalem of the first-temple period the hymns of Zion celebrated the peace and security associated with the presence and actions of the Lord. Such a state of affairs is portrayed as palpable in the city and as something to be recognized throughout the earth. It is this state of affairs in Jerusalem—known to the eyes of faith—that the Lord will bring to fruition in the latter days, including the nations. Psalm 46, for example, extols God as the refuge of his people and the city of God (Jerusalem/Zion) as the illustration of his care. In this context worshipers are called to take note of his work in the earth (46:9–11):

> He makes wars cease to the end of the earth; he shatters both bow and spear; he consumes the shields with fire. "Be still, and know that I am God! I am exalted among the nations, I am exalted in the earth." The Lord of Hosts is with us; the God of Jacob is our refuge.

Similar affirmations are made in Ps 48. The city's architecture and defenses are visible signs of the security provided by the Lord (vv. 3, 12–14). The kings of the earth cannot prevail against the Lord. His praise and renown extend through all the earth (vv. 4–11).

Hymns such as Ps 46 and 48 did not originate as eschatological beacons, as if their first task is to hold forth the transformative era to come. In the first temple period they indicate instead what the Lord provided for his people and demonstrated in their history through the institutions of royal city and holy temple. Nevertheless, the hymns note that the Lord, whose "house" is in Jerusalem, is the God of the whole earth and is to be recognized as such by all inhabitants.

The latter day vision of Isaiah and Micah builds on the related patterns of what might be called collectively the theology of Zion[10] and the ways of the Lord's self-revelation from there. The future conversion of the nations follows the patterns set for Israel and portrayed in Jerusalem. They may be listed here by way of summary:

First, Jerusalem is the city of God, his "dwelling place" and the location of his "house." Worship of the Lord and receipt of his revelation occur here. In the latter days Jerusalem will also be central for apprehending the divine will and presence.

Second, just as God's people would come up to Jerusalem or pray toward its temple, so in the latter days the nations will come up to Jerusalem to receive instruc-

---

10. See further J. J. M. Roberts, "The Davidic Origin of the Zion Tradition" and "Zion in the Theology of the Davidic-Solomonic Empire," in his *The Bible and the Ancient Near East: Collected Essays* (Winona Lake, Ind.: Eisenbrauns, 2002), 313–30 and 331–47, respectively.

tion from the Lord. That foreigners could and would pray to the Lord at the first temple is a sign of things to come.

Third, in Jerusalem God provides for the security of his people and can bring war to an end, including judgment upon recalcitrant nations. In the latter days, the Lord will establish a peaceable kingdom in which the nations will not war against each other.

One of the striking things about the theology of Zion and its influence on the prophetic depictions of transformation is the pride and particularity of place. Jerusalem is not only the place where Israel finds its spiritual home in the days of the kings and prophets, it is also the place in the latter days where the worship of the Lord will draw in other nations as well. This pride of place continues in Jewish teaching and in early Christianity, even when the eschatological horizon has been extended. This is not the place to develop the connections in detail, but suffice it to say that the New Testament references to the Jerusalem that is above, the heavenly city (Gal 4:26; Heb 12:22; 13:14; Rev 21–22), continue to draw upon the particularity of place as central to divine presence and communal well-being. Perhaps this is most notable in the concluding vision of the Apocalypse where the heavenly Jerusalem comes down from heaven as the home of the faithful in the new heavens and the new earth. In that place the redeemed from other nations find their home and healing (Rev 21:22–27; 22:2). John's portrayal captures much of the varying strands of prophetic vision regarding a transformed future, tying them together in the heavenly city of the Lamb.

Ruth

Although it is not clear how much emphasis on her religious status is intended by the compiler(s) of the story of Ruth, there are several indications in the book that she qualifies as an individual convert to Israel's faith in the Lord, however that might be interpreted in ancient Israel. As will be discussed below, her status as a convert to Yahwism certainly plays an important role in the fascinating history of the book's interpretation. Readers of the narrative are quickly introduced to Ruth's impassioned speech to Naomi her mother-in-law (1:16–17), where she declares that Naomi's "God will be her God" and she utters a self-imprecation to the effect that the Lord (= Naomi's God)[11] would deal harshly with her should anything, even death, sepa-

---

11. Naomi's God is the Lord (YHWH), the God of Israel, whom she acknowledges in both blessing (2:30) and anger (1:21). Cf. also 4:14.

rate her from Naomi. Later, when Boaz first encounters Ruth gleaning in his field, he offers a hope for her that "the Lord reward you for your effort and may your 'wages' be full from the Lord, the God of Israel, under whose wings you have come to seek refuge" (2:12). The metaphor of seeking refuge under the Lord's wings is commonly used in the Psalter and elsewhere to refer to those who put their trust and hope in the Lord (e.g., 2 Sam 22:3, 31; Ps 5:11; 7:2; 11:1; 16:1; 36:7; 57:2). As the terminology is associated frequently with David in the OT, one wonders if its use by Boaz in speaking to Ruth (David's ancestors) is a narrative artist at work, an intended echo on the part of the compiler(s) to show the providential link between the later king of Israel and his great-grandparents. Whatever the answer to this question, the role of the Lord in the events narrated, including the life of Ruth, is paramount to the account as we have it. It is fair to say, however, that Ruth's status as a worshiper of the Lord is not developed in the canonical account. It is rather assumed, and the account concentrates on her actions and those of the Lord, who is at work behind the scenes.

Two forms of a genealogy conclude the book. They indicate the significant future to which the efforts of the major characters and the providence of God lead. The longer of the two genealogies indicates that the family of Boaz (and thus that of Naomi's husband) is part of the line of Perez, known from the book of Genesis as a son of Judah (Gen 38), and that David, son of Jesse, is the fourth generation in succession from Boaz and Ruth. This is persuasive evidence for many readers that the story rendered in the book was preserved, at least in significant measure, because it illuminates the family of David. There are no external controls by which the factual accuracy of the story can be measured, but it is not likely that an account of David's Moabite ancestry would have survived as part of a larger national epic were there not persistent data in the tradition to support it. It is true that nothing is made of this connection in either Samuel or Chronicles, though the incidental comment in 1 Sam 22:3–4, that David sent his parents to stay with the king of Moab when he was under duress from Saul, is consistent with such a connection. So the book of Ruth stands in the canonical tradition as the account of a Moabite woman who came to take refuge under the wings of the Lord, the God of Israel, who married into the tribe of Judah and the family of David.

From the perspective of later Jewish interpretation, Ruth is a scriptural example of a convert to Judaism. In the Aramaic Targum Ruth's impassioned speech—that Naomi's God will be her God (1:16)—is answered by Naomi with a reminder that there are 613 commandments in the Torah that she must know and observe (cf.

Midr. Ruth 2:21–22). This is a wonderful illustration of reading an account of conversion, however understood in ancient Israel, from the perspective of a later age. In rabbinic Judaism observance of the Torah was the mark of an observant Jew. So the rabbis apparently reasoned, Naomi followed the expected protocol in instructing Ruth on her new privileges and responsibilities. Had Ruth been a man, one wonders if circumcision would have been mentioned explicitly in the midrash as the duty of a convert!

The liturgical use of the book in Judaism is also relevant to the interpretation of Ruth's conversion. In medieval Judaism the book of Ruth found a secure place for reading in the Festival of Weeks, also known as First Fruits. It is one of the three major festivals in the Pentateuch (Lev 23:15–21). Its roots are in the agricultural setting of spring harvests. Greek-speaking Jews in antiquity and Christians know the celebration as Pentecost. The historical reasons behind this eventual placement of the book as a liturgical resource for the Festival of Weeks are, however, unfortunately obscure. The practice is not noted in the Talmud, so the fixed liturgical tradition of reading the book in its entirety during the festival celebration is later than 500 CE, although the association of the book with the festival in some circles may be considerably earlier. One reason to associate the story of Ruth with the spring Festival of Weeks is internal to the book itself. The bulk of the narrative is set at the time of barley harvest (Ruth 1:22), which typically overlaps with the occasion of the festival. The latter is fixed at seven weeks after the Passover sacrifice. This connection, however, does not assist in determining the origins of the liturgical practice of reading it in the synagogue during the festival celebration.

The connection of the festival and the book of Ruth is possibly the result of another development in the festival calendar of Judaism, when the Festival of Weeks became the occasion to celebrate the giving of the Torah to Israel at Mt. Sinai. Again, there is a biblical reason to connect Sinai and festival, even though it is not explicit in the Pentateuchal instructions. According to Exod 19:1, the Israelites arrived at Mt. Sinai in the third month after departing Egypt. The text can be interpreted in a variety of ways, chronologically speaking, but the connection between the Festival of Weeks and the Sinai revelation goes back at least as far as the book of Jubilees.[12] In post-biblical Judaism the Festival of Weeks has not only an agricultural setting but also provides an occasion to celebrate the giving of the Torah to Israel. Among the traditions of Judaism associated with the revelation at Mt. Sinai is the belief that God

---

12. On these details see the recent work of Sejin Park, *Pentecost and Sinai: The Festival of Weeks as a Celebration of the Sinai Event* (New York: T. & T. Clark, 2008).

will eventually speak his word to other peoples. This is a form of Jewish eschatology. It is interesting to consider Luke's presentation of Pentecost in Acts 2:1–36 in light of these developing Jewish traditions, where he describes people from all over the world hearing the Christian message in their own language. Perhaps the reading of the book of Ruth at Pentecost is also linked to this conviction that God will speak his word to Gentiles, so that they too, after the manner of Ruth, can dwell under the wings of the Lord (Ruth 2:12).

As indicated, the book of Ruth has a fascinating place in the history of biblical interpretation. However it is to be explained, the Moabitess becomes an example of a convert in Judaism. In this regard we should not overlook her place in Matthew's Gospel (1:5), which has its origins in early Jewish Christianity. Ruth is one of only four women included in the genealogy of Jesus in Matt 1:1–17. The others are all men. Tamar, Rahab, and Bathsheba are named in addition to Ruth. As interpreters have long noted, there are problems associated with each of the women in terms of their sexual history. Two (Rahab and Ruth) of the four are also Gentiles, and Tamar may be considered one as well. In any case, all four must have been considered adherents to the faith of Israel and women who played vital roles in the Lord's work in Israel, irrespective of what might have been thought by some regarding their sexual histories. In this respect they are like Mary, the mother of Jesus. For those who rejected the Christian message of Jesus' supernatural conception, some among them would doubtless have claimed that Mary's "explanation" was a fraud, designed to cover-up an affair or other illicit activity. Those who maligned Mary, however, were going against God's past actions in using women, even Gentiles, with surprising sexual histories.

Conclusion

If one first thinks of conversion in the individual sense of a person embracing a new faith, then the vast riches of the OT have some perspective to offer. If, on the other hand, one thinks in terms of conversion more broadly as the promised transformation of the cosmos, including Israel and other nations, then one looks toward a future that is central to the OT and the matrix for much of what the NT says about the eschaton.

RESPONSE TO DEARMAN

Rajkumar Boaz Johnson

Prof. Andrew Dearman has done us a great service in outlining the parameters of the discussion related to the conception of "conversion" in the OT. He defines "conversion" as a "fundamental change and transformation" and outlines the OT conception of conversion under three rubrics. One, he discusses the relationship between Israel and the nations as a background to the conception of conversion. Two, he outlines conversion in relation to a transformation which takes on national and environmental connotations. And, three he takes the story of Ruth's conversion as an example of a Gentile conversion to the biblical faith. The eschatological dimension, the social and religious dimension, and the personal dimension are crucial to note.

Dearman observes in the first part of his analysis that stories of individual transformation, i.e. conversion, are very few. He writes, "If one thinks more specifically as the turning of an individual to God, perhaps in rejecting former commitments or in an initial exercise of faith and trust, or even as acknowledgement of divine power, then the OT is also relevant. Such examples, however, are infrequent compared to the emphases on the transformation of cosmos and communities, and few details regarding their 'conversions' are provided." He mentions Rahab, Naaman, and Ruth among the handful. The last part of his paper deals with the story of Ruth and the interpretation of this conversion story in Jewish liturgy and tradition.

Perhaps it is because I approach the OT from the perspective of the third world that I see the picture differently. I was myself quite influenced by OT characters in my conversion from Hinduism to the God of the Bible, and I have seen amazing stories of conversion from Hinduism, Islam, and Buddhism to the God of the Bible as a result of the Hebrew Bible narratives. Therefore, I see the OT as being replete with examples of individual and collective transformation which become models for NT conversion stories.

Please take my comments in that vein. I am of the opinion that some of the best conversion studies have yet to emerge out of the Hindu, Muslim, and Buddhist worlds. This is perhaps a part of Lewis Rambo's indication that conversion studies need to be looked at from a global dimension (see his paper in this collection). In some of these places new Christians and the church regularly confront issues such as anti-conversion laws. In these places one has to address issues about who is or is not a Christian. Jewish followers of Messiah in Israel have to ask the question, "Am I a Jew, or am I a Messianic Jew, or am I a Christian?" Ethiopian Jewish Christians have to ask the question, "Am I an Ethiopian Jew, a Falasha, or am I an Ethiopian Christian?" In India, Nepal, and Sri Lanka a Hindu follower of Jesus has to ask the question, "Am I a Hindu follower of Christ, or am I a Christian? In India, Bangladesh, Pakistan, Afghanistan, Iran, and similar countries a Muslim follower of Jesus—the word "Muslim" means, "one who has submitted himself or herself"—has to ask the question, "Am I a Christian, or am I a true Muslim, a true submitted one?"

Perhaps the answers to such questions will have to emerge from the countries that have been the cradle for these religions or the focal point—unfortunately, many times the very violent focal point—of confrontation between religions.

Of course, for the Christian church the Bible must be the source of answers to many of these questions. The questions are complex, and the answers by their very nature will need to be phenomenological.

With this in mind I ask questions of the Western church and of Dearman's paper as we take a closer look at the Hebrew Bible's perspectives on conversion.

Dearman observes that Ancient Near Eastern society portrays the "identity of a person being defined by membership in extended family, clan, and/or tribe." This, I suggest, is the model of conversion in the Hebrew Bible. The Abrahamic narratives are a paradigm for the rest of the book of Genesis, the Pentateuch, and the story of Israel. Abram's conversion in Gen 12:1–3 becomes a paradigm for the rest of the Hebrew Bible, and indeed for Pauline thought. Genesis 12:1 reads, "Now the Lord said to Abram, 'Go from your country and your kindred and your father's house to the land that I will show you.'"

It is a break with whatever defines one's identity in religious, social, economic, geographic, and other categories. To unpack all those categories is to describe a phenomenological conversion, the kind of conversion Lewis Rambo describes as taking on "a new complex matrix of the group into which the individual is converted." It is James Fowler's description of taking on a "new set of master stories." In the realm of liturgy this is reflected in the person belonging to the new community who recites the Shema.

The person who belongs to the new Abrahamic community says on every day of firstfruits when he brings the firstfruit offerings into the temple, "A wandering Aramean was my father . . . he went down . . . we cried . . . the Lord heard . . . he brought us to this place . . . So now I bring the first of the fruit . . ." (Deut 26:5–11).[1] The conversion experience of Abraham becomes the conversion experience of the new convert and the conversion experience of the new community. The individual conversion, the community conversion, and the historical conversion all get wrapped up into one at that liturgical moment.

The leaving (*hālak*) motif in the Abrahamic text is central to conversion in the OT. Every time there is a conversion to God, it is a movement (*hālak*) towards God. This is the portrayal of the Exodus narrative. People are told to walk (*hālak*) into the presence of God (Exod 3:18, 19, 21, et al.). The people encounter God at Mount Sinai.

It is interesting to note that both Abraham and the Abrahamic community in going towards God also go towards "the place" (*māqôm*) of encounter, the place at Shechem (Gen 12:6). Dearman notes that this motif of "the place" is central to understanding the concept of conversion in the OT. The "place" is the focus of conversion because this is the locus of the presence of the name of God. In the Abrahamic narrative *māqôm* is often a focus. For example, in Gen 22 Abraham is told to go "to the place" where God had told him (Gen 22:3). This focus appears repeatedly in the narrative of the Akedah of Isaac (Gen 22:3, 4, 9, 14), which concludes with Abraham naming the place "the Lord sees" (Gen 22:14). Focus on "the place" (*māqôm*) continues in other texts. In the Song of Moses, which in the compositional structure of the Pentateuch is central to understanding the Exodus motif, the destination of the Exodus community is defined as this place (Exod 15:16, 17). The temple is constructed at the place, and the Holy of Holies is constructed at the place where the Ark of the Covenant is placed (1 Kgs 8:6, 7, 21, 29, 30, and 35). This is the place towards which not just the Jewish people but also the non-Jewish people may pray. This is the place of redemption and transformation. The place throughout the Hebrew Bible is the nucleus towards which conversion takes place. It is as if it were a centripetal force taking the converted one through a set of concentric circles towards the middle.

The Abrahamic model also shows us that when human beings depart from this nucleus, they are departing from the holy presence of God. This is essentially what Abram does in Gen 12. Abram's response to the famine, just like the response of the sons of Jacob (Gen 42:2, 3) and the response of the apostate Israel was to "go down" (*yārad*; Deut 28:43 and 52). This is the opposite of conversion; it is de-conversion. In the Prophets and the Writings this is the term used when a person or community goes away from the presence of God. This, for example, is what happens to Jonah

---

1. Unless otherwise stated, all biblical quotations are from NRSV.

when he does not "arise" (*qûm*) into God's presence and obey his injunction to go to Nineveh (Jonah 1:1–3). Instead of arising, he goes down. In the Hebrew Writings the logical consequence of going down is going down to the grave (Pss 9:15; 28:1; 30:3, 9; Job 17:16; 33:24, et al.).

The antidote to de-conversion is "going back up" to the place of encounter (*ʿālāh*). This is essentially what Abram does (Gen 13:1). "Going up" becomes the paradigm of all conversion narratives in the Hebrew Bible. In the narrative of the Aqedah of Isaac this is what Abraham constantly does when he goes up to the place of encounter (Gen 22:2, 3, 6, 7, 8, and 13). This is what describes the salvation of the people from Egypt. Yahweh says to Moses, "I will bring you up (*ʿālāh*) out of the affliction of Egypt" (Exod 3:8, 17; et al.) In the Prophets also this is the motif of conversion. Dearman refers to the Gentiles who in the eschaton will convert to Yahweh. They will say, "Come, let us go up to the mountain of Yahweh, to the house of the God of Jacob" (Isa 2:3). In the Hebrew Writings also the theme of going up describes people who are saved from death and destruction and who move into the presence of God. For example, the psalmist cries out, "O Lord, you have brought up my soul from Sheol; you restored me to life from among those who go down to the pit" (30:3). However, this is not merely a futuristic thing. The Prophets and Writings give examples of this conversion as a present day reality. The stories of Gentile strong women like Tamar, Rahab, Ruth, and the wife of Uriah the Hittite are examples of this. It is significant that the NT text begins with underlining the conversion of these strong women in Matt 1. It is as if these Gentile women are portrayed as models of NT conversion to Christ.

Another metaphor for conversion in the Hebrew Bible is that of return or repentance (*šûb*). Abram's restoration is depicted by the motif of repentance and restoration (Gen 20:7, 14). The motif of restoration is also the story of the other patriarchs (Gen 31:3, 13; 32:1, 7, 10, et al.). In Leviticus the theme of repentance is a return back to the original order of creation. It is return back from de-creation to re-creation (Lev 25). In Deuteronomic history repentance becomes the motif of the day of the blowing of the shofar and the year of the blowing of the shofar. In the Prophets and the Writings this motif is shown as being available not just to the covenant people but also to the Gentiles. This is the main thesis of the narrative of Jonah, which has become a text for Yom Kippur and Minchah, the afternoon service on the Day of Atonement. The reason Jonah became a Yom Kippur text has been debated by rabbis for a long time. What becomes clear is that Jonah is paradigmatic of the covenant community. He does not repent. Yet, the people of Nineveh repent when they hear and believe God (Jonah 3:5, 8, 9). Interestingly, all the Gentiles of

Nineveh, which includes all sections of society, repent and convert. This conversion is not just limited to all sections of Gentile society; it also includes the animal kingdom (Jonah 3:7–9). This aspect of conversion is seen in the call of Jonah to the Gentile community, "Forty days and Nineveh will be overturned"—converted from the inside out (3:4; cf. Pss 41:4; 66:6 et al.).

This is the kind of conversion which was not seen in the covenant community of Israel. The Gentile Ninevites become the Abrahamic conversion community while the covenant community of Israel is portrayed as the non-Abrahamic, non-conversion community.

Returning back to my original contention with Dearman's analysis of conversion in the OT, it seems clear to me in the light of the above brief analysis that individual conversion in the OT is paradigmatic of the corporate conversion. It seems to me that Western theologians have viewed conversion as a highly individual act. Therefore, as noted by Dearman, there is very sparse evidence of OT conversion stories. I would contend that the individual conversion stories of the kind I have outlined above are paradigmatic of corporate conversion. As an eastern OT reader I would contend that individual conversion and corporate conversion are inter-paradigmatic. The theology of conversion is therefore intrinsic to the theology of the Hebrew Bible.

In conclusion, another aspect of conversion deserves mention. Conversion in the Abrahamic narrative is always portrayed as a double conversion: when Abraham returns and converts, God also returns and converts. This is what happens when God fulfills his promise to give Isaac to Abraham and Sarah (Gen 18:1, 33, 10, 14). In the Jonah narrative God saw the conversion of all sections of society and the animal kingdom, and he also converted (Jonah 3:10). It seems clear that conversion in the Hebrew Bible is always a two way thing. The people—Jews and Gentiles—and creation are supposed to convert; in response God also converts. Unfortunately, Jonah, who is paradigmatic of the covenant community, sees this theology to be a very evil thing (Jonah 4:1). Sometimes I wonder if the Western church would see the conversion of world society and call it "evil"! The thesis of the book of Jonah seems to be just this: God converts when human beings, Jews or Gentiles, of all strata of society convert. This also results in environmental conversion. When this happens, there will be "the new heaven and the new earth" of Rev 21 and Isa 65, which Dearman calls an eschatological transformation.

THE CONVERSIONS OF SIMON PETER

Markus Bockmuehl

This article arises out of an ongoing attempt to produce a book about Simon Peter, written in a kind of "back-to-front" approach that orients its study from the perspective of Peter's living memory in the immediately following generations. I am interested in seeing how the canonical impress of that memory may be not merely (and unsurprisingly) distorted, but also illuminated by the ways in which Petrine memory developed in the East and the West over the first two Christian centuries.

I wish to offer a case study that applies features of this "back to front" Petrine memory to the exegesis of the New Testament, specifically in areas pertinent to conversion. In the larger study on Peter, I hope to illustrate how attention to such early Christian "anamnetic" reception enhances our understanding of the "historic" Peter, the narrated and remembered and emulated apostle whose complex life stands at the fountainhead of such richly variegated rivulets and streams of Petrine tradition. The text's "living footprint" may grant insights that remain inaccessible to the grammarian and archaeologist.

I take my point of departure from a puzzling lacuna in the development of a conversion theme as part of Peter's profile in Luke and Acts. From this we will attend to early Christian reflection on the surrounding gospel narratives (not just in Luke) to see how our New Testament author at this point in fact draws to his readers' attention a theme that is then filled in and illuminated by the wider context of Petrine memory.

For students of the life of St. Paul, the question of his "conversion" is of course a standard topic, indeed fundamental for any understanding of early Christianity. It has featured in hundreds of scholarly articles, books, and dissertations, and it has been the subject of countless student essays. It has long seemed a self-evidently appropriate chapter in a life of Paul, from whichever angle one approaches it—indeed it has often functioned as the paradigm for popular notions of Christian conversion more generally.

In this present study, however, I wish to consider instead the "conversion" not of Paul but of Peter, a topic that in modern criticism receives virtually no significant attention, even taking into account the much smaller body of literature on Petrine subjects. I know of no books on the subject, and at best a handful of articles.

Preliminaries

Given the prominence of the topic in Pauline study, a degree of methodological throat-clearing is inevitable—enough, at any rate, to see that the definition of "conversion" is itself so contested and problematic to suggest that we are well advised to begin not from a supposedly well-known conceptual definition but from the biblical texts. It is to the latter rather than the former task that the present study aims to make its main contribution.

Following the classic individualistic-psychological analyses of William James and Arthur Darby Nock who were in different ways indebted to the romantic tradition,[1] a generation ago the New Testament scholar Krister Stendahl famously pointed out the absence of conversion language from the Pauline and Lucan references to the apostle's Damascus road experience. This observation led Stendahl to lay stress on the language of "calling" rather than "conversion."[2] Stendahl was soon taken to task for a blunt and anachronistic view of "conversion" as a change from one "religion" (an equally modernist term) to another.[3] In furthering this critique, scholars increasingly placed emphasis on categories drawn from social-scientific studies of conversion. They preferred to speak in terms of an individual's "cognitive shift,"[4] a radically reconstructed identity,[5] a socially recognized transformation of the self in newly structured relationships,[6] or (in my view perhaps less plausibly) on

---

1. William James, *The Varieties of Religious Experience: A Study in Human Nature: Being the Gifford Lectures on Natural Religion Delivered at Edinburgh in 1901–1902* (New York: Longmans, Green, 1902); Arthur Darby Nock, *Conversion: The Old and the New in Religion from Alexander the Great to Augustine of Hippo* (Oxford: Clarendon, 1933).

2. Krister Stendahl, *Paul Among Jews and Gentiles, and Other Essays* (Philadelphia: Fortress, 1976), 7–8 and *passim*.

3. For the conceptual problems of the notion of "religion" see especially Nicholas Lash, *The Beginning and End of "Religion"* (Cambridge: Cambridge University Press, 1996).

4. Beverly Roberts Gaventa, *From Darkness to Light: Aspects of Conversion in the New Testament* (OBT 20; Philadelphia: Fortress, 1986).

5. Alan F. Segal, *Paul the Convert: The Apostolate and Apostasy of Saul the Pharisee* (New Haven, Conn.: Yale University Press, 1990), 29 and passim. See my remarks in Markus Bockmuehl, Review of Alan Segal, *Paul the Convert*, JTS 43 (1992): 191–96.

6. Stephen J. Chester, *Conversion at Corinth: Perspectives on Conversion in Paul's Theology and the Corinthian Church* (London: T. & T. Clark, 2003), 13, 41 and passim.

a change of patronage, clientele, and loyalty to a patron deity.[7] Others have argued that Paul's language seems to use precisely the language of "calling" to denote what popular convention might regard as "conversion."[8] Other, more communally constructed ideas of conversion are increasingly *de rigueur*,[9] and Lewis R. Rambo has influentially clarified the extent to which, phenomenologically, conversion is always in the eye of the individual as well as the communal beholder.[10]

At one level that seeming neglect of Peter's story of faith is of course entirely as we should expect. You might say that the surface reading of the New Testament narrative itself hardly makes a dramatic "conversion" narrative a promising line of inquiry! Peter is a Galilean fisherman, called to follow Jesus. His life story certainly features some significant bumps and scrapes, but no dramatic conversion. Peter remains in the Jesus movement until the death of the founder, escaping a sticky confrontation at the trial by the skin of his teeth. He is evidently restored to prominence after the resurrection, and he exercises a temporary role in the missionary leadership of the Jerusalem church before disappearing from view. Aside from this, the New Testament contains two letters attributed to Peter, and other epistles suggest a sometimes testy relationship with Paul. The early Christian tradition of Peter's death in Rome is not explicit in the New Testament, but has often been argued to be compatible and even implied in it.[11] None of this, however, requires or even suggests for Peter anything like a Pauline conversion, even if we were to construe that in terms of radical *social* rather than religious discontinuity.

Some might think that ought to be the end of the discussion. Here, however, I want to take a step back from social-scientific analysis, valuable though it has been in understanding the phenomenological dynamics of "conversion" in significant ways. For my present purposes a somewhat less meta-discursive approach may prove heuristically more effective. In keeping with the perspective of the texts' larger

---

7. Zeba A. Crook, *Reconceptualising Conversion: Patronage, Loyalty, and Conversion in the Religions of the Ancient Mediterranean* (Berlin: W. de Gruyter, 2004).

8. So esp. Chester, *Conversion at Corinth*, 153–59 (and cf. others cited at 154 n.17).

9. I wonder if I am wrong to think that collective or "tribal" patterns of conversion have received much less attention than they should. In relation to ancient cities like Edessa or even ancient nations like Armenia these social phenomena would hold considerable historical interest. Equally important later historical examples could be added—and many a chapter of contemporary Christian missiology in relation to strongly socialized people groups especially, perhaps, in the Islamic world.

10. Cf. Lewis R. Rambo, *Understanding Religious Conversion* (New Haven, Conn.: Yale University Press, 1993) and his contribution to this issue of *Ex Auditu*.

11. Cf. on this my further discussion in Markus Bockmuehl, "Peter's Death in Rome? Back to Front and Upside Down," *SJT* 60 (2007): 1–23.

footprint, I shall examine how the biblical and early Christian sources *themselves* describe Peter in the language of conversion or calling, of turning or repentance.

Peter's ministry is all the more striking when one considers the stark contrast to the presentation of Paul in the early church. Paul's "conversion" story of course is dramatic and even picturesque, which has encouraged considerable artistic and theological reflection. We might assume there is little to be said about Peter apart from his call narrative by the Sea of Galilee. What is interesting, however, is that the case of Peter does not lag behind in early Christian *art* and theology. As we shall see, Peter in fact appears quite characteristically and consistently in connection with narrative or artistic motifs of repentance and "conversion," so much so that he serves as a paradigm in his own right, not just once converted but repeatedly converting and repeatedly called.

Converting Simon? The Problem of Luke 22:31-32

To set the stage, we will start with a puzzle raised by a particular text in Luke 22. Following the Last Supper, Jesus bestows on the Twelve the kingdom he has received from his Father, and in which they will sit on thrones judging the Twelve tribes of Israel. He then turns to Peter with a saying that is unique to Luke (22:31-32):

> Simon, Simon, behold, Satan demanded to have you (*humas*, pl.), that he might sift [you] like wheat, but I have prayed for you (*peri sou*, sg.) that your faith may not fail. And when once you (*su*, sg.) have turned back, strengthen your brothers.

What might this mean? Scholarship has obviously had much to say about this logion, which is without parallel anywhere else in the gospel tradition.[12] Interpreters generally stress the contextual emphasis on the severity of the coming conflict with Satan, in which Simon Peter will be challenged to the utmost. And he will not be beyond error, which is why there is a reference to future turning.[13] ("When you have turned *again*," as several modern translations have it, is linguistically inap-

---

12. A whole book on this passage was published over forty years ago. See Benedetto Prete, *Il primato e la missione di Pietro: Studio esegetico-critico del testo di Lc. 22, 31-32* (Supplementi alla Rivista Biblica 3; Brescia: Paideia).

13. Source-critical commentaries also tend to worry about the extent to which the vague reference to "turning" may compensate for this tradition's lack of an explicit connection with the prediction of Peter's denial in v. 34. See the commentaries; also, e.g., Wolfgang Dietrich, *Das Petrusbild der lukanischen Schriften* (BWANT 94; Stuttgart: Kohlhammer, 1972), 121-22, 133 and n.238 for earlier, esp. German scholarship.

propriate: it might seem to imply a previous turning, which is without support in the Greek.)[14]

On balance the language here is pretty significantly Lucan, with characteristic choices of vocabulary and expression. And it is Luke's point that primarily concerns me here: only Luke among the Synoptic gospels leads his readers to expect such a *future* turning (although John offers an important analogy, as we shall see).

Luke is particularly fond of this verb *epistrephō*, "to turn" or perhaps "convert," accounting for fully half of its 36 New Testament uses (7 times in Luke, and 11 times in Acts, compared to just 3 times in all of Paul).[15] While it sometimes denotes a straightforward return to a point of origin,[16] early in this gospel we find the word *epistrephō* used twice in the transitive sense to denote a moral and spiritual re-orientation. John the Baptist's birth is heralded as the arrival of one who will "*turn* many of the children of Israel to the Lord their God," and more specifically "*turn* the hearts of the fathers to the children, and the disobedient to the wisdom of the just" (1:16–17). And that of course is what, according to all four gospels, John the Baptist in due course sets out to do. In that respect his role is characteristic of the Old Testament prophets, who are explicitly said to seek Israel's "turning" (*epistrephō*): "Yet he sent prophets among them to bring them back to the LORD. These testified against them, but they would not pay attention" (2 Chr 24:19 LXX).[17] The LXX also distinctively uses this verb to speak of Manasseh's repentance or "conversion."[18] Paul, in what is perhaps the classic New Testament definition of how *Gentiles* come to faith, describes how the Thessalonians *turned* (*epistrephō*) from the worship of idols in order to serve the true and living God (1 Thess 1:9–10).

---

14. Unless otherwise stated, all biblical quotations are from ESV. The final sentence of this quotation is adapted to avoid the erroneous translation "turned again."

15. The fullest study of *epistrephō* in Luke 22:32 remains Prete, *Il primate e la missione di Pietro*, 103-35; cf. Benedetto Prete, "Il senso di epistrepsas in Luca 22,32," *Atti della XIX Settimana Biblica* (1967): 113-35.

16. Luke 2:39; 8:55; 17:4 (though this might imply repentance), 31.

17. Similarly Neh 9:26; there are over 100 pertinent instances in the Latter Prophets. *Epistrephō* is also used of repentance or conversion more widely in the Former Prophets and Writings, as well as, e.g., in Sir 5:7; 17:25, 29; Jdt 5:19; Tob 13:6; 14:6–7 (of Gentile conversion). Unusually for the Pentateuch, Deuteronomy uses the word of "turning" to the Lord to obey his voice (4:30; 30:2, 10; cf. 4:39, 30:8). Such "conversion," however, can also be to other gods (Deut 31:18, 20) or else back to slavery in Egypt (Neh 9:17).

18. 2 Chr 33:19 LXX *pro tou epistrepsai* (before he repented).

In our present context, Luke's Jesus predicts that only Peter's "turning" will place him in a position to "strengthen" his fellow disciples.[19] But when, where, or how does that anticipated "turning" or "converting" (as the Vulgate calls it)[20] occur?

One surprising implication of Luke 22:31–32 is that even on the last night of Jesus' ministry the evangelist evidently regards Peter's "conversion" still to be *in the future* rather than the past. Peter is already a disciple, one of those who have "left everything" (5:11; cf. 18:28), "stood by Jesus in his trials," and will sit on thrones judging the Twelve Tribes of Israel (22:28–30); and even here he is said already to have faith (*pistis*), however challenged it may be. So why does he still need to "turn"? Certainly it is interesting that Luke's talk of turning or even repentance is at no previous point in this gospel associated with Peter.

The call narrative of Luke 5 is worth rehearsing briefly to illustrate this point. The Marcan and Matthean Peter is called to discipleship when he first encounters Jesus together with Andrew while they are standing in the shallow waters and fishing with cast-nets. No boat is mentioned; in fact outside Luke there is nothing to suggest that Peter owned or could afford a boat.[21] In Luke, by contrast, Jesus has already met Simon and in fact healed his mother-in-law (4:38–39); so this is no unheralded encounter. Peter is called to discipleship after being humbled by a miraculous catch of fish from his own boat. He leaves everything to become a fisher of people. But while this is clearly a dramatic and decisive call, Luke does not apply to it the language of "turning" or repentance that for him appears still to denote an action in the future in 22:31–32.

So where else might we find Peter's conversion? Strikingly, there is no reference in any of the gospels to Peter being baptized, either by Jesus or by John the Baptist (although matters may by implication be different for his brother Andrew, evidently the Baptist's disciple: John 1:35–40).[22] Even 1 Pet 3:21, which explicitly discusses baptism under a Petrine heading, does not speak of Peter's *own* experience of it:

---

19. A point rightly stressed by Dietrich, *Das Petrusbild der lukanischen Schriften*, 133–34.

20. *Et tu aliquando conversus* (And when once you have converted . . .)

21. Various patristic texts assert the poverty of Peter's background.

22. In the Fourth Gospel there is perhaps a sense that Peter has in fact been baptized and "cleansed': at the foot-washing Jesus tells Peter, "The one who has bathed (*leloumenos*) does not need to wash, except for his feet, but is completely clean. And you are clean, but not every one of you" (13:10). John 15:3, like other Johannine passages, may imply that in the Fourth Gospel the disciples have no need for the sacraments, including baptism, while Jesus is with them: "Already you are clean because of the word that I have spoken to you." No hint of Peter's repentance or conversion is, however, developed in these contexts.

"Baptism . . . now saves you, not as a removal of dirt from the body but as an appeal to God for a good conscience, through the resurrection of Jesus Christ."

Another possibility might be Peter's famous confession in Luke 9, which unlike the other two synoptic gospels Luke does *not* locate at Caesarea Philippi: when Jesus asks the disciples who the people say that he is, Peter replies, "The Christ of God" (9:18–20). Yet Luke's focus in this story is considerably less Petrine than in Matthew or Mark, and there is no hint of a "conversion experience."

The Transfiguration story a few verses later (9:28–36) may seem to have more potential, since Peter's misapprehensions about Jesus' meeting with Moses and Elijah are corrected and he obviously comes to a better understanding of Jesus' significance. More to the point, perhaps, 2 Pet 1 draws extensively on the Transfiguration to establish Peter's intimate connection with the revelation of the gospel in the person of Jesus.

Luke's narrative of Peter's denial might be a more obvious place to look. As in all four gospels, Peter denies Jesus until the rooster crows. As in Matthew, this causes him to flee the scene and weep bitterly (Luke 22:62, par. Matt 26:75). However, while this act of shame and remorse eloquently speaks of Peter's weakness and fallibility,[23] interestingly Luke nowhere describes it as repentance or "turning," even though v. 33 might lead us to expect that. In fact, given Luke's fondness for the "turning" terminology it is striking that in this context of denial the language of "turning" applies not to the apostle but only to "the Lord" (*kurios*), who hauntingly turns (*strapheis*) and looks straight at Peter, thereby convicting him without a word (22:61).[24]

No turning of Peter is reported in the remainder of the Gospel. He next appears on Easter Sunday, where as in the Fourth Gospel he is seen running to see the empty tomb before going home (Luke 24:12; cf. John 20:6, 10). It is this same Simon to whom the risen Lord is later said to have appeared (24:34), although that appearance itself of course is *not* actually narrated in Luke. Luke 22:31–32, in other words, leads us to expect an event that is then never explicitly related in the gospel.

In Acts Peter, like Paul, preaches "conversion" in the language of Luke 22:32, but now he seems in fact to be "strengthening his brothers" from the start, beginning

---

23. Cf. already Ambrose on Luke 10:52: "We can imitate the Lord but not equal him, not even Peter. I do not criticize Peter's denial, but I praise his weeping." Ambrose of Milan, *Exposition of the Holy Gospel according to Saint Luke; With Fragments on the Prophecy of Isaias* (trans. Theodosia Tomkinson; Etna, Calif.: Center for Traditionalist Orthodox Studies, 1998), 405 quoted in Arthur A. Just, *Luke* (ACCS, NT 3; Downer's Grove, Ill.: InterVarsity, 2003), 337.

24. For the rich Lucan texture of *kurios* language see esp. Kavin C. Rowe, "Luke and the Trinity: An Essay in Ecclesial Biblical Theology," *SJT* 56 (2003): 1–26; Kavin Rowe, *Early Narrative Christology: The Lord in the Gospel of Luke* (Berlin: W de Gruyter), 2006.

arguably before Pentecost, with Acts 1:15–26—and thus apparently he is presented as having "turned" *already*. Significantly for our purposes, the same word *epistrephō* is repeatedly used in the apostolic preaching to call *Peter's audience* to repentance and conversion.[25] In response to his sermon at Pentecost the audience is "cut to the heart" and moved to action (Acts 2:37). The final paragraph of Peter's sermon in Solomon's Portico exhorts his audience to "repent therefore and turn (*metanoēsate oun kai epistrepsate*), that your sins may be blotted out" (3:19), closing with the assurance that God raised his Son and sent him "to bless you by turning (*apostrephein*) every one of you from your wickedness" (3:26). Residents of Lydda "turn to the Lord" in response to Peter's preaching (9:35) as do those of Antioch in response to Jerusalem's scattered Hellenistic believers (11:21); indeed the eschatological phenomenon of Gentiles "turning to God" is at the heart of the Jerusalem Council's agenda (15:19).

This preaching of conversion is equally prominent in the Pauline mission, as is "strengthening" the fledgling believers.[26] Preaching to Gentiles at Lystra, Paul and Barnabas employ an evangelistic appeal strikingly reminiscent of the classic Pauline conversion text in 1 Thess 1:9: the gospel is "that you should turn from these vain things to a living God who made the heaven and the earth and the sea and all that is in them" (14:15).[27] In his defence before King Agrippa, Paul describes his mission as being sent to the Gentiles "to open their eyes, so that they may turn (*epistrepsai*) from darkness to light and from the power of Satan to God" (26:18 cf. 26:20). In an echo of Mark 4:12 (where the verb also occurs), Paul's final warning to the Jewish community at Rome also cites Isa 6:9–10 using the same word *epistrephō* of the possibility of Jewish repentance (28:27).

But where does Peter himself "convert" or "turn" in the sense that Luke 22:32 leads us to expect? In seeking evidence of Peter's "conversion" in Acts, one might perhaps think of his vision at Joppa before the visit to the house of Cornelius in Acts 10. Indeed, Acts 10 is emphatically affirmed as "Peter's conversion" by a leading scholar like James D. G. Dunn, for example.[28] It is culturally fashionable to imagine Peter in this chapter undergoing a kind of 'taboo-toppling' fundamental religious

---

25. The only examples of more straightforward spatial usage are at 9:40; 15:36; 16:18.

26. See *epistērizō* in Acts 14:22; 15:32, 41; 18:23.

27. Acts 14:15, "turn (*epistrephein*) from these worthless things to the living God," cf. 1 Thess 1:9, "you turned (*epestrepsate*) to God from idols to serve the true and living God."

28. Most insistently James D.G. Dunn, *Beginning From Jerusalem* (Christianity in the Making 2; Grand Rapids: Eerdmans, 2009), 394–96. Cf., e.g., Ettore Malnati, *"Simone detto Pietro," nella singolarità del suo ministero* (Pro Manuscripto 13; Lugano: EU Press FTL, 2008), 55.

shift or conversion away from the practice of the law.[29] The text itself, by contrast, describes a vision whose *only* explicit interpretation is that Peter should not call any fellow *human being* common or unclean (10:28). In particular, it is certainly *not* the case that Peter or for that matter Luke concludes from the vision, either here or in subsequent references to it, that this was the formal "abolition" of all laws of purity or that Peter should now "eat unclean meat with a clear conscience."[30] The change is a gain in *understanding* about Gentiles: "God has shown me that I should not call any person common or unclean" (10:28); "now I truly understand" (10:34 *ep' alētheias katalambanomai*; cf. 11:12; 15:9). The language of turning and repentance is indeed applied to this narrative; it pertains, however, not to Peter but only to Cornelius and his household: it is they who receive the Spirit, and they who are baptized. More specifically, at Peter's rehearsal of his experience in Jerusalem the believers there quite clearly conclude from his report that "*to the Gentiles* God has granted the repentance (*metanoian*) that leads to life" (11:18). Similarly, Peter himself identifies the upshot of his vision to be that God makes no distinction between Jews and Gentiles in the gift of his Spirit, but cleanses the Gentiles' hearts by faith (15:9-11); for this reason *they* (not "we") should be seen as under no obligation to the law. James too recognizes the issue raised by Acts 10 to be the "turning" of *Gentiles*, rather than of Peter (*epistrephousin*, 15:19).

At the end of this short excursion through Luke and Acts, then, we return without obvious answers to the question I posed at the outset of this section: given that after the Last Supper the Lucan Jesus evidently looks *forward* to Peter's "conversion" as something in the future, where might Luke consider this to have taken place?

---

29. Thus explicitly in a popular account Charles Edward van Engen, "Peter's Conversion: A Culinary Disaster Launches the Gentile Mission: Acts 10:1—11:18," in *Mission in Acts: Ancient Narratives in Contemporary Context* (ed. R.L. Gallagher and P. Hertig; Maryknoll, N.Y.: Orbis, 2004), 133–43; note esp. 141–42 n. 3.

30. Thus explicitly Dunn, *Beginning from Jerusalem*, 395, 394. His somewhat offhand dismissal (395 n.75) of careful (if admittedly tentative) arguments like that of Clinton E. Wahlen, "Peter's Vision and Conflicting Definitions of Purity," *NTS* 51 (2005): 505–18 by appealing to the supposed (italicized!) "therefore" in Lev 20:25 collapses in the absence of any such "therefore" in all known ancient Hebrew, Greek, Aramaic, or Latin versions of that passage: contrast more accurately NJB. Read contextually, Lev 20:22–26 asserts that Israel's distinction between clean and unclean animals symbolizes its separation from the abhorrent practices of the nations (v. 23).

Three Clues: Hagiographical, Allegorical, Exegetical

It seems clear that while Luke deliberately raises that question, he does not really provide an unambiguous answer. He is thereby implicitly encouraging his readers to supply the conclusion, quite possibly because (as elsewhere) they already know things about Peter that are not explicitly related in Luke or Acts. Among these aspects may be above all the question of what happened to the apostle after his disappearance "to another place" (Acts 12:17)—perhaps paralleling what happened to Paul after the end of Acts. To help explore this question further, therefore, I propose to draw on the early footprint of this text in the first two or three centuries of Christian reflection and appropriation. The key principle here is simple but important for this project: *if Luke is tacitly inviting his readers to reach certain conclusions, one of our best available exegetical guides may be to consult the conclusions the earliest readers did in fact reach.* So the procedure I adopt here is to take three snapshots of the imprint left by our text on early Christian reception, moving in reverse chronological order from third- and fourth-century visual interpretations to second- and then first-century texts.

We shall see that a range of early Christian sources show the answer to our question to be intimately linked both with Peter's experience during the passion and resurrection of Jesus, and with certain patterns of his own subsequent mission and martyrdom. In this way the effective history of Luke 22 will be seen to shed light on its meaning.

The Cock's Crow in Christian Art

One of the most striking phenomena in the early effective history of our text is the appearance in the third century of artistic representations featuring Christ facing Peter in highly symbolic poses that reflect but often heighten the themes of the biblical narrative. The earliest of these representations are early third-century wall frescoes, beginning around A.D. 230 at the simple Christian chapel in the cosmopolitan Hellenistic city of Dura Europos on the upper Euphrates, in Syria. In addition to other paintings including the Good Shepherd and the healing of the paralytic, we find the first known visual depiction of Christ and St. Peter. More directly relevant for our purposes is a large third- and fourth-century group of images on catacombs and other wall frescoes, ivories, and especially sarcophagi that depict Peter and Christ together with a cock—sometimes on the ground, sometimes on top of a pillar, but always prominently positioned and clearly of enormous iconographic significance.

A 1984 dissertation at the University of Utrecht produced a catalogue of well over 120 such items,[31] including several particularly attractive and telling examples.[32]

St. Peter's Denial

Catacomb of St. Commodilla

Catacomb of St. Cyriaca

31. Paulus Gijsbertus Johannes Post, "De haanscène in de vroeg-christlijke kunst: een iconografische en iconologische analyse = La scène du coq dans l'art paléochrétien: une analyse iconographique et iconologique" (DD Diss., Schrijen-Lippertz/Katholieke Theologische Hogeschool Utrecht, 1984), 24–42.

32. Particularly clear examples are found at nos. 23 (Sarcophagus Lat 174), 30 (Dellys sarcophagus), 32 (wooden panel on the door of Santa Sabina), 33 (miniature panel from the 5th c., Maskell Ivories, London British Museum). Catacomb frescoes include especially no. 35 (St. Cyriaca, arcosolium; cf. Josef Wilpert, *Roma sotteranea: Le pitture delle Catacombe* (Rome: Desclée, 1903), 2.242), which is depicted above. The other illustration is the arcosolium from the Catacomb of St. Commodilla, which appears here by kind permission of the Pontificia Commissione di Archeologia Sacra.

Much discussion has swirled around these fascinating images, and here I have neither leisure nor expertise to offer a detailed art-historical account.[33] What we can do here is simply to interrogate this evidently influential and important motif for its *exegetical* significance. As is the case for the "labelled" saints in classic orthodox icons, the image invites the viewer to participate in the reality identified in the word, while the word makes unambiguous the signification of the image.

In this case, the visual image encapsulates the narrative of the trial scene—not, to be sure, exclusively in its Lucan form, but perhaps in a more synthetic canonical outline. Arguably, however, that canonical shape nevertheless encompasses Lucan features such as the challenge of Peter's repentance and the Lord's turning to look at Peter (22:61; cf. above n.23).

The chief point to notice is fairly simple: a surface reading might incline the viewer to see in these depictions primarily the prediction of Peter's denial together with a hint of its fulfilment, or perhaps—in its Lucan version of Jesus looking at Peter—a narrative encapsulation of the denial itself, culminating in the cock's crow.[34] In that sense we would not need to find much of either "conversion" or "calling." If that self-contained vignette were all that is meant, however, it would not explain the frequency with which this motif occurs, nor the graphic prominence and position regularly assigned to the cock: he is displayed larger than life, almost turkey-sized, on top of a pillar, or with a finger pointing at him. What is going on here must be more than merely narrative representation. We are meant to appreciate the deeper significance of this animal. Iconographic studies have not been slow to point out where this significance lies: whereas in pagan art the cock tends to symbolize light, victory and sometimes immortality, Christians unsurprisingly tend to link this with the theme of Christ's resurrection.[35] Most influentially, perhaps, this comes to powerful expression in the fourth-century hymnody of Ambrose (*Aeterne rerum conditor*) and Prudentius (*Ales diei nuntius*). Ambrose memorably celebrates the "herald of the day" whose voice restores health, hope, and faith, and at whose crowing the very Rock of the Church himself washed away his guilt: as Jesus turns to look at us

---

33. See the full discussion in Post, "De haanscène in de vroeg-christlijke kunst = La scène du coq dans l'art paléochrétien; also P. C. J. Van Dael, review of Post, *VC* 45 (1991), 96–101 and previously Sv. Aage Bay, "Die Hahnszene der Sarkophage," *ST* 35 (1981): 107–35.

34. Somewhat as envisaged by Josef Wilpert, *Roma sotterranea*, 1.329–31.

35. This is all the more significant in view of the fact that the "scene of the cock" (*scène du coq/Hahnszene*) is itself a Christian innovation without iconographical precedent, as Bay, "Die Hahnszene der Sarkophage," 112 also notes.

at cock's crow, our sins leave us and our guilt is washed away in tears.[36] Prudentius, from whom we get some familiar hymns like "Of the Father's love begotten," similarly develops the theme of the cock as symbolizing redemption and new life.

While the precise nuance of this artistic motif may be open to a range of interpretations (e.g., whether it involves elements of a theophanic encounter with the risen Christ or not),[37] it is clear that for a third- or fourth-century context the themes of denial, remorse and repentance, resurrection and renewal are all prominently encapsulated here—heightened, no doubt, by the readmission of penitent believers who had lapsed under the duress of persecutions from Decius to Diocletian.[38] The moment of Peter's threefold denial is read here, in a fashion telescoping Luke 22 together with an anticipation of his threefold restoration in John 21, as the single point of his repentance and the promise of his rebirth to new life in Christ. The point of Peter's fall and remorse becomes here (unlike for Judas) the point of Peter's conversion: the cock's crow projects into the dark night of Maundy Thursday the bright daylight of Easter Sunday renewal.

Conversion and Subversion in the Acts of Peter

A lot more could no doubt be said about this popular third- and fourth-century artistic theme. In the third section of this study, I now want to turn the clock back to a *literary* sort of vignette in the latter half of the second century: the *Acts of Peter*. Critical problems abound in any serious discussion of this puzzling, not to say infuriating, document that mixes an ounce or less of collective memory with many a pound of wild fancy. The conventional date for the composition of the Petrine *Acts* has been around A.D. 190, and I continue to think that most likely. It is true that a recent monograph argues firmly for a date of the so-called Vercelli manuscript in the fourth century,[39] but this may be indicative more of the editorial state of that particular manuscript than of the stage at which the core narrative outline begins to take shape. For example, another recent study appears to document a partly al-

---

36. See online text and translation at http://medieval.ucdavis.edu/20A/Music.html (accessed June 19, 2009). Prudentius' text with translation by J.M. Neale is at http://www.preces-latinae.org/thesaurus/Hymni/AlesDiei.html (accessed June 19, 2009).

37. See, e.g., Van Dael, review of Post, 98 *contra* Post, "De haanscène in de vroeg-christlijke kunst = La scène du coq dans l'art paléochrétien," 164.

38. Cf. Bay, "Die Hahnszene der Sarkophage," 119–21.

39. Matthew C. Baldwin, *Whose Acts of Peter? Text and Historical Context of the Actus Vercellenses* (WUNT 2:196; Tübingen: Mohr Siebeck, 2005)

ternative textual tradition in a previously unknown manuscript.[40] Given the signs of familiarity with that outline in late second-century documents like the *Acts of Paul* and the *Acts of Andrew*, it remains in my view reasonable to suppose that the story of Peter's upside-down crucifixion at the hands of Nero was known in Rome no later than the mid-second century, apparently along with diversely articulated convictions about preceding conflicts with the enemies of the church that were personified at least symbolically in Simon Magus, the arch-fiend and anti-Christ of Acts 8.

However one decides to place it, the *Acts of Peter* remains a complex and confusing document. What matters here is that conversion is an intriguingly important theme from the start—highlighted in Paul's preaching (1:2) as much as in Peter's attempts to win the church of Rome back from its beguilement by Simon Magus. Early on, Peter acknowledges his denial of Jesus "not once only, but three times"—a fall that he attributes to the subverting work of Satan by means of the "wicked dogs" of Ps 22:17, and which he uses as an incentive to encourage his audience to "change your hearts" and be strong in "the Father of our Lord Jesus Christ" (3:7). Over the subsequent chapters a series of paradoxical and exotic miracles ensue in Peter's contest with Simon Magus, including such party pieces as a talking dog, a swimming smoked mackerel, the killing of a boy by Simon's word and his resuscitation by that of Peter, a flying contest, and a good deal else. Finally a plot on Peter's life is revealed and the fellow believers urge him to leave the city. Peter at first rejects this suggestion, saying, "Shall we act like deserters, brothers?" (35:6), as if reflecting on what the disciples did when Jesus was arrested. Famously, he then agrees to his friends' request and leaves the city in disguise. As he leaves the gate he sees Jesus entering Rome and greets him with the words, "Lord, where are you going?" (That at least is the more famous version of the Vercelli MS; another and perhaps more original version has "Lord, why have you come?" or "why are you here?").[41] Jesus replies, "I am coming to Rome to be crucified." Peter asks him, "Lord, are you being crucified again?" And Jesus answers, "Yes Peter, I am being crucified again." Coming to himself, Peter sees the Lord ascending into heaven, but he himself turns back (*hupestrepsen*) to the

---

40. Otto Zwierlein, *Petrus in Rom: Die literarischen Zeugnisse. Mit einer kritischen Edition der Martyrien des Petrus und Paulus auf neuer handschriftlicher Grundlage* (Untersuchungen zur antiken Literatur und Geschichte 96; Berlin: W. de Gruyter, 2009). For an older critical edition of the *Acts*, see Léon Vouaux, ed., *Les actes de Pierre: introduction, textes, traduction et commentaire* (Paris: Letouzey et Ané, 1922).

41. See Zwierlein, *Petrus in Rom*, 82–92 and *passim*, noting additional internal support for this reading in the wording of Jesus' reply in the MS and in Origen.

city to face his fate (35:6),⁴² which turns out to be a crucifixion that is carried out upside down at his own request (37:8—38:9). The symbolism of this upside-down crucifixion is clearly vital to the author, as the dying Peter delivers a long speech on this subject from his cross: he explains that the manner of his crucifixion expresses sinful Adam and the new Adam's subversion of all secular human values,⁴³ to which the hearers' response must be to "leave your former error and turn back" to the cross of Christ (38:9).⁴⁴ The nail in the middle of the cross symbolizes the point of man's conversion (*epistrophē*) and repentance (*metanoia*).

The *Acts of Peter*, in other words, bring together Peter's evangelistic and apologetic preaching with the theme of repentance and conversion in his own life. Early on, this theme features briefly and in passing in relation to the gospel narrative of Peter's denial of Jesus and subsequent remorse. It is then developed rather more emphatically in relation to Peter's own martyrdom as the antithesis and redemption of that earlier episode. Where once he denied and then deserted in remorse when the Lord turned to look at him, so now he flees but turns back when he meets Christ in order to share his fate, just as Jesus predicted in John 13:36 and 21:18–19. He is presented as the converted apostle, the one who turns and is faithful the second time round, the one who shares his master's fate upside down, the one for whom the cross is the crown and quintessence of conversion from the powers of the world to the God and Father of Jesus Christ. Where he fails miserably before the resurrection to keep his promise to Jesus, after the resurrection he becomes faithful to the end.

The New Testament's Born-Again Peter

In light of these second- and third-century illustrations it now makes sense to open our eyes to other New Testament passages that may help shed light on the incomplete Lucan talk of Peter's conversion. Two such texts are particularly relevant in confirming the understanding of a Petrine conversion as linked to the cross and resurrection.

---

42. *Kai elthōn eis heauton ho Petros kai theasamenos ton kurion eis ouranon anelthonta, hupestrepsen eis tēn Rōmēn agalliōmenos kai doxazōn ton kurion, hoti autos eipen, Stauroumai, hoeis ton Petron ēmellen ginesthai.*

43. A point also developed in interesting political and culture-critical terms by János Bolyki, "'Head Downwards': The Cross of Peter in the Lights [sic] of the Apocryphal Acts, of the New Testament and of the Society-Transforming Claim of Early Christianity," in *The Apocryphal Acts of Peter: Magic, Miracles and Gnosticism* (ed. J. N. Bremmer; Studies on the Apocryphal Acts of the Apostles; Leuven: Peeters), 3:111–22.

44. *Lēxantes tēs prōtēs planēs epanadramein opheilete.*

1 PETER 1

This is hinted at, first, in the opening verses of 1 Peter: the otherwise Pauline-sounding[45] opening benediction of "the God and Father of our Lord Jesus Christ" is here grounded specifically in the fact that "by his great mercy he has given us a new birth into a living hope through the resurrection of Jesus Christ from the dead." The unusual maternal language of "giving renewed birth" (*anagennaō*) occurs in biblical Greek only here and at v. 23, where it similarly contrasts the readers' pre-Christian life with their imperishable new life in the gospel. This "new birth" is evidently a matter of moral and spiritual transformation, as the author reflects that the readers have "purified your souls by your obedience to the truth so that you have genuine mutual love" (v. 22). The use of the first person plural implies that in 1:3 the Petrine author includes himself in the moral and spiritual "new birth into a living hope" that God has granted through the passion (vv. 2, 11, 19) and resurrection of Jesus Christ. Such renewal in obedience and love, then, is at its root not a matter of human agency but of the divine gift of new life in Christ's death and resurrection. Read in the context of chapter 1, Peter is presented as having experienced through the passion and resurrection of Christ both penitent turning from false hopes and rebirth to a true hope and obedient love. In some respects, therefore, 1 Peter parallels Luke's move from Peter's predicted "turning" and denial (Luke 22:31-34) via the Emmaus disciples' dashed hopes (24:21) to the risen Lord's appearance to them and to Simon (24:34)—culminating in their imminent "clothing with power" in the Spirit (24:49).[46]

JOHN 21

Our second text is presented as the final resurrection appearance in John's gospel, which serves as an extended meditation on the post-resurrection apostolic commission of Peter and the Beloved Disciple. (It may or may not be relevant for our discussion that commentators have sometimes noted links between the Lucan and Johannine passion narratives, and echoes of John 21:2-14 in Luke's otherwise unique alternative Petrine call narrative of Luke 5:1-11). At the opening of the chap-

---

45. E.g. 2 Cor 1:3; Eph 1:3, cf. Rom 15:6; 2 Thess 1:1; Eph 1:17.

46. A little later in the letter, the Petrine author specifically identifies *baptism* as of saving significance and spiritual purification of the resurrection of Christ (3:21)—though on this occasion, the application is in the second person plural and does not include himself.

ter Simon Peter appears as yet somewhat "unrenewed": he instigates the decision to go fishing, even if there is perhaps no decision here to return to his former life.

What follows is a story with elements reminiscent of the miraculous catch of fish in Luke 5. Jesus, who is here on the shore (rather than in the boat), instructs Peter after a night's unproductive fishing to cast the net on the other side. The disciples immediately enclose a great quantity of fish: for John, "153" fish that cannot be hauled in but must be dragged to shore (21:6, 8, 11). Here I think it is not crucial to decide if there may be an oral link or shared tradition between Luke and John at this point. But it is perhaps significant that both John's and Luke's version culminate in a contrite fisherman by the Sea of Galilee being called to follow his Lord.

In John, this unique commission of Peter appears here for the first time. He is newly appointed (not "restored"!) to a pastoral role by his threefold declaration of love, corresponding to the gravity of his threefold denial. This of course has long been a favorite topic of preachers and exegetes. And the link between the two scenes seems strikingly underscored even by the intriguing detail that the Greek word *anthrakia* used for the warming coal fire in high priest's courtyard (18:18) recurs only once more in the entire OT or NT—namely to denote Jesus' coal fire by the sea of Galilee (21:9).[47] Having thrice denied and thrice "turned" from that denial, Peter is ready to share his master's task and his master's fate. He is appointed as undershepherd, assigned to share his master's work of "strengthening" and "pastoring" his fellow believers, and predicted like Jesus to lay down his life for the flock on a cross (21:19, 22; cf. 13:36–37 with 10:11). In other words, the death and resurrection of Christ have become for Peter the point of his conversion from denial to love, and to an apostolic office incorporated into Christ's own.

It is worth noting a valid exegetical insight in traditional Roman Catholic talk of Peter as in some sense the "Vicar of Christ" (*vicarius Christi*, i.e., his representative), in that the task and path of the earthly Christ is indeed now entrusted to the earthly Peter to carry on.[48]

---

47. The term *anthrakia* does, however, appear in a similar sense at Sir 11:32 and 4 Macc 9:20.

48. A similar point could be asserted in relation to Matt 16:16–18, as Hans Ludwig Windisch, *Paulus und Christus: Ein biblisch-religionsgeschichtlicher Vergleich* (Untersuchungen zum Neuen Testament 24; Leipzig: Hinrichs, 1934), 13–14 rightly noted (I owe this reference to Jane Heath). N.B. Tertullian still used the phrase *vicarius Christi* of the Holy Spirit: *Praescr.* 28 (*Christi vicarius*, PL 2.40b); *Virg.* 1 (*ab illo vicario Domini*, PL 2.889b). (This is of course an entirely separate question from that of whether specifically the Bishop of Rome should rightly be regarded as inheriting that role, as has been claimed controversially since the sixth century. That question depends largely on whether one regards Peter's role somehow uniquely vested in the Roman Episcopal succession, a point strongly contested in antiquity by Origen, Cyprian and others; and furthermore, to what extent a "vicar of Peter" can really be said

The idea that the narrative of John 21 captures what Luke's Jesus predicts as Peter's "conversion" is not of course a new insight. The fourth-century commentator Apollinaris of Laodicea cites precisely Luke 22:31 in this connection, to indicate that just as Jesus is inviting Peter to reciprocate his teacher and Saviour's unwavering love for him, so also Peter should imitate Christ's care for him by strengthening his brethren and shepherding his sheep. The three affirmations of love match the three denials.[49]

One final point is worth noting. While critical scholarship has tended to suspect in such links between the Lukan and the Johannine passion narratives signs of a *compositional* connection, the example of Apollinaris also bears witness to the synthetic, *canonical* coherence of Petrine memory.

Conclusion

I began with the observation that the theme of Peter's conversion or repentance has been remarkably underplayed in scholarship, even if we allow for Paul's historically greater influence and biographically more dramatic change of direction. In both cases, prevaricating talk of the importance of "calling" rather than "conversion" may obscure rather than enlighten the key issue. We found in Luke 22:31–34 the evangelist's surprisingly clear anticipation that at some point, not in his Galilean past but in his apostolic and episcopal future, Peter would indeed "turn back" and, as a result of this "conversion," assume a charge of strengthening his brothers. Ironically, however, Luke never explicitly identifies that anticipated point of conversion either in the gospel or in Acts; and texts like Acts 10 that are sometimes cited in fact fall considerably short of any language of Peter's "conversion" or repentance.

Taking our cue from the early effective history of this text, therefore, we noted the great artistic importance of the cock's crow motif for Peter's conversion as closely identified with Christ's death and resurrection, and we found the motif of the apostle's own subsequent conformity with his Lord's passion powerfully refracted in the narrative context of the so-called "Quo Vadis" episode in the *Acts of Peter*. Returning to the New Testament, we were able to identify in 1 Peter 1 and John 21 traces of this same understanding of the conversion of Peter as focused in his own rebirth to new life in the resurrection of Jesus. From that perspective, perhaps the closest

---

to be "vicar of Christ" in substantially the same sense.)

49. Apollinaris, *Frag. In Joh.* 155 (John 21.15–17) in *Johannes-Kommentare aus der griechischen Kirche* (ed. Joseph Reuss; Texte und Untersuchungen zur Geschichte der altchristlichen Literatur 5 Reihe Bd. 34; Berlin: Akademie-Verlag, 1966).

Luke comes to filling his own silence on this matter is in the unnarrated resurrection appearance at 24:34: "The Lord is risen, and has appeared (*ōphthē*) to Simon." It is Jesus' looking at Peter (22:61) that convicts Peter of his guilt, and Peter's "rising" (*anastas,* 24:12!) to run to the tomb and above all his "seeing" of Jesus (24:34) that marks his turn from darkness to light. The cock symbolizes the entire narrative, declaring the end of night and heralding the beginning of dawn.

Simon Peter, then, was seen as the follower of Jesus as a Galilean fisherman who was transformed—"converted"—from denial and despair to a confessing hope. As a result he received a unique ministry of pastoral strengthening that allowed him to serve the servants of Christ as a representative of Jesus' continued ministry on earth. In his preaching as well as in his very biography, the remembered Peter became a man of conversions, a "converting" disciple whose faith begins in Galilee but grows in "convertedness." In early Christian memory Simon Peter embodies, for individual discipleship as much as for the church, what it means to turn—from denial to faith, from despair to hope, and from deserting Christ to shepherding his flock.

RESPONSE TO BOCKMUEHL

Michael J. Gorman

Markus Bockmuehl has provided us with a very fascinating approach to a very much neglected subject: the conversion(s) of Simon Peter. He offers it as a "case study" in what he calls a "back to front" approach: using the early "effective history" of a text—its impact on Christian perception and memory—to help us interpret a topic or text, in this case one with an apparently insoluble exegetical puzzle. When and also how was Peter converted? More specifically, when was Luke 22:31–32, Jesus' prophecy of Peter's failure and return (turning, *epistrephō*), fulfilled? Bockmuehl argues that early Christian art and texts point to Peter's encounter with the resurrected Jesus as his conversion. He also contends that early Christian art and theology portray Peter as "an apostle of conversion, not just one converted but repeatedly converting and repeatedly called."

This brief response is divided into four interrelated areas: (1) definition and methodology; (2) identifying Peter's conversions; (3) similarities and differences between the conversions of Peter and Paul; and (4) reflections on the ongoing meanings of conversion in light of all this.

Definition and Methodology

Two main points need to be made with respect to definition and methodology. First, early in the paper Bockmuehl suggests, for his purposes, that we move beyond both "individualistic-psychological" and "social-scientific" approaches to conversion to look at the actual early Christian language of "conversion or calling, of turning or repentance." This move may be fine in principle, but I am not sure that the resulting strategy of first looking for another occurrence of *epistrephō* associated with Peter in Luke-Acts is a good way to begin. For one thing, it forces Bockmuehl to deny that Peter's call was a conversion, at least not for Luke, and to deny that another major transformation of Peter—the vision at Joppa—was not a conversion, only a "gain in understanding."

It is interesting to contrast the position of Bockmuehl with that of James Dunn in his new book *Beginning from Jerusalem*, in which he calls Acts 10:1–11:18, in part, the account of Peter's "conversion."[1] Dunn writes:

> The revelation which Peter receives and the new conviction which comes to him were neither so dramatic nor so traumatic as in the case of Saul (ch. 9). But it was every bit as much a conversion as in Saul's case—a conversion from traditional and deeply rooted convictions which, according to Luke's telling, had completely governed his life till that moment (10:14–15, 28).... The fact that it took the further event of the Spirit's coming upon Cornelius in such an unexpected, unprecedented way to complete Peter's conversion indicates Luke's appreciation of just how major a transformation had taken place in Peter and how epochal a step was being taken by the new movement.[2]

Similar to Dunn's view are those of three well-known authors on conversion in the New Testament, Beverly Gaventa, who says that there was a more "wrenching change" to Peter et al. than to Cornelius; Ronald Witherup, who writes of the "double conversion" in the Acts narrative; and Scot McKnight, who argues that the Joppa experience was part of Peter's "process" of conversion.[3]

Bockmuehl's fixation on *epistrephō*, and the consequences of that methodological move, seem especially ironic because he wants to argue—and in fact concludes the paper by saying—that Peter's conversion was in fact multiform, even plural: "In his preaching as well as in his very biography, he [Peter] became a man of conversions, a 'converting' disciple whose faith begins in Galilee but grows in 'convertedness.'"[4] If we posit the presence of *epistrephō*, and/or a form of the words "repent/repentance," as the requirement for identifying a conversion, whether generally or with respect to Luke, then our ability to describe and define conversion is greatly constrained and in fact distorted. Indeed, based on those criteria, not even Zacchaeus, arguably one

---

1. James D. G. Dunn, *Beginning from Jerusalem* (Christianity in the Making, vol. 2; Grand Rapids: Eerdmans, 2009), 389–96.

2. *Beginning from Jerusalem*, 389–90.

3. Beverly Roberts Gaventa, *From Darkness to Light: Aspects of Conversion in the New Testament* (OBT 20; Philadelphia: Fortress, 1986), 109; Ronald D. Witherup, *Conversion in the New Testament* (Collegeville, Minn.: Liturgical, 1994), 70; Scot McKnight, *Turning to Jesus: The Sociology of Conversion in the Gospels* (Louisville: Westminster John Knox, 2002), 172. Interestingly, these three authors are mainline Protestant, Roman Catholic, and evangelical Protestant, respectively.

4. In discussion, Bockmuehl balked at my use of this term to characterize his pursuit of occurrences of the verb *epistrephō*. While I do not think the word mischaracterizes his paper, I would be willing to substitute "strong interest."

of the most converted figures in the Gospel of Luke (Luke 19:1–10), was not converted.[5] It seems to me that the term "conversion" needs to be defined, not primarily in terms of vocabulary used to describe an experience, but in terms of the correspondence between an experience and a theological understanding of conversion/transformation gained from the texts yet not dependent solely, or even primarily, on one or two lexical items.

Second, Bockmuehl wisely asks us as theological interpreters to takes seriously the various strands of early Christian memory that implicitly suggest that Peter's conversion occurs in his encounter with the risen Lord, especially as narrated in John 21. His argument, in a nutshell, is that all roads lead to resurrection, or perhaps better said, to death and resurrection. Although I think he is right, I wonder two things. First, does this confluence of interpretive strands tell us anything at all about what Jesus in Luke (or Luke) wanted us to understand? A very brief reference in Luke to Jesus' appearance to Peter (Luke 24:34)—without any language of conversion—may not suffice. Second, is such a definition of conversion—from death to resurrection—so generically Christian that *any* account of Christian transformation could be seen as Petrine and vice versa? Perhaps the first question will not matter to many people, though I myself am not prepared to discard it. As for the second question, it makes Bockmuehl's phrase "In some respects . . . 1 Peter parallels Luke's move from Peter's predicted 'turning' and denial," seem undeniably true, but not necessarily directly relevant. *Any* change in Peter, or in anyone else who is or becomes a Christian, is going to be narrated by Christians in their language and thus something like this.

Identifying Peter's Conversions

I have already raised the issue of identifying Peter's conversions, or points of transformation, or whatever we wish to call them. But now I wish to extend our memory of the memory of Peter in early Christian literature to include the writings of Paul, and specifically Galatians, which Bockmuehl does not discuss. Here we have the memory, not merely of a "testy" relationship between Paul and Peter, but also, from Paul's perspective, of another kind of conversion, a change in the wrong direction, an anti-conversion, or "backsliding." Here is Paul's memory:

> [11]But when Cephas came to Antioch, I opposed him to his face, because he stood self-condemned; [12]for until certain people came from James, he

---

5. I am aware that the claim that Zacchaeus needed to be, or was, converted is not universally accepted. See the discussion by Wyndy Corbin Reuschling in this volume.

> used to eat with the Gentiles. But after they came, he drew back and kept himself separate for fear of the circumcision faction. ¹³And the other Jews joined him in this hypocrisy, so that even Barnabas was led astray by their hypocrisy. ¹⁴But when I saw that they were not acting consistently with the truth of the gospel, I said to Cephas before them all . . . (Gal 2:11–14a)

This memory suggests that Peter's conversion was either not permanent or not perfect. Paul is sure that God called and used Peter as much as God used Paul himself (God "worked through Peter making him an apostle to the circumcised [and] also worked through me in sending me to the Gentiles"—Gal 2:8). But Paul is no less sure that Peter is now led astray, hypocritical, and acting antithetically to the gospel. (Parenthetically, we may add that Dunn comes to Peter's defense, making a "case for Peter,"[6] even though he [Dunn] ultimately sides with Paul's position. Dunn also believes that Peter, not Paul, "prevailed" at Antioch.)[7]

This strengthens my earlier suggestion, if we look at the larger tableau of all early Christian memories, that Peter's Joppa vision was indeed a conversion, a point of transformation, and one that was vulnerable to undoing, no less so than his original call/conversion could be undone, or at least temporarily undone, by a threefold denial of his Lord.

In the end, my argument actually confirms Bockmuehl's main thesis—that Peter is a man of conversions, who in some sense repeatedly must move from death to resurrection and may, at times—like all of us—move in the opposite direction.

Similarities and Differences between the Conversions of Peter and Paul

I do not wish to be misunderstood. I am quite certain that the early church rightly remembered that Peter's encounter with the resurrected Jesus changed his life and took him from denial, death, and despair to hope, new life, and ministry. Bockmuehl's contention that this encounter is in fact a conversion, or at least the major conversion in a series of conversions, is persuasive. As I have already hinted, this encounter/conversion is not completely dissimilar from other Christian conversions or specifically from Paul's.

For both Paul and Peter, conversion involves an encounter with the resurrected Jesus. It is a kind of dying and rising with Christ, to use Pauline language. And if we think about Scot McKnight's reminder, grounded in the work of James Fowler,

---

6. *Beginning from Jerusalem*, 481–82.
7. *Beginning from Jerusalem*, 489–94.

that one definition of a conversion is adaptation of a new master story, or (better) incorporation into a new master story, then we can say that that both Paul and Peter have been drawn into a new master story, that of Christ's death and resurrection, and that each of them, in unique ways, has experienced precisely that—death and resurrection. This similarity might not just be a generic similarity to ignore, as I could be understood to have said earlier, but might in some profound way be the very core of Christian conversion.

Yet there are still dissimilarities. Paul's conversion was instantaneous (more or less), or at least it is narrated that way in both Acts and the letters, whereas Peter's was prolonged—from call to denial to restoration to ministry to betrayal to . . . ? (I am sure that plenty of people felt that Paul had need of reconversion on various occasions, even though he himself seems to have seen the process more in terms of daily "living into" the initial experience and moving constantly forward [Phil 3:7–14]). Peter's was more of a process, with more points, more time needed to become incorporated and re-incorporated into the master story/stories.

Reflections on the Ongoing Meanings of Conversion

The church in its wisdom celebrates Peter and Paul on two days in the same month, days that now open and close (January 18, 25) the week of prayer for Christian unity, and again in June on the same day (June 29) to remember their martyrdoms. Perhaps, in addition to symbols of Jewish and Gentile unity, and maybe today also especially Catholic (Peter) and Protestant (Paul) unity,[8] these symbols of unity can also celebrate the unity-in-diversity of two sorts of conversion: the instantaneous, more or less, and the prolonged, or the one that has several significant moments of transformation. This too may represent a more Protestant versus a more Catholic understanding of conversion, on the whole, though there are plenty of Catholics with Paul-like stories and Protestants with Peter-like stories.

Perhaps we can learn from one another on this matter of Petrine-Pauline similarity and difference. Conversion is incorporation into the master story of Christ's death and resurrection and thus into God's own story. It can happen instantly, or in fits and starts. In either case it either is, or becomes, a process of ongoing death and resurrection, of living into the initial experience, whether we identify that ini-

---

8. I do not mean to leave the Orthodox out, but the Peter-Paul dichotomy in the church is sometimes analogous to the Catholic-Protestant division.

tial reality as baptism or conversion or salvation or being born again or whatever.[9] Even Paul acknowledged the need for ongoing conversion, both for his churches (especially the Corinthians, as Stephen Chester has shown)[10] and, in some sense, for himself: "I die every day; I press on" (1 Cor 15:31; Phil 3:12–14). And this means also for us.

---

9. Elsewhere I have spoke of initial and ongoing cruciformity. See Michael J Gorman, *Cruciformity: Paul's Narrative Spirituality of the Cross* (Grand Rapids: Eerdmans, 2001).

10. Stephen J. Chester, *Conversion at Corinth: Perspectives on Conversion in Paul's Theology and the Corinthian Church* (London: T. & T. Clark, 2003).

ZACCHAEUS'S CONVERSION
To Be or Not To Be a Tax Collector
(Luke 19:1–10)

Wyndy Corbin Reuschling

Introduction

Every summer I attended Vacation Bible School at the Mentor Baptist Church in Mentor, Kentucky. Each day, sitting in the small wooden pink chairs, we would learn a new song that would become part of the repertoire for the final program in front of adoring parents and grumbling siblings who were required to attend. One song still sticks with me. You may know it, motions and all:

> Zacchaeus was a wee little man, and a wee little man was he.
> He climbed up in a sycamore tree for the Lord he wanted to see;
> And as the Savior passed that way, He looked up in the tree,
> And he said, "Zacchaeus you come down for I'm going to your house today. For I'm going to your house today."[1]

This ditty is based on the story of Zacchaeus in Luke 19:1–10 which was the lesson for the day reinforced by the song we just memorized. We were taught the basic lessons of this Bible story. In order to find Jesus, we must search high and low for Jesus. The Savior is looking for each of us as he passes by, and is waiting for us to respond. Zacchaeus was a tax collector, a sinner and bad person. No one, therefore, is too bad or too sinful for Jesus. Jesus loves all persons, including unlovable tax collectors. Salvation had come to Zacchaeus and could come to us if we, like Zacchaeus, searched and waited for Jesus, and responded by trusting him to forgive our sins just as he did for this tax collector. In doing so, we would be converted and, hence, saved.

I do not remember much being made about what it meant to be a tax collector. Locating tax collecting within the political structures and social practices of the first century was not on the minds of those who had volunteered for one week during

---

1. Anonymous. http://kidsongs.wordpress.com/2006/08/04/zacchaeus.

the summer to corral and teach fifty antsy children, all the while ensuring the snacks were served on time and there were appropriate activities during the day to keep us enrapt and entertained. I also do not recall any reference to the *ordo salutis,* or order of salvation, in this story.[2] The story line was a simple one: Zacchaeus met Jesus, Zacchaeus was converted, which meant he "became a Christian," and was saved from judgment for his sins. This is the first and only time we meet Zacchaeus since Luke is the only one to include this story in the Gospels. I can't help but wonder what ever happened to Zacchaeus. How was Zacchaeus's life different after this encounter with Jesus? Zacchaeus might have been saved as I was taught, but was he converted? Did he remain a tax collector? Could he have kept collecting taxes? *Should* he have remained a tax collector? It is these questions I want to explore in this paper pertinent for our theological engagement with Scripture on the theme of conversion.[3]

A few caveats are in order before proceeding. First, I am a Christian social ethicist so I approach this topic with an interest in the moral dimensions of conversion, and, in the case of Zacchaeus, how conversion impacts and informs our vocational choices and ways of earning an income. My aim is to reflect on this text in light of two primary notions of conversion. The first is an understanding of conversion as a one-time decision, an event simply equated with "getting saved." The second views conversion as an on-going process of change, reorientation and moral formation.

---

2. The *ordo salutis* is an attempt to delineate the order of salvation, typically starting with and involving such terms as effectual calling, conviction of sin, regeneration or conversion, faith, justification, sanctification, and union with Christ. The order and emphasis may vary depending on historical and theological trajectories. See the following standard works in Protestant theology that include an *ordo salutis:* Donald G. Bloesch, *Essentials of Evangelical Theology* (2 vols.; New York: HarperCollins, 1978); Miyon Chung, "Conversion and Sanctification," in *The Cambridge Companion to Evangelical Theology*, (ed. Timothy Larsen and Daniel J. Treier; Cambridge: Cambridge University Press, 2007); Millard J. Erickson, *Christian Theology,* (One volume edition; Grand Rapids: Baker , 1992); Justo L. González and Zaida Maldonado Pérez, *An Introduction to Christian Theology* (Nashville: Abingdon, 2002); Stanley J. Grenz, *Theology for the Community of God* (Grand Rapids: Eerdmans, 1994); Shirley C. Guthrie, *Christian Doctrine* (Louisville: Westminster John Knox, 1994); and Daniel L. Migliore, *Faith Seeking Understanding: An Introduction to Christian Theology* (Grand Rapids: Eerdmans, 2004).

3. The conversations on conversion at the 2009 Theological Interpretation of Scripture at North Park Theological Seminary were rich and invited more substantive thinking about conversion from many disciplines. It was a privilege to participate and I am especially grateful for the probing and thoughtful response to my paper offered by Elizabeth Musselman Palmer. I will note, as appropriate, how her questions helped me in thinking further about Zacchaeus's conversion. The questions which students posed have also prodded me to think about conversion in the very concrete dimensions of pastoral practices and church leadership.

This "thicker"[4] concept takes into consideration how an on-going process of conversion informs *and* changes how we live, the choices we make, and the work we do.

Second, I am keenly aware that the ability and opportunities to pursue my vocation as a teacher and scholar are made possible by the work of others. My job and salary are supported by student tuition, generous donors, and foundations that fund theological education and research. It is an odd and troubling thing, something that produces various degrees of angst for me, to critique and chastise our economic and employment systems and the means by which income is earned while accepting the fruit of others' labors that make my own possible. Therefore, I hope my proposals and conclusions reflect my own ambiguity and tentative judgments about the kinds of work people do simply to survive.[5]

Finally, I also recognize the complexity of labor, employment, economic systems and practices in a global economy. It is difficult to have discussions "from nowhere." We are all located in an intricate web of economic and political relationships and structures that are interdependent and complex with multiple points of complicity which makes no participation almost, if not, impossible. I am not an economist, a human resource manager, a labor relations expert, a social policy guru, or even a biblical scholar. I am a theological ethicist with an interest in social ethical issues who works more with normative points of reference and social analysis as we engage with Scripture and theological claims pertinent for the Church as an "agent of the Kingdom of God,"[6] so that we might discern and work out the creative and faithful living of Christian faith in complex moral contexts. I tend to work with the idea of "middle axioms"[7] that acknowledge that I speak as a Christian theologian and ethicist, hopefully humbly, with a desire to think about moral norms inherent in Christian faith and practice and how they might be brought to bear on various

---

4. See Clifford Geertz, *The Interpretation of Cultures* (New York: Basic, 1973), 14. Geertz's concept of "thickness" necessitates multi-dimensional perspectives and descriptions for comfortably working with complex issues such as conversion. This Symposium made important contributions for gaining "thickness" in exploring conversion.

5. See chapter 2, "Five Faces of Oppression" in Iris Marion Young, *Justice and the Politics of Difference* (Princeton, NJ: Princeton University Press, 1990). The five faces are exploitation, marginalization, powerlessness, cultural imperialism, and violence. I am especially indicted by Young's category of powerlessness in contrast to my vocational privileges of autonomy in managing and directing my own work, decision making, use of time, position of authority, and opportunities to engage in reflection and leisure as opposed to the powerless who have few or none of these benefits in employment.

6. Howard Snyder, *The Community of the King*, (2nd rev. ed.; Downers Grove, Ill.: InterVarsity, 2004), 14.

7. John C. Bennett, *Christian Ethics and Social Policy* (New York: C. Scribners' Sons, 1946).

issues in conversation with other disciplines and areas of expertise. I desire to offer ways in which, as Christians, we can reflect on and discern our vocational choices and their moral dimensions in light of our conversions and the continual living out of our Christian commitments.

I will start with a brief hermeneutical exploration of Zacchaeus's encounter with Jesus in the context of Luke's Gospel as a form of conversion in that Zacchaeus did something and made changes when he met Jesus. I will limit my exploration to the story of Zacchaeus while recognizing that Jesus had other encounters with tax collectors recorded in the Synoptic Gospels. Given the scope and purpose of this paper, my questions are focused on the particular story of a particular tax collector in light of the theme of conversion. I will also explore various notions of conversion and come back to the text with two primary questions. Could Zacchaeus have remained a tax collector or *should* Zacchaeus have remained a tax collector? I will conclude by offering linkages between conversion and ethics particularly as they relate to concrete practices in choosing and living out our vocations.

The Context and Text of Zacchaeus's Conversion: Luke 19:1–10

The story of Zacchaeus is recorded in the Gospel of Luke. It is widely held among scholars that the main themes and theological concerns of Luke's Gospel are the call to salvation and discipleship, the stewardship of money and resources, practices of justice and mercy as marks of true piety, and the inclusivity and extension of God's Kingdom to all through faith and repentance.[8] The inclusive nature of the Kingdom of God in Luke's Gospel explains the perpetual invitation to the marginalized and the examples of faith offered by those unlikely to be acknowledged by religious elites as exemplars of piety and true religion such as tax collectors, women, Samaritans, prostitutes, beggars, social outcasts due to illness, and children (Luke 4:14–19; 5:12–16; 7:36–50; 10:25–37; 13:10–17; 14:15–24; 16:19–31; 21:1–4; 24:1–12). Becoming and being a disciple of Jesus Christ by responding to the call to salvation through repen-

---

8. See the following sources: Paul J. Achtemeir, Joel B. Green and Marianne Meye Thompson, eds., *Introducing the New Testament: Its Literature and Theology* (Grand Rapids: Eerdmans, 2001); David A. deSilva, *An Introduction to the New Testament: Contexts, Methods and Ministry Formation* (Downers Grove, Ill.: InterVarsity, 2004); Joel B. Green, *The Gospel of Luke* (Grand Rapids: Eerdmans, 1997); Halvor Moxnes, *The Economy of the Kingdom: Social Conflict and Economic Relations in Luke's Gospel* (Philadelphia: Fortress, 1988); Luke Timothy Johnson, *The Writings of the New Testament: An Interpretation* (Philadelphia: Fortress, 1986); Sharon H. Ringe, *Luke* (Louisville: Westminster John Knox, 1995); and John T. Squires, "The Gospel According to Luke," in *The Cambridge Companion to the Gospels* (ed. Stephen C. Barton; Cambridge: Cambridge University Press, 2006), 158–81.

tance implied a conversion, a change to a different kind of a life and a responsibility to this new community of disciples. Unlike some modern conceptions of conversion which are personal and private, "between an individual and his or her God," Luke's portrayal of salvation and conversion is communal and "ecclesiological—concerned with the practices that define and the criteria for legitimating the community of God's people, and centered on the invitation to participate in God's project."[9] This new life was to be characterized by justice and right relations among persons in this new social order of Christ's disciples, which was to stand in marked contrast to the prevailing mores and social strata of the first century. As Joel Green notes, "it is not too much to say that the Lukan narrative is an invitation to embrace an alternative worldview and to live as if the reign of God had already revolutionized this age."[10]

This age that was revolutionized by this new community of disciples was first century Palestine which was pervasively influenced by the power of Greco-Roman culture. John Squires reminds us that in Luke's Gospel, "discipleship takes place within the realities of life in the Roman Empire."[11] Palestine at this time was a colony, an outpost of Rome, and existed to bolster the material and political privileges of the Empire and to expand its reach. This provided a mixed blessing to the inhabitants of first century Palestine. Being a part of the Roman Empire secured certain benefits like possible citizenship, military protection, personal status, trade, transportation systems and access to roads, and overall political stability. Yet this did not come without a cost. As Luke Timothy Johnson notes, "the empire grew by conquest . . . and two significant aspects of life within it were shaped by that fact."[12] The first aspect, according to Johnson, was the growing social unrest caused by dissidents of Rome and the congregation of displaced persons in urban centers which drew the attention of the military to quell disturbances.[13]

The second significant aspect "was the constant pressure of taxation of the provinces"[14] in order to feed people and to support the machinations and spread of the Roman Empire; taxes which Johnson notes were especially severe for subjected persons, thereby furthering their oppression and subjection. Tax collecting was a complex system that involved taxation in three areas: on land, on "heads" or persons

9. Green, *The Gospel of Luke*, 22.

10. Ibid., 11.

11. Squires, "The Gospel According to Luke," 160.

12. Johnson, *The Writings of the New Testament: An Interpretation*, 26.

13. Ibid.

14. Ibid.

in a household, and on goods, or the customs tax.[15] It was a system largely detested by Roman subjects and viewed with suspicion, as were the agents, or tax farmers and collectors, who perpetuated the taxation system and "were despised for their collusion with Rome."[16] It was particularly the practice of collecting the customs tax from economically vulnerable and traveling persons seeking to sell or acquire basic goods that was reviled. In this practice, the collecting of taxes was farmed out to the highest bidder, creating "tax farmers" whereby "Rome received its money in advance, and the tax collector made his living from commissions on tolls and customs."[17] Not only were goods excised by Rome but additional amounts, often in large sums, were added to pay the commissions of tax collectors which created a form of "institutionalized robbery."[18] Tax collectors collected more for themselves than what was required by Rome. This system thrived on dishonesty, exploitation, overcharging, and abuse of those being taxed which lined the pockets of these tax collectors. It is no wonder that tax collectors were universally reviled, were viewed as the worst of all sinners, and were often characterized as unclean by religious leaders as well as were those who associated with them, such as Jesus.

This brings us to the meeting between Jesus and Zacchaeus in Luke 19:1–10. Jesus was passing through Jericho on his way to Jerusalem when he met Zacchaeus. Starting at the end of Luke chapter nine and through to the end of chapter nineteen, we have a collection of parables, teachings, meetings, examples, and events where Jesus is stressing the imperatives and cost of discipleship to his listeners, perhaps in light of his impending trial and execution. Luke indicates that Zacchaeus was a "chief tax collector" and very wealthy (19:2), two dubious attributes for characterizing persons in Luke's Gospel. As a chief tax collector, Zacchaeus was responsible for supervising other tax collectors, which was further indication of his wealth and power. When Jesus entered Jericho, Zacchaeus went to great lengths to see who Jesus was and did so by climbing up a tree because the crowd obstructed his view, which Green surmises may have been intentional given the negative assessment of Zacchaeus.[19] In a way that had become typical of Jesus, he spots Zacchaeus and invites himself to Zacchaeus's home much to the chagrin of "all the people" who sup-

---

15. Thomas E. Schmidt, "Taxes," in *Dictionary of Jesus and the Gospels* (ed. Joel B. Green and Scot McKnight; Downers Grove, Ill.: InterVarsity, 1992), 804–7.

16. Ibid., 806.

17. Ibid., 805.

18. Ibid., 806.

19. Green, *The Gospel of Luke*, 670.

posedly were there to see Jesus as well. It is no surprise by this time that Jesus spent time with tax collectors who appeared quite receptive to him and that it continued to raise the ire of those who observed Jesus' interaction and fellowship with such sinners like Zacchaeus (19:7). Zacchaeus's response was equally shocking: "Look, Lord! Here and now I give half of my possessions to the poor, and if I have cheated anybody out of anything, I will pay back four times the amount" (19:8).[20] This was a public declaration made in the presence of "all the people" and before Jesus. It is likely that many whom Zacchaeus had cheated were among "all the people," and we can only imagine their cynicism and disbelief when they heard this. Imagine their double shock when they heard Jesus' response to this tax collector, acknowledging Zacchaeus as a son of Abraham for this act of faith and justice. It was after this that Jesus pronounced, "Today salvation has come to this house" (19:9).

This story indicates that salvation had come to Zacchaeus like it had to so many in Jesus' ministry who seemed beyond the pale of God's grace, love, and forgiveness, and that Zacchaeus responded by announcing changes to his practices, much to the surprise of all those who knew this chief tax collector. According to Green, we ought to be cautious, however, in reading this narrative as a "story of conversion" since Luke "mentions nothing of Zacchaeus's need for repentance, act of repentance or faith, nor of Jesus' summons to repentance . . ."[21] But what we know from the story is that something changed for Zacchaeus. He acknowledged Jesus as Lord (19:8) and sought to make things right by rectifying the economic wrongs he had done. In response, Jesus proclaimed salvation had come to Zacchaeus, signifying "Zacchaeus's vindication and restoration to the community of God's people . . . Zacchaeus thus joins the growing rolls of persons whose 'repentance' lies outside the narrative, who appear on the margins of the people of God, and yet who possess insight into and a commitment to the values of Jesus' mission that are exemplary."[22]

While Zacchaeus's repentance may lie outside the narrative, his acknowledgement of Jesus as Lord and the effect which this had on Zacchaeus may be construed, I think, as part of a conversion experience that resulted in new commitments, allegiances, and practices that took Zacchaeus in new directions, even though the narrative does not contain the theological language or process we have become accustomed to in describing conversion. The story of Zacchaeus gives us clues about the effects which his encounter with Jesus produced, an important and often

---

20. Unless otherwise noted, all biblical quotations are from NIV.
21. Green, *The Gospel of Luke*, 672.
22. Ibid.

neglected aspect of conversion. Zacchaeus experienced a profound change in attitude *and* behavior related to the practices and purposes of his occupation as a tax collector. Was this an external manifestation of an internal change that had already occurred as part of his anticipated meeting with Jesus? Was this an act of repentance, or an assuaging of a guilty conscience? Was this to appease the maddening crowd? Who could ever know the motives behind experiences like this? But what we do know is what we observe: Zacchaeus's behavior changed.[23]

Zacchaeus's wealth was likely obtained through the unjust practice of tax collecting so it is quite amazing that his first observable act was to give back money and possessions unjustly obtained. Sharon Ringe suggests Zacchaeus was following standard practices of almsgiving and restitution.

> The distribution of half of his goods, although falling short of what was required of the rich man seeking eternal life (18:22), more than meets the standards of almsgiving that have been so important earlier in the Gospel (12:13-21 ; 16:19-31). Concerning the second part of his promise, Torah and custom provide that if anyone has defrauded another and offers to make amends, the one who has done wrong must make restitution of the original, plus an additional 20 percent (Lev. 6:5; Num. 5:7).[24]

Perhaps Zacchaeus took to heart John the Baptist's earlier response to tax collectors who came to be baptized, telling them to stop collecting more taxes than they were required to collect (Luke 3:12-13). Others suggest that Luke is contrasting Zacchaeus's attitude and actions with those of the Rich Ruler in Luke 18:18-30 who refused to sell his possessions to follow Jesus, thereby shunning the costs of discipleship. Zacchaeus and the Rich Young Ruler offer contrasting role models of how we should view money and possessions, with Zacchaeus offering the positive type for the wealthy to emulate.[25] David deSilva describes Zacchaeus as "the model convert," who does not sell all his possessions "but he does sell half of them and gives the proceeds as alms for the poor."[26] In this way, Zacchaeus is offering us a prototype

---

23. In her response to my paper, Elizabeth Musselman Palmer asks the question: "Is there always a visible component of conversion?" I would like to think so because of the relationship between repentance and conversion which calls persons to a new way of life which necessarily involves changed behavior.

24. Ringe, *Luke*, 232.

25. Squires, "The Gospel According to Luke," 175.

26. David A. deSilva, "The Gospel According to Luke," in *An Introduction to the New Testament: Contexts, Methods and Ministry Formation* (Downers Grove, Ill.: InterVarsity, 2004), 326.

of concrete practices for fulfilling obligations as converts of Jesus Christ when it comes to our attitudes towards, and use of, money. While many of us are not in the position to give up all of our resources we are obligated to steward them justly. As deSilva notes,

> In a way Zacchaeus poses a much more potent challenge to the reader than the rich young man. While few if any could sell *all* their possessions and give to the poor, it would be possible, though difficult, for many to give away a large portion of their possessions and still provide for their necessities, making it all the more real a challenge.[27]

Alan Mitchell suggests the story of Zacchaeus reflects a vindication of his job as a tax collector not a change of direction. According to Mitchell, Zacchaeus was simply confirming what he already was as a son of Abraham when he stated in v.8 that he would give half of his possessions to the poor and pay back anyone he had cheated. This "iteration" indicated that Zacchaeus was already following the prescriptions of the Torah in his attitudes and practices toward wealth and possessions.[28] Zacchaeus's statement in v. 8, therefore, ought to be read as a defense or vindication affirmed by Jesus before the "murmuring crowd" as opposed to a resolution made by Zacchaeus to a new way life.[29] Zacchaeus demonstrated his righteousness as son of Abraham by stating what he had done by giving half his possessions to the poor. He also offered to give back to anyone *if* he had cheated, implying the possibility that Zacchaeus had not cheated anybody in the collection of taxes. For Mitchell, Zacchaeus's statement in v. 8 was not a resolve to do good works from here on out since Zacchaeus was already doing good works of justice and hospitality as indicators that he was a true son of Abraham whom Jesus recognized as such when they met. In other words, Zacchaeus was already "converted" in that he was declared righteous by Jesus and was already doing what was required as a son of Abraham. "To that end Luke 19, 1–10 should be understood as a story about Zacchaeus, a rich toll collector, a Jew to whom Jesus came to bring salvation *because* he was a son of Abraham."[30] This interpretation serves Luke's purposes according to Mitchell, one of which was

> . . . to challenge the view that Christianity in his day should not be associated with the rich, with toll collectors, or with certain pious Jews simply

---

27. Ibid.

28. Alan C. Mitchell, "Zacchaeus Revisited: Luke 19, 8 as a Defense," *Biblica* 71 (1990): 153–76.

29 Ibid., 162.

30. Ibid. (emphasis mine).

because they were members of those groups. Basically it is a matter of who can be saved, and Luke wanted to show that anyone who fulfills the mandate of the gospel can be saved, regardless of his or her status. In the case of Zacchaeus he seems to be answering the question whether a pious Jew, who is also a toll collector, can have material possessions and the associations his business requires, and still be saved.[31]

Contrary to Mitchell's theory of vindication, Fernando Méndez-Moratalla believes that we do have a story of salvation and conversion in Luke 19:1–10.[32] According to Méndez-Moratalla, vindication theories, such as Mitchell's, enable Zacchaeus to remain a tax collector since Jesus' pronouncement of salvation to Zacchaeus's household was made while he was still collecting taxes.[33] In the vindication theory, Jesus offers no condemnation of Zacchaeus's job. Therefore Zacchaeus was not a sinner as a tax collector since Luke's purpose in vindicating Zacchaeus was to serve "the underlying purpose . . . to make acceptable in the Christian community the presence of those who, although having socially despised occupations, were faithful believers."[34] For Méndez-Moratalla, this interpretive conclusion goes against the thrust of the passage and the overall purposes of Luke to portray the immediacy of salvation, a reversal of priorities and commitments, and evidential changes in attitudes toward wealth and possessions. The story of Zacchaeus does contain evidence of conversion which Méndez-Moratalla defines as starting with divine initiative and the desire to seek Jesus resulting in a life-changing encounter. This life-changing encounter had a direct correlation on how Zacchaeus obtained his wealth and what he resolved to do with it in the future. The giving back of unjustly gained wealth was an act of repentance for past actions which would have implications for any future actions related to the obtaining and use of wealth and possessions. It is only then, in an act of acceptance and fellowship, and after Zacchaeus's promise of change, Jesus announces salvation to Zacchaeus.[35]

I do take seriously Green's earlier caution that we ought not to read the story of Zacchaeus as an obvious story of conversion as Méndez-Moratalla does. I do not

---

31. Ibid., 163.

32. Fernando Méndez-Moratalla, *The Paradigm of Conversion in Luke* (London: T. & T. Clark, 2004).

33. The same kind of vindication could also be made of all tax collectors since John the Baptist in Luke 3:12–13 did not instruct hearers to stop collecting taxes but to stop collecting more than required. By way of reminder, I am exploring a particular tax collector, Zacchaeus, and not tax collecting.

34. Méndez-Moratalla, *The Paradigm of Conversion in Luke*, 159.

35. Ibid., 160–78.

think we can find in or force on the story the *ordo salutis* or derive a standard formula for conversion. There is no overly familiar linear process that enables us to be clear about what conversion actually should be, functioning as some kind of test to measure the validity of a person's conversion. I recognize the sometimes hegemonic ways in which our obsession for orderly systems of theology control our reading of Scripture and force on texts paradigms that hide and tame Scripture's power and possibilities.[36] However I do think we learn something about what it means to encounter Jesus and how this encounter changes or converts us in very tangible ways as it did for Zacchaeus, contrary to Mitchell's reading of Zacchaeus's vindication *as* tax collector.

The story of Zacchaeus's encounter with Christ begs for an "analogical imagination"[37] in our interpretation and reading whereby we pose new questions and wonder about the possibilities of these kinds of stories for our own lives; for our purposes in particular, how this story might challenge our accepted notions of what conversion is and how it might relate to where and how we spend the majority of our time (i.e. working) and the means for earning incomes. So, this is where the story of Zacchaeus takes me and the questions with which I am left. Whatever happened to Zacchaeus? How did this initial encounter, this seminal change of attitude and behavior, result in further conversions of attitudes and behaviors? What did this initial change of heart and action mean for subsequent changes, particularly as they related to tax collecting knowing what we know about the practices and purposes of tax collecting? Could Zacchaeus have continued collecting taxes? *Should* Zacchaeus have continued collecting taxes? Our answers will likely depend on how we understand not only Zacchaeus's conversion but our own, and how we might imagine the possibilities of where our conversions may take us.

---

36. See Trevor Hart, *Faith Thinking: The Dynamics of Christian Theology* (Downers Grove, Ill.: InterVarsity, 1995), 137–9. Hart offers an important warning about reading Scripture at the two extremes of objectivism and relativism. Objectivism insists on one meaning and only one way of reading Scripture, which closes one's self off from any other readings and fresh possibilities which Scripture, the Spirit, and Christian community offer. Hart is also critical of relativism in our reading of Scripture in that there are no constraints in our interpretation. We become free to read Scripture as we want, with no stable reference points beyond our own proclivity for comfortable and comforting renderings of texts. Both are a "taming of the text" that ultimately fails to take Scripture seriously.

37. See William Spohn's rich insights on analogical imagination in *Go and Do Likewise: Jesus and Ethics* (New York: Continuum, 2007), 61. See also Richard Hays, *The Moral Vision of the New Testament: Community, Cross and New Creation* (San Francisco: Harper, 1996), 3–7, and John McIntyre, *Faith, Theology and Imagination* (Edinburgh: Handsel, 1987) for other helpful insights on the relationships between Scripture, faith, theology and imagination.

Two Notions of Conversion

Conversion is a word that describes an experience of change, or a turnaround in belief, attitudes, and behavior. It may involve the rejection of one set of religious beliefs and practices, or no belief, and the adoption of another. It may entail a drastic reversal of direction in favor of a new way of life or something more gradual. In Christian theology, conversion is a term used to describe various elements and aspects of a person's encounter with Christ that result in an awareness of sin, an acceptance of Christ's work on the cross, and a response of saving faith in Christ as fundamental aspects of being converted, or turning from one way of life and accepting the new life which Christ offers. A person is therefore, converted, or changed in the past tense. Often conversion is equated with salvation, and points to the past and looks forward to the future. A person turns from one way of life, or converts, and therefore one will be saved. A person points backward to the date, time, and place, often excruciatingly specific, when she or he accepted Christ as her or his Savior, was converted, and therefore will be saved from the judgment of God for sin. This past action has bearing for the future in that a person's decision of conversion guarantees a place in heaven.

This first notion of conversion places an emphasis on the past event "getting saved" and the future reward of "being saved" as both a result and benefit of conversion. It equates being converted with getting saved as the ultimate goal of one's life that was accomplished through a one-time decision to convert.[38] While this first notion of conversion may reflect aspects of the biblical witness and contemporary experience in that people do have dramatic encounters with Jesus that change them forever and offer hope and promise for the future, it misses some fundamental notions of conversion that have implications for the here and now, the important times of our lives between the then of the past and the then of the future. This first notion of conversion as one-time event enables us to read Zacchaeus's story as a tale of conversion in that Jesus was searching for Zacchaeus; Zacchaeus had an encounter with Jesus that elicited a response that could be interpreted as repentance; and with the result of the inclusion of Zacchaeus into the people of God. The past event and

---

38. See Wyndy Corbin Reuschling, *Reviving Evangelical Ethics: The Promises and Pitfalls of Classic Models of Morality* (Grand Rapids: Brazos, 2008), 99–100. See also the essay by Luke L. Keefer, "What is Conversion?" in *Brethren in Christ History and Life* 30 (Apr 2007): 63–84; and Gordon T. Smith, *Beginning Well: Christian Conversion and Authentic Transformation* (Downers Grove, Ill.: InterVarsity, 2001).

the future promise assure us Zacchaeus was converted, and hence fulfills our desire for a tidy explanation of how one is converted to Christ.

Yet this first notion of conversion leaves me troubled in a number of ways. It still does not explain the difference that this encounter with Jesus made in Zacchaeus's life in the every day and over the long term, and on his vocation as a tax collector. Do we only encounter Jesus once and experience a life change upon conversion only once? This bi-polar view of conversion, that emphasizes the past and the future and compartmentalizes the here and now, fails to recognize that authentic conversion is on-going and progressive,[39] and should impact all areas of our lives, the spiritual, intellectual, and vocational[40] and, I would add, the relational, social, and moral. This first notion of conversion tends to relegate our experiences and encounters with Christ to some kind of ethereal sphere which privileges the spiritual over the material aspects of our lives. This brackets the very concrete and social dimensions of our lives, such as our vocations, ways of earning and using money, the ethical demands of Christian discipleship and our responsibilities to others, from pertinent moral critique that come from the commitments we have as followers of Jesus Christ. Morality becomes bifurcated from conversion, discipleship from salvation, and beliefs from practices, since all that matters is that we *were* converted and we *shall be* saved.

It is the second view of conversion, a "progressive understanding"[41] that I find more apt for exploring how conversion is on-going and how it might impact our vocational choices. Instead of seeing conversion as a one-time encounter of "getting saved," might it better to see conversion as continual posturing and willingness for change and formation that can be gradual,[42] but may be as cataclysmic as a first encounter with Christ? In other words, even as Christians, we can be converted again and again when encountering the demands and implications of the Gospel that may put us on a different course. Seeing conversion not as the end of Christian life but its beginning may enable us to make stronger connections between conversion, moral

---

39. Luke L. Keefer, "What is Conversion?" 73.

40. Ibid.

41. Ibid.

42. This gradual kind of formation is akin to sanctification. I am avoiding this word while recognizing it is theologically rich and important in Christian faith. I want to keep the focus on conversion in order to stress that even in the process of sanctification we might be "re-converted" in a radical turn-around as opposed to a gradual formation forward.

formation, discipleship, and choices throughout the course of our lives. Should we not always be converting to the ways and purposes of Christ?

In light of these possibilities, I offer this tentative definition of conversion as an *ongoing socialization and formation by and into a Christian narrative for all dimensions of life*.[43] I realize that it is difficult to talk about conversion without talking about the work of the Triune God in the economy of salvation and the important role of the Holy Spirit.[44] Due to the limits of this paper and the topic of our conversation, I want to focus on conversion "as the human activity that enables us to appropriate the justifying work of God."[45] I will expand on this definition and the human side of conversion and then return to Zacchaeus for possible answers to my questions about his vocation as a tax collector in light of the on-going nature of conversion.

Conversion is not simply an event or a one-time encounter with Christ. Conversion is the beginning of a new life, the acceptance of a new life story, an invitation into a new community and a new way of seeing the world that is now informed by the love, mercy, and reconciling grace of God on behalf of the world. This involves processes of socialization by learning and practicing the demands of this new life in Christ. It is what Nicholas Taylor and Joel Green call an "autobiographical reconstruction."[46] This reconstruction of our selves is on-going, personal and communal. Who we understand ourselves to be changes and how we conceive of our lives before God and with others radically shifts. We no longer exist for ourselves and because of this we need to learn ways of relating to God and others that reflects our

---

43. This definition has been informed by the following works: Beverly Roberts Gaventa, *From Darkness to Light: Aspects of Conversion in the New Testament* (OBT 20; Philadelphia: Fortress, 1986); Joel B. Green, *Body, Soul, and Human Life: The Nature of Humanity in the Bible* (Grand Rapids: Baker Academic, 2008); Scot McKnight, *Turning to Jesus: The Sociology of Conversion in the Gospels* (Louisville: Westminster John Knox, 2002); Wayne A. Meeks, *The Origins of Christian Morality* (New Haven, Conn.: Yale University Press, 1993); Lewis R. Rambo, *Understanding Religious Conversion* (New Haven, Conn.: Yale University Press, 1993); Tobias Rink, "An Interdisciplinary Perspective on Conversion," *Missionalia* 53:2 (August 2007): 18–43; Nicholas H. Taylor," "The Social Nature of Conversion in the Early Christian World," in *Modelling Early Christianity: Social Scientific Studies of the New Testament in Its Context*, (ed. Philip F. Esler; London: Routledge, 1995), 128–38; and Jim Wallis, *The Call to Conversion: Why Faith is Always Personal but Never Private* (revised and updated edition; New York: HarperSanFrancisco, 2005).

44. I agree with Elizabeth Musselman Palmer in her response to my paper in that God's grace and initiative is the starting point for any understanding of salvation, and hence conversion.

45. Gordon Smith, *Beginning Well*, 10.

46. Nicholas H. Taylor, "The Social Nature of Conversion," 134; and Joel B. Green, *Body, Soul, and Human Life*, 129. Both Taylor and Green are using insights from social theory, particularly the works of Peter Berger and Thomas Luckmann, and David Snow and Richard Machalek.

acceptance of this new Christian narrative. Processes of socialization require a community where we learn what it means to be a Christian and what attitudes, behaviors and commitments are consistent with Christian faith and practice.[47] Concerned with overly personal and sentimental understandings of conversion that do not make a lasting impact on our lives, Gordon Smith seeks to highlight the deeply communal and on-going nature of conversion and the necessity of a community in which the language and practices of Christian faith are learned on a continual basis. Without this social dimension, conversion is incomplete. Smith writes,

> In the community of faith we learn the language of faith and conversion through sermons, hymns, prayers and readings of Scripture. But we also learn this faith language through ongoing conversations day in and day out in the context of both play and work. This communal language enables us to make sense of and give definition to our human predicament, the longings and aspirations of our hearts, the reality of God and the work of the Spirit in our lives.[48]

Smith goes so far as to suggest that without Christian community conversion is not possible. It is the Christian community that mediates and communicates through the language of faith this new interpretive framework that reinterprets and reorients our lives. It is the community of faith which socializes us and helps us to learn the "rules" of Christian faith through its liturgy, worship, teaching, mission, and ministries of service. It is the Christian community where we learn to live out our salvation (Phil 2:12–18), and which provides the environment and means for continual conversion to the purposes of God through its preaching and embodiment of the story of God. As Taylor notes, "resocialization, therefore, is integral to the conversion process, particularly in societies where human identity is essentially social."[49] Since we are social creatures, conversion is never just a personal or private decision even though these aspects are important. Conversion is social and embodied, and is lived out through the adoption of "requisite beliefs and practices"[50] that are found in a Christian narrative.

---

47. See Tod E. Bolsinger, *It Takes a Church to Raise a Christian: How the Community of God Transforms Lives* (Grand Rapids: Brazos, 2004).

48. Smith, *Beginning Well*, 41.

49. Taylor, "The Social Nature of Conversion," 136.

50. Ibid.

This on-going socialization in a process of conversion requires the assumption of a "master attribution,"[51] "a new conceptual scheme,"[52] a new story, or narrative by which we interpret and orient our (new) lives. If Alasdair MacIntyre is correct that we all have and need narratives by which to live, then it matters which narrative we believe and embody.[53] For those converted and continually converting to Christ, this narrative is the Kingdom of God, which involves a

> ... total relocation from which we see the world. True conversion is the radical reorientation of our lives according to our membership, our new citizenship in the Kingdom of God. Conversion is not just or only "getting saved" as the end of Christian life. Conversion is both an entry point and the continual process by which we actualize the story of Jesus, develop virtues, and engage in ethical practices. [54]

Conversion transfers us "from darkness to light" (1 Pet 2:9) and disrupts and recreates commitments, belongings, loyalties, and identities. This "total relocation" may likely cause dissonance between what we believe and what we do, and the commitments we have already made and the ones we should make. Conversion relocates us as members of God's Kingdom, where we are now co-participants in God's purposes of justice, mercy, restoration, community, and service to others. As we grow in "actualizing the story of Jesus," and continually change in our perceptions, attitudes, and behavior, we will be confronted with choices in such practical areas as our vocations as means of serving the purposes of God.

This is what is hopeful and morally rich about the nature of on-going conversion that takes seriously the here and now of our lives. We can continually examine our choices and our practices in light of what we believe; we can continue to rely on our communities of faith for wisdom and direction; and we can also hold onto the

---

51. Ibid., 134.

52. Green, *Body, Soul and Human Life*, 126–27.

53. Alasdair MacIntyre's work in *After Virtue* (Notre Dame, Ind.: University of Notre Dame Press, 1984) has been influential in Christian ethics and has resulted in a recovery of narrative, virtue and teleology in moral deliberation. See the following as examples: Stanley Hauerwas, *A Community of Character: Toward a Constructive Christian Ethic* (Notre Dame, Ind.: University of Notre Dame Press, 1981) and *The Peaceable Kingdom* (Notre Dame, Ind.: University of Notre Dame Press, 1983); Stanley Hauerwas and Charles Pinches, *Christians Among the Virtues: Theological Conversations with Ancient and Modern Ethics* (Notre Dame, Ind.: University of Notre Dame Press, 1997); Nancey Murphy, Brad Kallenberg and Mark Thiessen Nation, eds., *Virtues and Practices in the Christian Tradition: Ethics After MacIntyre* (Notre Dame, Ind.: University of Notre Dame Press, 1997); and Samuel Wells, *Improvisation: The Drama of Christian Ethics* (Grand Rapids: Brazos, 2004).

54. Corbin Reuschling, *Reviving Evangelical Ethics*, 100.

hope that we are always being formed, always changing, always converting in fundamental and dynamic relationships with the Triune God and with others.[55] So as Green asks and answers, "Who, then is a convert? The simple answer would be, one who has undergone a redirectional rotation and is on the move in faithful service to the purpose of God as this is revealed in Jesus Christ and underwritten by the Spirit of God."[56] Continual conversion involves faithful movement forward and a willingness to have our lives disrupted again and again by the call and challenges of the Gospel for the way we live and for what we do. This on-going process of conversion, when "transposed into narrative and embodied in tradition, can make possible other conversions"[57] and produce profound changes and redirections in every aspect of our lives, as we hope it did for Zacchaeus.

Zacchaeus's Conversion: To be or Not to be a Tax Collector

In his article, "What is Conversion?" my colleague, Luke Keefer, recounts the story of New Testament scholar, Etta Linnemann.[58] He notes a crucial juncture in her own faith, a dramatic encounter with Christ that caused her to call into question her commitments to historical biblical criticism under the tutelage of Rudolph Bultmann. Linnemann's initial dramatic conversion prompted yet another one, "a crisis of faith. Could she continue to employ her critical approaches to Scripture without offending the Lord who saved her?"[59] Apparently she decided she could not, publically announced her conversion and denounced her previous scholarship. Keefer goes on to note additional dimensions to Linnemann's conversion.

> This change in scholarship brought about a further vocational choice. Could she continue to teach in an educational system that fostered doubt in those who were being trained for ministry? She decided she could not and resigned from her teaching position. Subsequently, she followed the

---

55. See Jeannine K. Brown, Carla M. Dahl, and Wyndy Corbin Reuschling, *Becoming Whole and Holy: An Integrative Conversation About Christian Formation* (Grand Rapids: Brazos, forthcoming).

56. Green, *Body, Soul, and Human Life*, 135.

57. Brian V. Johnstone, C.Ss.R, "The Dynamics of Conversion," in *Spirituality and Morality: Integrating Prayer and Action* (Mahwah, N.J.: Paulist Press, 1996), 40–41.

58. Keefer, "What is Conversion?" 72–73. See Etta Linnemann, *Historical Criticism of the Bible: Methodology or Ideology?* (trans. Robert Yarbrough; Grand Rapids: Baker, 1990; Repr. Grand Rapids: Kregel, 2001).

59. Keefer, "What is Conversion?" 73.

leading of the Lord to a Bible school in Indonesia, where pastoral candidates were being trained to proclaim the gospel.[60]

Conversion for Linnemann brought about a change in vocation. Did it do the same for Zacchaeus? It is important to remember that we meet Zacchaeus for the first and only time at a point of encountering Christ. We do not know how things turned out for him. We can imagine and hope that Zacchaeus willingly and joyfully entered into an on-going journey of formation and conversion. I would like to imagine that this initial encounter and subsequent ones did cause degrees of dissonance and discomfort with his job as a tax collector so that Zacchaeus himself wondered if he could be both a tax collector and an on-going convert of Jesus Christ.

Could Zacchaeus have remained a tax collector? I posed this question in a Sunday school class I was teaching at church. This was a class of older adults who had been involved with this church for years. Many had grown up in this church along with their children and grandchildren. These were faithful saints who had met Jesus, who knew the Bible, and who retold various experiences and stories of God's faithfulness to them. A number of people in the class took issue with this question for a variety of reasons. Some were successful business people who saw their honest business activities as a means of honoring God and blessing other persons with jobs. Some saw work as a gift and command from God. No matter what kind of work we do, we should "work at it with all your heart, as working for the Lord not men" (Col 3:23). Work is amoral; it is our attitude toward work that concerns God. Others were puzzled by this question because salvation and conversion were spiritual matters that accomplished the main purposes which God had for their lives. There were very little connections made between how conversion might reshape our very notions of work, how it is done, why it is done, and whom it serves. Topics such as work were not viewed even as a spiritual issue, let alone a moral one that had much to do with conversion to Christian faith which, it was believed, was about spiritual matters. I found this a bit surprising given the extraordinary amount of time we spend working and forming relationships with those with whom we work. Work takes up a lot of our time and energy, yet this group of faithful church goers had a difficult time making connections between their own faith commitments, the purposes of their work, and the kinds of work in which they participate. For many, conversion and work belong to two different spheres.[61]

---

60. Ibid.

61. This was a Protestant church informed by streams of Anabaptist pietism and American evangelicalism. Some of these comments reflected an appropriation of the "two kingdoms" inherited from the

In light of this common scenario and perceptions about work and conversion, the answer to the question about whether or not Zacchaeus *could* have remained a tax collector, could be yes, but with a number of conditions which the members of this Sunday school class would affirm. At a minimum, Zacchaeus's conversion and new citizenship in the Kingdom of God should have resulted in changed behaviors and new priorities. While conversion has important spiritual dimensions given the work of the Holy Spirit, conversion also involves visible changes in attitudes and behaviors. The story of Zacchaeus gives us a glimpse of this. He recognized wrong and made adjustments in the way he collected taxes, in his attitude and use of wealth, and his response to those he had exploited. Zacchaeus would need to cease collecting more taxes than he was required (Luke 3:12–13) and stop using his position to exploit others for his own benefit. Zacchaeus could be an honest tax collector and a generous one; using the wealth he had gained honestly to help others. We do see a tangible change, observable by those who witnessed the interaction between Zacchaeus and Jesus. We have a glimpse of what Zacchaeus stopped doing, such as exploiting people and dishonestly collecting taxes. This is an important but incomplete aspect of conversion because it still leaves open the question of Zacchaeus's participation in an enterprise that thrived on exploiting others and maintained oppressive conditions for a majority of people.

This is why the more interesting question for me is *should* Zacchaeus have remained a tax collector? If we have an understanding of conversion as on-going socialization by and into a Christian narrative, I think the answer is no. Zacchaeus should not have continued to be a tax collector for the long term. Zacchaeus's continual conversion must have created levels of dissonance as he confronted competing obligations and loyalties as a disciple of Christ, and as a member of this new community, with his service to Rome. If Christian conversion is an on-going socialization process by and into the purposes and values of the Kingdom of God, then decisions about ways of earning an income are not merely individual. They are communal and may often place converts such as Zacchaeus at odds with ac-

---

Protestant Reformer, Martin Luther. See "Secular Authority: To What Extent It Should be Obeyed" in *Martin Luther: Selections from his Writings*, (ed. John Dillenberger; Garden City, N.Y.: Anchor, 1961), 363–402. In this treatise, Luther articulates the two spheres of the Kingdom of Christ and the kingdom of the world which have different sets of responsibilities ordained by God. Christians belong to both and will often have dual and competing loyalties. For some, the result has been a separation between spiritual matters and "earthly" concerns such as work, political authority, use of the sword, economics, etc., that are given a separate sphere in which to operate. The use of Luther's "two kingdoms" in certain segments of Protestantism has contributed to a bracketing and division that further removes issues such as work, military participation, politics, and economics from Christian moral critique.

cepted customary practices such as tax collecting. To think that there may have been no conflict between Zacchaeus's conversion and the purposes and practices of tax collecting reveals "thin" notions of conversion that are private and personal, and limited to a one-time event of "getting saved" with very little change or conflicts of conscience. As Lewis Rambo notes, conversion is far more complex and has implications for our moral commitments and "sociopolitical engagement." He writes,

> Genuine conversion requires that the person move and grow beyond mere personal conversion. Engaging the social institutions and systems of the wider world requires yet another level of conversion, and entails acknowledging accountability and taking responsibility, to the fullest degree possible, for the quality of life produced by these institutions. While the substance of the other forms of conversion are important, the core evaluation of social conversion is justice for all. For Christian converts, then, challenging institutions to live according to the ethics of Jesus would be a consistent, logical goal.[62]

An understanding of conversion that is continual and has moral implications affirms this important social dimension of conversion, in that "transformation cannot be a purely interior phenomenon; the energy it generates radiates out and modifies social structures."[63] While tax collecting provided basic amenities and services to persons, the means and ends of tax collecting could also be at odds with the moral vision of God's Kingdom of justice, mercy, and generosity. Tax collecting served the kingdom of Rome and ensured Rome's continual power and presence. Certain persons benefitted from tax collecting at the expense of those who become more impoverished and more vulnerable as a result of the system. Many of these were members of Zacchaeus's new community of Christian disciples. This placed

---

62. Lewis R. Rambo, *Understanding Religious Conversion* (New Haven, Conn.: Yale University Press, 1993), 147. Rambo is building on Donald Gelpi's proposal for five dimensions of conversion: affective, intellectual, ethical, religious, and social. I have a more modest expectation that institutions can live according to the ethic of Jesus but I appreciate and take seriously the challenge this notion of conversion presents to social ethics. See also the interesting essay by Stephen Long, "Corporations and the Ends We Serve," in *Calculated Futures: Theology, Ethics and Economics* (eds., D. Stephen Long and Nancy Ruth Fox, with Tripp York; Waco, Tex.: Baylor University Press, 2007). Long writes, "No one should expect members of a corporation to begin their day by citing the Nicene Creed . . . The point is not to turn the corporation into a confessional institution; it is to recognize that, for the baptized, their work in the corporation must be able to be offered to God's glory. No neutral space exists outside the vocation to offer our labor as such a gift. At the minimum, this requires that we not let our labor produce vices in us or others. At a maximum, we should not be surprised if opportunities arise to receive gifts of faith, hope, and charity through our daily labor" (127).

63. Johnstone, "The Dynamics of Conversion," 37.

Zacchaeus right in the middle of serving two masters and two kingdoms that at some point would need to be reconciled if conversion was to have a morally forming impact on his choices, practices, and commitments to the new community of Christ followers, and if his work was to reflect the priorities of the Kingdom. He could have been a good Christian trying to make a difference in a complex system or working to subvert it from the inside out. Or he could have been a part of propping up a system, engaging in practices, and serving ends, that belied the narrative to which he had been converted and the One to whom he made his confession of conversion.

Conclusion

My hope in this paper was to raise the possibility that conversion is on-going and has tangible effects on our attitudes and behaviors in such important areas like occupations and work. A progressive understanding of conversion helps us continually examine our choices, practices, and commitments in all areas of our lives. Our occupations are not in separate spheres or beyond the purview of moral critique. I realize there are no "pure" vocations devoid of conflict, dissonance, and ethical conundrums due to the complexity of economic and political structures. But I do want to hold out the possibility that there are some occupations which we just should not pursue and ones we should leave because, according to Miroslav Volf, they do not serve the purposes of God's "new creation."[64] Work that serves God's new creation is work that is "related to the goal of all history, which will bring God, human beings, and the nonhuman creation into 'shalomic' harmony."[65] Since conversion is the entrance and acceptance into this new creation, how we think about our work in light of our conversions and God's desires for creation is important.

What might be some questions for reflecting on the implications of our conversions and Christian commitments for the kinds of vocations we pursue and the work we do? The story of Zacchaeus makes a claim on us because it is in the sacred Scriptures that we see as authoritative and normative for Christian faith and practice. Even though we can only speculate on how it all turned out for Zacchaeus, we can

---

64. Miroslav Volf, *Work in the Spirit: Toward a Theology of Work* (Eugene, Ore.: Wipf and Stock, 2001; previously published by Oxford University Press, 1991), 79–85. Volf's theology of work arises out of the complex nature of employment in industrial societies which are very different from the context first century Palestine. Volf notes this difference (77), as do I. However Volf's proposals help us think about our work in light of our Christian commitments and the on-going realization of God's good purposes for the world.

65. Ibid., 85.

pose questions and exercise theological imagination.[66] If our work is an important means for serving God and reflecting God's intentions for creation, discerning the *kind* of work that contributes to God's "shalomic harmony," and what we should do in and through our work is important. As my pastor, the Rev. Jim Cox, reminded us in a recent sermon, "God is not indifferent to how we make money and how we spend money."[67] How does Christian faith guide our vocational choices? Who benefits from our work? Who is harmed by our work? How does the actual conducting of our work reflect the virtues and vision of the Kingdom of God? How does our work form us into more faithful disciples of Christ? How are our salaries obtained and invested, and resources shared with others in acts of justice and compassion? These questions simply offer a start to think about work in light of what it means to be a convert of Jesus Christ, invited in by the work of the Holy Spirit to participate in the good work of God in the world.

So, even as Christians, we still need to be continually converted. We will always need a radical reorientation of our lives to the purposes of God. We need to name the dissonance and conflicts between what we do and what we believe, particularly as they relate to such important activities as work. *Should* Zacchaeus have remained a tax collector? I don't think so. But should I continue to do what is acceptable, customary, and convenient in my work? I don't think so, especially if I am willing to be continually converted by the Gospel of Christ for the purposes of the continual conversion of God's creation toward "shalomic harmony" of justice and peace.

---

66. This point was made by Elizabeth Musselman Palmer since Luke does not give us the end of the story. Even though we cannot answer the question with assured definitiveness of whether or not Zacchaeus *should* have remained a tax collector, we are still left with a story that has implications for us which is the point.

67. This was part of a sermon series at Christ United Methodist Church in Ashland, Ohio, on *The Social Principles of the United Methodist Church, 2009–2012* (Washington, D.C.: United Methodist, 2009).

RESPONSE TO CORBIN REUSCHLING

Elizabeth Musselman Palmer

Having attended a Lutheran elementary school, I too grew up singing the Zacchaeus song, always in a classroom with twenty other young Lutherans. Our favorite line was always, "Zacchaeus, you come down," in part because children are so rarely allowed to address adults in the imperative mood while finger-wagging, but also because we saw in that moment of encounter with Jesus a relationship elicited by divine grace that we too hoped to be a part of. Any adult who climbs a tree must be very desperate, and as children we could relate to those feelings of desperation and powerlessness. And what made us love the story was the delightful fact that Zacchaeus gets *more* than he asks for—he gets not only to *see* Jesus, but even to talk to Jesus and invite him into his home. As little Lutherans we were taught that the story of Zacchaeus is about the generosity of divine grace. It was only when I was much older that I recognized that this story might also teach us something about conversion; that conversion itself is a manifestation of the generosity of divine grace.

I believe that Corbin Reuschling is right to locate Zacchaeus's conversion not in a single moment, but rather in "an on-going process of formation by and into a Christian narrative," which exists in and for "all dimensions of life." However, I'm not as convinced as Corbin Reuschling is (or as Fernando Méndez-Moratalla is) that Zacchaeus changed his behavior tangibly after seeing Jesus. In both the Greek New Testament and the Latin Vulgate, the verbs in Luke 19:8 are in the present tense ["I *give* to the poor, I *restore* fourfold to anyone"]. Although the present tense occasionally takes on a future meaning in Greek, nevertheless it is plausible to argue, as many exegetes have, that *before* his encounter with the Christ, and even before he thinks of climbing the tree to see Jesus, Zacchaeus is *already* being generous with the poor and restoring wealth to anyone he might have cheated. There is no unambiguous textual evidence for the supposition that he changes his behavior in this way only after meeting Jesus. And yet, as Corbin Reuschling demonstrates, we read the Zacchaeus story always with the hope of identifying tangible and immediate ways in which the encounter with Jesus changed his behavior. Even if we identify the tax collector's conversion as an ongoing process (which began long before the narrative moment at which Luke picks up the story and continued throughout Zacchaeus's life), nevertheless, we want Zacchaeus's conversion to be visible and identifiable. This is why some interpreters have gone so far as to suggest that the sycamore tree typifies the cross of Christ—and that in climbing the tree Zacchaeus immerses himself into the death of Christ, almost baptismally, thus entering into the salvation that the cross event effects. We want the moment in the tree to have the same theological and ethical *gravitas* that we seek in our own conversion stories.

Despite grammatical signs to the contrary, I don't believe that Corbin Reuschling is entirely mistaken in claiming that Zacchaeus "recognized wrong and made adjustments in the way he collected taxes, in his attitude and use of wealth, and his response to those he had exploited." After all, the meaning of a story is always located in its history of interpretation as well as the intent of the author. Zacchaeus is not only a first-century man who climbed a tree and spoke of his righteous behavior in the present tense; he has also functioned in the history of exegesis as a symbol of what it means to seek God and find God, to be called in an instant and converted over a lifetime, and to turn radically toward new life and new community. And if the story of Zacchaeus functions theologically in this way, Corbin Reuschling is right to suggest that the *where and when* of Zacchaeus's conversion are less significant for the life of the church than the ethical questions: *could* he have remained a tax collector and *should* he have remained a tax collector?

The answer to the former question (i.e., the *could* question) is speculative and is intertwined with larger questions about the nature of God and human nature as well as the relationship between divine activity, human activity, and human passivity. One who holds to a very low anthropology—like a Luther, or the late Augustine—would probably take issue with Corbin Reuschling's optimistic conviction that Zacchaeus could have fulfilled his putative promise to reform his work practices, and might instead question: *To what extent could Zacchaeus have hoped to change his behavior, given the reality of human failure*? Similarly, one who believes in predestination might ask: *By what (or whose) agency could Zacchaeus have reformed his life*? A question then arises for Corbin Reuschling: what is your theological anthropology, and how is your desire to identify tangible changes in Zacchaeus (whether gradual or sudden) informed by such anthropology? The more nuanced *could* questions do not necessarily change one's answer to the *should* question, but they do highlight the complexity of the theological issues at stake in ethical reflection for the life of the church. Further, they might add another *should* question: *Whether he remained a tax collector or not, what should Zacchaeus have done in each of those moments in his life when he failed to live righteously?* Corbin Reuschling hints at this question at the end of the paper when she suggests that perhaps we all fail in our vocations by upholding the status quo.

Identifying the particularities of Zacchaeus's post-tree behavior serves an important ethical function in the life of the church, but I wonder if there may be some significance also in the fact that Luke doesn't give us the end of the story. This is where Luke differs from John in the structure of conversion narration. In the great conversion story of John's gospel, the reader's uncertainty about the extent of Nicodemus's conversion is left unresolved as Nicodemus goes off into the night at the end of chapter three. But by the end of John's gospel Nicodemus has returned to the passion narrative twice: once to defend Jesus in front of the Pharisees and then again to take his body down from the cross, anoint it, wrap it in linens, and carry it to the tomb. That's exactly the kind of tangible evidence of conversion that Luke *does not* provide in the story of Zacchaeus. With Luke we are left hanging, not knowing the end of the conversion story.

But perhaps this is precisely the point. If Corbin Reuschling is right that in Luke-Acts the whole of the Christian life is a turning and a re-turning, if Zacchaeus's story is our story, and if this intersection of stories is meant to elicit in us ethical transformation then perhaps the end of Zacchaeus's life needs to remain unwritten. However he did or didn't reform his behavior and transform his vocation, we trust that Zacchaeus, that wee little man, is *now* in the presence of God with all the saints and sinners, seeing God face to face, living fully in the kingdom of justice and mercy that is so elusive on this earth. We trust that this will be the end of our story too, but in the meantime, as Corbin Reuschling stresses, *how* we negotiate the tensions of living responsibly under the burden of our failures has yet to be written and is of vital importance for this broken world. Called and converted, righteous and sinful, turned and turning, we negotiate the complexities of privilege and power; we forgive out of our goodness; and we seek forgiveness for our continuous deep failures. None of this is meant to be easy. The good news is that Zacchaeus most likely failed again and again, just as we will, and still God is calling us, inviting us to embody a narrative that is greater than any written story.

TOWARDS INDIVIDUAL AND COMMUNAL RENEWAL
Reflections on Luke's Theology of Conversion

Frank D. Macchia

I vividly recall answering the telephone one sunny afternoon in our small Swiss apartment located not far from the University of Basel. I was a doctoral student at the University hard at work on a seminar paper when I paused to take the call. A friendly female voice on the other end asked me if I was a Christian. I said that I was but that I also wanted to know why she was interested. The woman informed me that calling people at random for the purpose of bearing witness was her mission. I wished her well but before I had the chance to hang up she pressed the question as to how I *knew* that I was a Christian. Was I "born again"? A bit irritated at this point, I quickly responded, "Are you?" "Yes!" she enthusiastically answered and then promptly began to tell me her story. Sensing that I was getting more deeply involved in this call than I wanted to be, I took advantage of a pause in her narration to jump in with words of appreciation for her new life and mission. Yes, I assured her, I am indeed born again. This confession allowed me to hang up without further questions or insult either from her to me or from me to her. The major problem that I had with her call was the implication (real or merely perceived as such) that she had arrived and wanted to know if I had as well.

In fact, all that my uninvited caller wanted to know is whether or not I was among the *awakened*. Implied in her call was a desire to free me from a life of godlessness or of various aberrant forms of Christian faith, perhaps from a nominal Christianity devoid of a personal relationship with Jesus Christ. A clear consciousness of conversion was for her the hallmark of genuine Christianity and the dividing line between the true essence of Christianity and any counterfeit claims of Christian faith that might lead people astray. This call illustrates the ambiguity of conversion as a theological emphasis in the churches.

The Ambiguity of Conversion

This brief story reveals what turns many off within the churches today to the entire issue of "conversion." Highlighting conversion as a dividing line between true and false forms of Christian faith can sound narrow, judgmental, and elitist. Those who do so are pejoratively labeled "pietistic," "revivalistic," or an advocate of "born again Christianity." Among such folk as these the body of Christ can be superficially bifurcated between the truly awakened and the slothful in ways that serve the interests of (and elevates in significance) a particular church or family of churches. A focus on conversion can also lead to forms of evangelism by Evangelicals and Pentecostals towards those of the historic churches in ways that denigrate or ignore the historic witness of these churches to Christ in the world, a sore spot within ecumenical relations. Christian groups that highlight conversion in this way even tend to quarrel with each other as to the proper steps to be taken in the overall process of Christian initiation. If there are any doubts about this, just ask a group of Evangelicals from various denominations to explain the role of water and Spirit baptism in one's turn to Christ! Moreover, Christian movements that stress the experience of conversion can end up disrespecting people of other religions, since a conversion-driven mission sometimes leaves no place for valuing the religious journey of the other as a genuine seeker after God.

Furthermore, a preoccupation with conversion can lead to church services intentionally bent on manipulating people's emotions so as to gain a certain kind of religious (or financial!) response. Potential violence is done especially to young people or to children who might be coerced into psychologically premature or otherwise unhealthy forms of religious devotion. The significance of process and development in Christian conversion is often neglected. Even those otherwise sympathetic to born again Christianity detect a possible imbalance in a focus on conversion that accents the human response to God more than the activity of God in the world to liberate and to redeem the creation. This imbalance in favor of conversion is not exclusively an Evangelical problem, since one can argue that the Protestant Reformation sought to deliver folks from the medieval Catholic preoccupation with conversion and penance in order to place the emphasis back on the triumph of God's grace over sin and death in the crucifixion and resurrection of Jesus Christ. Some blame Protestant "pietism" and revivalism for an unhealthy return to a preoccupation with conversion or with inner piety. Often labeled "pietistic" in the pejorative sense, conversion has also tended to be highlighted among those churches that stress an individualistic relationship with Jesus Christ without much sensitivity to the significance of faith as a communal dynamic. It seems that there are numerous potential difficulties involved in an accent on Christian conversion.

How can it be otherwise? After all, conversion is not only dependent on a divine act; it is also a human reality with all of the ambiguities and potential abuses to which any human response to the Holy Spirit is vulnerable. As an act of God, conversion is a wonderful gift to be celebrated. But as a human turning, it is vulnerable to various dangers and misunderstandings. Yet, despite the dangers, we ignore the importance of conversion at our own peril. A certain attention to the reality of conversion is the correlate to the biblical conviction that creation has been made for something other than its current state of captivity to sin and death. Conversion is a necessary consequence also of the belief that God is the living God "who gives life to the dead and calls things that are not as though they were" (Rom 4:17).[1] In the light of these bedrock biblical truths, how can we avoid the reality of faith as a turning from death to life, the very life of the eternal God? As Karl Barth wrote concerning conversion:

> The witness of Holy Scripture is that God does this. We would have to reject its witness altogether if we were to deny that it is also the witness to this reality. What the church makes of this is another question. It has made of it many things—some good and some bad. It has often seemed not to know how to make anything of it at all. But it can never or never altogether, set it aside, or ignore or forget it.[2]

Since conversion is biblical, we would do well to explore its vital truth for our time. There are signs that the churches are desirous of this. The eighth assembly of the World Council of Churches in Harare in 1998 had as its theme, "Turn to God: Rejoice in Hope."

In general, it seems that we in the Evangelical churches require greater humility in how we talk about conversion. Rather than an individualistic claim on having been awakened in distinction from those who have not, we should strive instead to reach for a more holistic and process oriented understanding of conversion that sees conversion as both an event and a process in which one journeys with others towards greater understanding of what it means to follow Christ in the world. One has not yet "arrived." Conversion always catches us off guard and leaves us open to learn from others, including those from churches very different from our own.

---

1. Unless otherwise noted, all biblical quotations are from NIV.

2. Karl Barth, *Church Dogmatics* (eds. Geoffrey W. Bromiley and Thomas F. Torrance; vol. IV/2; Edinburgh: T. & T. Clark, 1958), 559.

We are not meant to forget that conversion is indeed an event. But this event also leads to a process. Something is always dying and being born in us as the circle of reconciliation expands within and among the churches. To explore this more corporate (relational) and ecumenically open understanding of conversion, I will look to Luke's missionary theology of the Spirit.

Conversion: A Lucan Theology

Luke shares with all four Gospels a focus on the Messiah's role as the coming One who will baptize in the Holy Spirit and fire (Matt 3:16-17; Mark 1:8; Luke 3:15-18; John 1:32-33). This is foretold by John the Baptist whose mission it will be to covert the wayward of Israel: "Many of the people of Israel will he bring back to the Lord their God. And he will go on before the Lord, in the spirit and power of Elijah, to turn the hearts of the fathers to their children and the disobedient to the wisdom of the righteous—to make ready a people prepared for the Lord" (Luke 1:16-17). The Old Testament contrasted physical and spiritual circumcision (e.g., Deut 30:6). In highlighting the Messiah as the Spirit Baptizer, John contrasted his material (water) baptism with the Messiah's spiritual baptism. The meaning of both contrasts is similar. Religious ceremony can be meaningful but only as a witness to a deeper work of the Spirit of God. The law can bear witness to life but only the Spirit can grant it. True conversion is only possible due to a deeper change of heart brought about by the Spirit of God. To prepare for the coming Spirit, John the Baptist asked the Jewish leaders to "produce fruit in keeping with repentance" (Luke 3:8), for the time is coming in which the winds of the Spirit will separate those who are turning to God from those who have not: "His winnowing fork is in his hand to clear his threshing floor and to gather the wheat into his barn, but he will burn up the chaff with unquenchable fire" (Luke 3:17). The same Spirit that will baptize those who repent will judge those who do not.

What is interesting about John's ministry was the fact that he called the "righteous" to convert along with the sinners, a point stressed further by Jesus. Jesus preached repentance and conversion, granting the grace to do so especially among the sick and the outcast. This focus sets the stage for audience *resistance* among the righteous to these conversions. A poor blind beggar (presumably Bartimaeus, Luke 18:35-43) and a rich tax official (Zacchaeus, Luke 19:1-9) both convert over the complaints of the righteous. The blind man is hushed when addressing Jesus by a messianic title and Jesus is accused of accepting hospitality from a sinner when he agrees to visit Zacchaeus. Jesus grants the blind man the dignity of addressing him messianically and heals him in his process of turning to Christ for help. The implication is that conversion is not just a cognitive process but also a turning to Christ for help in times of desperate need. Zacchaeus's conversion functions as proof positive that all things are possible with God, a point that Jesus makes after the rich young ruler turns away, thereby showing how hard it is for a rich man to enter the Kingdom of God (Luke 18:18–29). In both cases, the conversion of the outcast offends those considered accepted within the household of God. It seems that more than the unrighteous require conversion. So do those regarded as righteous. More to the point, conversion requires expansive forms of reconciliation within the community of faith, being a communal as well as an individual experience, an ongoing process as well as an event.

For Luke, this adventure in conversion will involve a new community that is reconciled and is reconciling. Jesus in fact reached out to both the outcast and the Jewish leaders *in relation to each other*, implying that conversion was a communal and not just an individual reality. Both those coming in and those already in (at least presumably) must change. The parable of the Lost Sons (not lost "Son" as our individualistic mindset would have it) of Luke 15 illustrates this point well. In the previous chapter, Jesus exhorted the Jewish leaders to invite the outcasts to their banquet table (Luke 14:12–14). It seems that this charge to accept the unclean outcasts at the banquet table was criticized at least by some. The next chapter is prefaced by the complaints being voiced by some of the Pharisees and teachers of the law concerning Jesus: "This man welcomes sinners and eats with them" (Luke 15:2). This complaint is the setting in which Jesus then tells the parable of the Lost Sons. In this parable, conversion is highlighted, since, unlike the Lost Sheep or Lost Coin, the errant younger son who squanders his inheritance in a distant land has a change of heart and returns to the household of his father. The younger son said to himself: "I will set out and go back to my father and say to him: Father, I have sinned against heaven and against you. I am no longer worthy to be called your son; make me like one of your hired men" (15:18–19).

Rather than receiving the wayward younger son as a household servant, however, the father receives him as a royal guest. The excessive grace of the father towards the outcast younger son, however, catches the elder son completely off guard. It overturned the system of punishment and reward upon which he had come to rely. Even though he had not received as much reward as he might have wished, he was at least able to comfort himself with the thought that he was better off than his outcast sibling. But the shameless display of grace poured out upon this undeserving wretch of a son was simply too much to bear! It must have appeared as the height of injustice. God's justice, rooted in mercy and fulfilled in redemptive grace, appears to those bound to systems of exchange as the height of injustice. As the father implores the elder son to join him at the banquet table, the elder son rebukes him for transgressing the rules of fair play: "Look!" he replies to his father, "All these years I've been slaving for you and never disobeyed your orders. Yet you never gave me even a young goat so I could celebrate with my friends. But when this son of yours who has squandered your property with prostitutes comes home, you kill the fattened calf for him!" (15:29–30). The father reminds him by way of response that their own relationship was rooted in grace: "You are always with me, and everything I have is yours" (v.31). He then reminds the elder brother (who had referred to his younger brother as "this son of yours" when speaking to the father) that "this brother of yours" now requires grace as well. Besides, love demands a celebration at the return of a lost family member: "we had to celebrate and be glad, because this brother of yours was dead and is alive again; he was lost and is found" (v. 32). Divine justice serves divine love. Love does the right thing when it shows mercy and celebrates its fulfillment in a repentant heart. Conversion depends on the grace of God from beginning to end. The end result is the needed conversion of both brothers in relation to each other.

Jesus in fact ends up in Luke's Gospel doing more than is indicated by the parable of the Lost Sons. As the faithful Son, he goes to the far country on the cross to give his life as a ransom for many in order to bring the outcast and the so-called righteous together to the banquet table. The disciples themselves only gradually became aware of the significance of what Christ had done for them, piecing it together only after the resurrection. The angel reminds the women at the empty tomb: "'He is not here; he has risen! Remember how he told you, while he was still with you in Galilee that the Son of Man must be delivered into the hands of sinful men, be crucified and on the third day be raised again.' Then they remembered his words . . ." (Luke 24:6–8, NRSV).

After Jesus' resurrection, Luke gives us a foretaste of how the community of faith will function as the womb of conversion in the story of the two men on the road to Emmaus (Luke 24:13–35). The risen Christ encounters the two men while they were discussing the events recorded in Luke's Gospel surrounding Jesus' unlawful crucifixion and the reports of the empty tomb. The irony is that they were discussing these events with the risen Christ! Christ took the time as they walked to explain the scriptural prophecies concerning his death. After agreeing to stay with them, he and they sat at the table to break bread together. After Jesus broke the bread, gave thanks, and gave it to them, their eyes were opened and they recognized him. He then vanished from their sight. They recalled afterwards, "Were not our hearts burning within us while he talked with us on the road and opened the Scriptures to us?" (Luke 24:32). They also explained later to the disciples "how Jesus was recognized by them when he broke the bread" (24:35). It seems Luke gives us an early indication here of how those who seek out the community of the Scriptures and of the grateful breaking of bread will discover within it the risen Christ. Conversion is not only an individual event but a communal journey in the Scriptures and at an expanding (increasingly diverse) table fellowship in communion with Christ.

Luke tells us that this community of the proclaimed Word and the broken bread will represent the occasion for conversion precisely as the dwelling place of the Holy Spirit, who is poured out from the exalted Christ on behalf of the heavenly Father (Acts 1:6-8; 2:4f; 2:33). The goal of the Spirit is to turn people to God so that they might become a living witness as a reconciled and reconciling community. The larger goal is that "everyone who calls on the name of the Lord will be saved" (2:21). The story of Acts is not only about the work of the Spirit in turning people to Christ through the living witness and proclamation of the church, it is also about the ongoing conversion of the community of faith as it expands to take in the "other." Philip and the Samaritans (Acts 8:4-13), Philip and the Ethiopian Eunuch (Acts 8:26-40), Paul under the ministry of Ananias (Acts 9:10-19), and Peter and Cornelius (Acts 10:1-48) are classic cases in point. This series of conversions serve Luke's overall narrative theology of the Holy Spirit. This theology moves on the conviction that the Spirit is meant to bring the good news to the "ends of the earth" through the witness of the church as part of the ever expansive reign of God in the world (1:3-8).

Acts 2 symbolizes this ever expansive and increasingly diverse missionary fellowship with the public event of speaking in tongues as the Holy Spirit fell upon the original company of Jesus' disciples in the world. These tongues recall for many the Tower of Babel incident of Genesis 11. Genesis 1:28 offers us insight into the divine mandate to multiply and to fill the earth. Genesis 11 grants us a contrary vision involving an effort of a people to centralize power and to focus on the task of achieving a name for itself. In confusing their tongues and in scattering them, they are forced to follow the mandate of Genesis 1:28, though not in the most ideal of circumstances. It is possible to argue that Luke has in mind the issue of a scattered people in his tongues narrative of Acts 2. Diaspora Jews from many nations come together to witness the tongues event. Luke, however, does not limit the plight of a scattered people to Israel. In Paul's sermon on Mars Hill (Acts 17:16–34), Luke seems to hearken back to Genesis 11 by reminding his readers that many peoples were scattered and needed to find their way back to God: "From one man he made every nation of men, that they should inhabit the whole earth; and he determined the times set for them and the exact places where they should live. God did this so that men would seek him and perhaps reach out for him and find him, though he is not far from each one of us" (Acts 17:26–27). Not only Israel but also the nations were scattered and Pentecost is the clarion call for them to return.

The tongues of Acts 2 symbolize the coming together of many scattered peoples, not only the Diaspora Jews but also the Gentiles. The diversified tongues are not the confused cacophony of Genesis 11 but rather a united witness to the risen Christ. They do not represent an expanding division and alienation but rather a reconciled community that is continuously reconciling. The diversity is not only a curse but now also a promise. The promise is that the Spirit of God that hovered over Israel is now to hover over the nations as well. Conversion will cause an increasingly expansive and diverse coming together of people from every nation. Unity will not be uniformity but rather a differentiated unity that respects otherness as much as commonality. Conversion will not only be an event but in some sense also a process, not only an individual but also a communal reality.

Luke prefaced the Acts 2 tongues event with the challenge to witness to Christ to the very ends of the earth (1:8). In chapter 2, the challenge is also to witness the eschatological horizon of the Spirit coming upon all flesh. But this "flesh" is not mentioned as a generalized or generic category. The term is granted specificity involving national and language groups, young and old, as well as male and female servants. Not only will others convert, but the community "converts" as well as it expands its borders to accommodate the unexpected newcomers. The greatest challenge, of course, will be the bringing together of Jew and Gentile, which is why the story of the household of Cornelius plays such a pivotal role in the narrative (occupying chapters 10 and 11 and setting the stage for chapter 15). But the diversity also includes the poor (2:18; 2:45), the young and the aged (2:17), women as well as men (2:17), and the possibly competing religious community devoted to John the Baptist (19:1–6). I wish briefly to discuss the major conversion cases of Acts in order to reveal both the individual and the communal aspects of conversion.

The church had just received a series of serious blows. The apostles had been arrested and put in jail (5:18). Peter and John were flogged and threatened (5:40). Stephen was stoned to death (7:54–59). It was on the heels of these threatening events, however, that Luke reports the church's greatest breakthroughs. Philip goes out to preach to the Samaritans, the very people that many Jews considered racially impure and religiously inferior. Many came to Philip seeking help from illness and demonic oppression. They expressed faith in the word of God and found deliverance: "With shrieks, evil spirits came out of many, and many paralytics and cripples were healed. So there was great joy in that city" (8:7–8). As under the ministry of Jesus, many converted in the midst of deliverance from disease and oppression. Again, conversion was not just a cognitive process but a deep and total transformation from "darkness to light."[3]

Peter and John soon arrived to pray for the Samaritan crowd. As with the earliest followers of Jesus in Jerusalem, the Samaritans received the Spirit (8:14–17). The symbol of these chief apostles laying hands on Samaritans implies that turning to the Lord implies an unexpected turning of alienated people to each other. Even Simon the Sorcerer prayed in a way that implied repentance (8:24). The word and spirit of God reached out to those who seemed to disgust the community of faith the most. They all joined the converted Jews in the missionary fellowship of the Spirit. The community of the Spirit or of the Messiah was expanding and converting to the expanding reign of God in the world.

Philip then encountered an Ethiopian eunuch in the desert. The man had been to Jerusalem to worship and, yet, he was also a foreigner from a far-off land. The eunuch had just read from Isaiah 53 and was struck by the moving lines depicting the despised and rejected servant of God: "In his humiliation he was deprived of justice. Who can speak of his descendants?" (8:33). There is little wonder that a eunuch would have been drawn to these lines. He himself had been set apart for his role as a eunuch in a way that he might have thought deprived him of the privileges of home and family. Perhaps he was in a unique position to understand the servant who was deprived of justice and of descendents. Philip immediately directed his attention to Jesus as that servant. Jesus was deprived of justice in his unlawful death, and yet God vindicated him and made him the means by which to redeem the world. The eunuch was able to identify with Christ. This foreigner without any descendents found a home in the family of God.

We then reach the extremely important account of Paul's conversion in Acts 9. Since this testimony is repeated in Acts (Acts 21:1–21, 26:1–18), it obviously played a significant role in the narrative. Luke accents the fact that Paul was an enemy of

---

3. Beverly Gaventa's accent in *From Darkness to Light: Aspects of Conversion in the New Testament* (OBT 20; Minneapolis: Fortress, 1986).

God and of God's people: "Saul was still breathing out murderous threats against the Lord's disciples" (9:1). Yet, Paul encountered the risen Lord in a blinding light. The Lord identified himself as Jesus whom Paul was persecuting. The injustice of the crucifixion (a major theme in Acts) is seemingly furthered according to Jesus in Paul's persecution of the Lord's body. The solidarity between Jesus and his community is powerfully expressed in this story. To convert to Jesus was to convert to his family and the family included in its ongoing movement from repentance to faith an acceptance of those who come to the Lord. The community of Jesus was both reconciled and reconciling (converted and converting).

After Paul converted to Jesus Christ, the community of faith was obviously stuck with a dilemma. Were they to trust this enemy of the faith? And, even if they trusted him, could they so easily forget what he had done to them? The act of Ananias in laying hands on Paul to pray for him across a gulf of misunderstanding and pain is symbolic of the fact that reconciliation with the Lord is a horizontal reality as well (9:17). Paul acknowledged as much when noting that he was not worthy of his calling: "For I am the least of the apostles and do not even deserve to be called an apostle, because I persecuted the church of God. But by the grace of God I am what I am, and his grace to me was not without effect" (1 Cor 15:9–10). Surely this grace included not only Jesus' acceptance but that of his body whom Paul persecuted.

We then come to the startling conversion of Cornelius (and Peter!). An important turning point for Peter will come in his mission to the household of Cornelius. Peter was prepared for the encounter with Cornelius by a vision containing an array of animals considered unclean for consumption. God told Peter to eat one of them, causing in Peter an unprecedented conflict between a command from God and Peter's understanding of the implications of Jewish ceremonial law. He felt at first forced to disobey the Lord's direct command: "Surely not, Lord!" (10:14). Then the Lord commanded him further: "Do not call anything impure that God has made clean" (10:15). The dream was repeated three times as a witness to Peter. As the Lord, God asserted sovereignty with regard to the fulfillment of the law. What God regards as clean is clean. Case closed! Even piety can turn into an idol if it leads to disobedience. Peter had to "convert" in his mission to convert Cornelius. The two conversions are not the same to be sure, but they are analogous. Something must continue to die and be awakened in the Lord's followers as they continue to turn away from their own selves in obedience to what God is doing in the world through the Spirit.

While still contemplating the meaning of the dreams, Peter was instructed by God to follow the visitors to Cornelius' household, for God regarded Cornelius as "a righteous and God-fearing man, who is respected by all the Jewish people" (10:22). Upon entering Cornelius's household, Peter's opening remarks in addressing the large gathering there focused immediately on his "conversion" with regard to the Gentile world: "You are well aware that it is against our law for a Jew to associate with a Gentile or visit him. But God has shown me that I should not call any man impure or unclean" (10:28). Peter elaborated: "I now realize how true it is that God does not show favoritism but accepts men from every nation who fear him and do what is right" (10:34–35). In the light of his newly expansive view of God's liberating reign in the world, Peter proclaimed Christ crucified and risen to his Gentile audience. As he was yet speaking, the Spirit came upon them as he had upon the Jewish audience at the beginning, including the speaking in other tongues (10:44–46; 11:15).

Apparently, the tongues event of chapter 2 signaled a move of the Spirit in the world more radical in implication than Peter had realized. In accepting Cornelius, Peter had radically to change his view of Gentiles. Luke even indicates that Cornelius's religious journey towards Christ was respected, for Peter recognized that God "accepts men from every nation who fear him and do what is right" (10:35). Later in Acts, Luke highlighted Paul's message that God had directed the paths of all peoples in the world "so that men would seek him and perhaps reach out for him and find him, though he is not far from each one of us. 'For in him we live and move and have our being.' As some of your own poets have said, 'We are his offspring.'" (17:27–28). In converting to God's reign among the Gentiles, Peter was turning towards a larger picture of the reign of God in the world, one implied in the tongues of Pentecost but which transcended Peter's former awareness. Though Peter's and Cornelius' conversions were obviously not the same, they were analogous, and the two men needed each other for them to occur. The parable of the Lost Sons takes on an expansive significance.

In all of these cases, it took all of the church's energy and effort to simply try to keep up with the work of the Spirit in the world. The reign of God in the world moved forward with the church lagging clumsily behind and struggling to die to former ungodly attitudes in order to awaken ever anew to more expansive horizons opened up by the work of the Spirit. For example, the decision of the church in chapter 15 to accept the cleansing and Spirit-filling of the Gentiles solely on the basis of their faith in Christ seems to be a ground-breaking event until one realizes that it occurs five chapters after the Spirit had already made their acceptance a foregone conclusion! The church in Acts moved like Socrates' clumsy steed spurred on by the voice of the Spirit and struggling to move ever more deeply towards God and away from its sin. This clumsiness can be seen in one sense as unfortunate but in another as promising. At least this church was on the move by God's grace towards the horizon of the Spirit! This movement is certainly preferable to the standstill or even wrong direction experienced among some churches today!

The many churches today that tout the "born-again" experience as a way of distinguishing themselves as the awakened ones from the "worldly" churches should take heed. Even the most awakened churches exemplified in Acts had to live from a perpetually painful and humbling conversion experience, one that caused them to depart from long held and even cherished beliefs. To use the born-again slogan as a cheap means for self-aggrandizement runs completely contrary to the true nature of conversion. Conversion should bring about humility, critical self-evaluation, and openness to the other to see what God would teach us about the expanding horizon of the Kingdom of God in the world.

The communal dynamic of conversion as a journey also helps us to understand Jesus' stinging words of Luke 6:37: "Do not condemn, and you will not be condemned. Forgive, and you will be forgiven." We often move quickly past such words with the assurance that our forgiveness is solely dependent on Christ in isolation from anything else. But in Luke's missionary theology, conversion is also horizontal. One's attitude towards Christ cannot be neatly separated from Christ's body. The risen Christ asked Paul on the Damascus Road, "Saul, Saul, why do you persecute me?" (9:4). There was no way that Paul could have embraced the risen Christ while still persecuting his body. Forgiveness involves a gift that is both received and given.

Concluding Reflections

Luke's missionary theology of the Holy Spirit implies that conversion is both individual and communal, an event of turning as well as an ongoing process of turning in obedience to Christ. It has its stages and growth. It must not be rushed or manipulated (after all, it's the Lord's work) but it must also not stall. It is also humble and open to God's work among the others who are different from us, even in piety. The community of faith in turning to Christ turns also towards the "other" with an offer of gracious hospitality. The offer is not given with a hidden agenda to do violence to the other by manipulating him or her to a group think. Otherness is respected in the offer of grace and the community is willing to "convert" in incorporating this other in all of his or her God-given uniqueness. The "all flesh" upon whom the Spirit will fall (and is falling) implies a journey of painful conversion by which Jews and Gentiles, young and old, rich and poor, find each other at the table of Christ and submit to one another out of reverence for him (Eph 5:21). They will constantly die to idolatrous attachment to any particular sense of self and will yield both to Christ and to what Christ is doing to form a diverse people. In yielding to Christ they yield to what his Spirit is doing among the increasingly diverse giftings arising in our midst.

The influx of diverse peoples into the community of faith will cause us to convert as we rejoice in their conversion. As Miroslav Volf notes, conversion does not annihilate the self. Our unique otherness is not sacrificed on the altar of conversion. For Luke, the many tongues of the nations are not dissolved but rather brought together in all of their colorful diversity into a unified witness to Christ. For Volf, the self is rather "de-centered" in conversion in order to yield the center to Christ. This yielding the center to Christ causes the self to yield also to the other who comes in Christ's name[4] (see, "Submit to one another out of reverence for Christ," Eph 5:21). The impulse to manipulate the other out of some self-serving motive is resisted. The other is respected and allowed to flourish in relation to me in his or her obedience to Christ. In short, in converting and continuing to convert to Christ, I am also converting in relation to the other. I cannot turn to Christ again and again without turning in love and grace to this other who stands with me in Christ's name. There is no conversion that exalts me or separates me from the other as spiritually superior. Conversion is continuously a humbling of the self in relation to Christ and the other.

The goal is that the people of God might then become the church for others in the world. The church's expanding unity in diversity is ultimately to provide a witness to the ends of the earth of the crucified and risen Christ. Hospitality is not confined to the household of faith but is also extended outward towards the others not of that household. Evangelism is a form of hospitality. We seek to be a source of grace to them while inviting them to join our table of fellowship so as to glorify Christ with their unique giftings in fellowship with us. In making this invitation, we are willing to die to whatever is within us that would resist what God is doing and wills to do in and through them. Cherished beliefs might have to die in the process. In submitting to Christ we must submit to them too, to that which manifests Christ in them. In turning to Christ we turn to that which Christ has done and is doing in

---

4. Miroslav Volf, *Exclusion and Embrace: A Theological Exploration of Identity, Otherness, and Reconciliation* (Nashville: Abingdon, 1996), 69–71.

and through them. The many tongues of Pentecost point to a painful but also richly rewarding process of converting so that the people of God can become the diverse chorus to Christ that God wills by the Spirit for them to become.

Reconciliation across deep gulfs of misunderstanding and even suffering is never easy. We should never take it lightly. The book of Acts shows us how difficult it can be. Conversion in the larger sense of the word is thus a journey fraught with both difficulty and promise. Volf reminds us that reconciliation in turning towards each other requires both parties to turn. Not only Luke but also Paul wrote about Jew and Gentile forming a new humanity through the obedience of both to the way of the cross (Eph 2:11–22) as well as to the transforming power of the Spirit that allows them to reflect the Lord to each other "from glory to glory" (2 Cor 3:18). Until such ongoing reconciliation is achieved and cultivated, we can at least hold out the will to embrace. The community of faith in its conversion to Christ holds out this will to embrace out of obedience to Christ. If terms like "conversion," "revival," and "born again" are ever to regain their usefulness in the larger body of Christ outside of the Evangelical movement as terms to celebrate and even highlight, we will need to approach them with all due humility, self-sacrifice, and love. Such terms cannot be used as weapons unjustifiably to exclude others or to lift some communities of faith up as a Christian elite. They must be used to explain the joy involved in following after Christ both as individuals and as communities. Accent upon it must be a source of ongoing self-criticism and renewal. If evidence of that renewal is clear from our communities, then the language that we use to explain this reality will mean something.

RESPONSE TO MACCHIA

D. Christopher Spinks

I do not think that Frank Macchia intended to recall for me my childhood days at Hickory Grove Baptist Church (HGBC) outside Kilgore, Tex. Indeed, he is quite clear about his topic—Luke's theology of conversion. But early in his essay he delineates five things that turn many off "to the entire issue of conversion." He notes how a focus on conversion too often leads to a "superficially bifurcated" body; how certain forms of evangelism within traditions that stress conversion can "denigrate or ignore the witness of [historic churches] to Christ in the world"; how churches that highlight conversion "even tend to quarrel with each other as to the proper steps to be taken in the overall process of Christian initiation"; and how a stress on the experience of conversion can disrespect people of other religions. These four things remind me of many of my experiences growing up as a faithful member of HGBC. It is what Macchia notes as a fifth result of a preoccupation with conversion, however, that fully opens the door to my memories of life there. He says that such a preoccupation "can lead to church services intentionally bent on manipulating people's emotions so as to gain a certain kind of religious (or financial!) response. Potential violence is done especially to young people or to children who might be coerced into psychologically unhealthy forms of religious devotion." After reading these lines, I was unable to continue the essay without memories of summer revivals, pulpit pounding, prolonged invitations with all six verses of "Just As I Am," and Sunday School role-playing to practice witnessing to friends at school.

I wish I had heard Macchia's words in those earlier days. They are words I wish folks at HGBC could hear—would be able to hear! I would like them to hear it said that "conversion has tended to be highlighted among those churches that stress an individualistic relationship with Jesus Christ without much sensitivity to the significance of faith as a communal dynamic," and be able to recognize themselves in those words. I would like them to hear how conversion is both a gift from God and "a human reality with all of the ambiguities and potential abuses to which any human response to the Holy Spirit is vulnerable." Macchia's survey of conversion in Luke-Acts would have helped me see much earlier that even the righteous require conversion.

His exploration of the story of the Lost Son(s) would have shown me the communal dimension of the conversion event that neither of my two revival-induced "conversions" ever demonstrated. It would have been nice to hear a revival preacher, influenced by Macchia's essay, use the Emmaus Road story to illustrate "how those who seek out the community of the Scriptures and of the grateful breaking of bread will discover within it the risen Christ," rather than the more typical appeal "to recognize Jesus as you walk down the road and turn your life over to him."

I've come a long way down the road to Emmaus since HGBC. I very much appreciate how Macchia's Lucan description of conversion rightly challenges many well-worn dyads. The individual/communal dyad is highlighted in the title of his essay. But the essay also calls attention to the dyads of vertical/horizontal, receiving/giving grace, spiritual/material transformation, one-time event/ongoing process, mental assent/lived reality, and repentance/faith. Like Macchia, I too want to see terms like "conversion," "revival," and "born again" regain their usefulness in the larger body of Christ. He does us a service by offering reparative notions of conversion through a more holistic account, but his is most often a repairing of evangelical types.

And, while you can take the boy out of Hickory Grove, you can't take Hickory Grove out of the boy. It is that part of me that recognizes well the needed words of Macchia's essay. But it is also that part of me that wonders what, if anything, is good and right about the evangelical use of conversion language. What contribution do the evangelical notions of conversion, which Macchia seems to be combating most, have to make to the conversation? There is, surely, much that I wish HGBC could hear, but I also wonder what the folks at HGBC might have to say to us on this topic.

As I grow further away from my days among those folks, I also recall a people—a family—who demonstrated a humility, self-sacrifice, and love that one young boy has rarely seen since. And though the language of "conversion" and being "born again" was too often shouted from the "revival" pulpit, the communal aspect of one's conversion experience was manifested in the way the converted grew to see life together in the joyful process of this community of faith caring for one another. Quite often those communities that emphasize conversion most strongly (even in unhealthy ways) are also the same communities that evidence the following of Christ most joyfully. I fear their voices may get muffled as our understanding of conversion broadens.

In addition to my recollection of younger days, I also could not help but read Macchia's Lucan survey with the eye of one who teaches a seminary course on Acts. I was pleased to read his conclusion that "Conversion should bring about humility, critical self-evaluation, and openness to the other to see what God would teach us about the expanding horizon of the Kingdom of God in the world." This echoes well the structure of Acts as a movement of the Spirit-led witness "in Jerusalem, in all of Judea and Samaria, and to the ends of the earth" (1:8).[1] Macchia highlights the "major conversion cases of Acts in order to reveal both the individual and the communal aspects of conversion." The conversions of Peter and Paul are taken up in other symposium papers, so I would like to turn our attention to Macchia's references to the Pentecost event in Acts 2. He says, "Acts 2 symbolizes this ever expansive and increasingly diverse missionary fellowship," and he makes the well-known and lectionary-supported move of connecting Acts 2 to Genesis 11 and the Tower of Babel incident. There is surely something to this connection and to the church's reading of this connection, especially given the scattering and coming together of many tongues. But it is not clear that Luke intended the connection or that the original audience would have made it. For one, the Babel event was what we might call a miracle of speaking—a people of one language becomes a people of many languages. The Pentecost event, though it records speaking in other languages, is more a miracle of hearing. The Jews of many nations *heard* the Galileans speak "in the native tongue of each" (2:6). It is still a people of many languages.

More significantly though, Mikeal Parsons suggests that there is more evidence for linking the Pentecost episode with the renewal of the Sinai covenant.[2] There is evidence in the book of *Jubilees* (1.1 and 6.1) and an explicit joining in later rabbinic literature (b. Pesaḥ. 68b) that Pentecost was associated with Moses's being given the law. The phenomena of sound, fire, and speech were associated with the Sinai theophany (Ex 19:16–19; cf. Philo, *Decal.* 9:33). And, the giving of a new covenant is something that Luke has already highlighted when, in Luke 22:20, Jesus refers to a new covenant in his blood (though, there is some textual question as to whether this portion is original). Furthermore, in the speech that follows the Pentecost event, Peter makes clear "that receiving the Holy Spirit at Pentecost is the fulfillment of the ancestral promise given to Abraham."[3] Pentecost, when viewed in its connection with the giving of the law and fulfillment of the promise to Abraham, is still an event

---

1. Unless otherwise noted, all biblical quotations are from NRSV.
2. Mikeal C. Parsons, *Acts* (PCNT 3; Grand Rapids: Baker, 2008), 36–37.
3. Ibid., 37.

symbolic of the "differentiated unity" of the early Christian community, but it is more importantly a part of Luke's larger ecclesiological purpose, as David Aune puts it, of addressing Christianity's need for definition, identity, and legitimation.[4]

We might also bring up here the claim that "the decision of the church in chapter 15 [was] to accept the cleansing and Sprit-filling of the Gentiles solely on the basis of their faith." While this statement is true in most respects, the Jerusalem council also writes, "For it has seemed good to the Holy Spirit and to us to *impose* on you no further burden than these essentials: that you abstain from idols and from blood and from what is strangled and from fornication. If you keep yourselves from these, you will do well" (15:28–29, my emphasis). Likewise, the Pauline notion of mutual submission in Eph 5:21, to which Macchia points toward the end of the essay, is followed by a rather exclusivist list of household codes (Eph 5:22–33). Those critical of Paul, who latch on to passages like this to build arguments for his patriarchal, even misogynistic, perspective, are at least right to notice Paul's recognition of and even tacit support of dividing walls. One can argue whether they are dividing walls of hostility, or if Paul is doing what he can to weaken the walls, but they are walls, nonetheless.

So while Macchia is right, in my estimation, to argue for an expanded view of conversion, there are still socially-defined boundaries at play. Elsewhere in the letter to the Ephesians we read that God, "has made known to us the mystery of his will, according to his good pleasure that he set forth in Christ, as a plan for the fullness of time, to gather up all things in him, things in heaven and things on earth" (1:9–10). It seems to me there is some distinction to be made between the gathering up or subsuming of "all" things and the death of "all" prejudice. How are we to situate the defining and identity-shaping of the early Christians and the dividing walls that still seem evident in Luke and Paul? More pointedly, if Christian community is to be distinctive, are there not boundaries or identity markers that must remain in place?

In the end, I am asking us to consider two things: firstly, the contribution of the folks at HGBC and other "born-again" types to this conversation about holistic conversion; and secondly, the dyadic relationship between conversion as inclusion in an "increasingly expansive" and yet *distinct* community.

---

4. David E. Aune, *The New Testament in Its Literary Environment* (LEC 8; Philadelphia: Westminster, 1987), 137.

WAS PAUL A CONVERT?

Scot McKnight[1]

Asking if Paul was a "convert" is a bit like asking if a tomato is a vegetable. I grew up being taught that tomatoes are vegetables and one reason I knew they were was because they grew in my father's vegetable garden. Everyone knows that fruits do not grow in vegetable gardens. Then one day my son came home from high school and calmly declared that tomatoes were fruits and he trotted out a reason or two. I have since pondered this question a few times and seen a few reasons to call into question my childhood learning, not the least of which was that Pietro Andrea Mattioli, an Italian physician and botanist, called a tomato a *pomo d'oro*, or "golden apple," and that meant he saw it as a fruit. Linnaeus, for his part, called it a "wolf peach" (*Solanum lycopersicum*), which adds weight now to the fruit classification of a tomato. Alongside these two notables is Wikipedia, which lodges yet another complaint against my childhood education: "Botanically, a tomato is the ovary, together with its seeds, of a flowering plant: therefore it is a fruit."[2]

Someone probably knows what this means. Still, one should not disagree with this triumvirate of witnesses, so I changed my mind. Tomatoes, let it be said, are a fruit and from now on should be served with apples and peaches for dessert instead of atop salads and other ruffage-forms of fuel. Caprese, my favorite *hors d'oeuvre* (or should I say *antipasto*?), has now become an after dinner delight, replacing our occasional visits to Culvers for custard. (I lie, of course.)

Yet perhaps I have been too hasty in reaching a conclusion. Tomatoes, the Wikipedia entry tells me in guarded tones that make me think we were right as kids, are not as sweet as fruits. In fact, we are informed that the category "vegetable" is a "culinary" classification. Now we are onto something postmodern—calling something a vegetable is in the eyes of the beholder and could be, if the right people start listening, an act of classificatory violence. Do you know that the US Supreme

---

1. I am grateful to my colleague, Joel Willitts, for his careful reading of this paper before my presentation; I have edited and adjusted at points in light of his suggestions. I am grateful also for the response by Eric Greaux.

2. http://en.wikipedia.org/wiki/Tomato (accessed March 2, 2010).

Court, in 1893, declared tomatoes were vegetables in accordance with popular usage and tomatoes were therefore subject to a tax on vegetables from which fruits were exempt? When taxing bodies start classifying foods we are going to get skeptical fast. As if to seal the point, New Jersey made the tomato the state *vegetable*. Arkansas, never quite sure where to stand, one-upped them and made the tomato the state vegetable and fruit! In 2009 Ohio, which likes to wait to render judgment so its decisions seem more significant, declared the tomato the State *fruit*. We are just about done with the Wikipedia entry but I quote this: "Due to the scientific definition of a fruit, the tomato remains a fruit when not dealing with US tariffs. Nor is it the only culinary vegetable that is a botanical fruit: eggplants, cucumbers, and squashes of all kinds (such as zucchini and pumpkins) share the same ambiguity."[3] And there we have something that scholars appreciate: ambiguity.

Readers may be wondering why a NT scholar is discussing tomatoes. What I am doing is setting the scene for the shock I experienced when I read NT scholars arguing that Paul was not in fact a *convert*. Once again, I went back into my history to recall that I was always told he was a convert. Furthermore, his story was the paradigm for conversion appeals in my church as a kid, and lots of folks converted because of Paul's conversion, including me, so he must have been a convert. At least we knew we were converts because we had an experience like Paul's.

That is until Krister Stendahl, a tall, lanky Church of Sweden New Testament scholar invented the new perspective before it was called that. Stendahl gave rise to ideas that were far more radical than those who are more often called new perspective scholars. Stendahl came to such conclusions in a Lutheran-shaped country and in world that had not yet re-examined what Judaism was like in the first century. No, in fact, Stendahl argued, Paul was not a convert. He was called to preach the gospel to the Gentiles and justification is not so much about personal guilt before God but about Gentiles being included in God's people.[4] Paul, he argued, did not change religions. He remained a Jew. Therefore, he was not a "convert." It made me wonder if I was saved when I read Stendahl. Although my eyes did not twitter and I did not see Jesus, my own conversion story was a radical break from the direction I was

---

3. These statements were part of the Wikipedia entry cited in the last note, but for unknown reasons are no longer included. They can be accessed, with Wikipedia referenced as the source, at http://uk.answers.yahoo.com/question/index?qid=20090617132619AAeWGvM (accessed March 2, 2010).

4. The farsightedness of Stendahl's work has been brought to the fore by Magnus Zetterholm, *Approaches to Paul: A Student's Guide to Scholarship* (Minneapolis: Fortress, 2009), 76–78, 97–100. See the seminal study of Krister Stendahl, *Paul Among Jews and Gentiles, and Other Essays* (Philadelphia: Fortress, 1976), esp. 1–77, along with 78–96.

headed and it sure seemed to me that Paul's story was mine, or at least like mine, and the similarity made me think I had experienced the real thing. Maybe, I thought, I was just "called" and not "converted." If that was so, I began to wonder when I was converted, and it was hard to find a really decisive moment. Well, enough of this. You get the point and the question: Was Paul a fruit or a vegetable? Was he a convert or was he only called from one form of Judaism to another or called to preach the gospel within Judaism? In these questions we can find the problem that I want to address. In the process of seeking to answer the question, "Was Paul a convert?" I will dabble in texts and topics that would take an article in and of themselves to resolve, and I will touch on texts for which there is scholarship of which I am entirely ignorant, but I want to make it clear that my goal is to tackle this one question about whether or not Paul was a convert. It is my hope that a sociological category will help us answer the question.

Conversion or Call: The Options[5]

Perhaps the most popular reading of Paul's story is that he was converted in (what is often said to be) an Augustinian and Lutheran sort of way. Many read Paul's story through the lens of Rom 7, or Gal 2:15-21, even if that reading of Paul is not embraced by the guild of Pauline scholars today, or for that matter by Augustine or Luther.

> Rom 7:14 For we know that the law is spiritual; but I am of the flesh, sold into slavery under sin. 15 I do not understand my own actions. For I do not do what I want, but I do the very thing I hate. 16 Now if I do what I do not want, I agree that the law is good. 17 But in fact it is no longer I that do it, but sin that dwells within me. 18 For I know that nothing good dwells within me, that is, in my flesh. I can will what is right, but I cannot do it.

---

5. I have relied here on the taxonomy of J. D. G. Dunn, "Paul's Conversion: A Light to the Twentieth Century," in his *The New Perspective on Paul* (rev. ed.; Grand Rapids: Eerdmans, 2008), 347–65, here 348–56. See also D. A. Hagner, "Paul as a Jewish Believer—According to His Letters," in *Jewish Believers in Jesus: The Early Centuries* (ed. O. Skarsaune and R. Hvalvik; Peabody, Mass: Hendrickson, 2007), 96–120, esp. 101–2; J. M. G. Barclay, "Paul among Diaspora Jews: Anomaly or Apostate?," *JSNT* 60 (1995): 89–120. Alongside these pieces, two books by Martin Hengel inform a variety of issues in this study: *The Pre-Christian Paul* (in collaboration with R. Deines; trans. J. Bowden; Philadelphia: Trinity, 1991); M. Hengel, with Anna Maria Schwemer, *Paul Between Damascus and Antioch: The Unknown Years* (trans. J. Bowden; Louisville: Westminster John Knox, 1997). A lucid sketch of the interpretation of Paul in the history of the Church can be found in B. Corley, "Interpreting Paul's Conversion—Then and Now," in *The Road from Damascus: The Impact of Paul's Conversion on His Life, Thought, and Ministry* (ed. R. N. Longenecker; Grand Rapids: Eerdmans, 1997), 1–17.

> ¹⁹ For I do not do the good I want, but the evil I do not want is what I do. ²⁰ Now if I do what I do not want, it is no longer I that do it, but sin that dwells within me. ²¹ So I find it to be a law that when I want to do what is good, evil lies close at hand. ²² For I delight in the law of God in my inmost self, ²³ but I see in my members another law at war with the law of my mind, making me captive to the law of sin that dwells in my members. ²⁴ Wretched man that I am! Who will rescue me from this body of death? ²⁵ Thanks be to God through Jesus Christ our Lord! So then, with my mind I am a slave to the law of God, but with my flesh I am a slave to the law of sin.[6]

Put simply, Paul struggled with a troubled, or "pricked" (Acts 26:14), conscience over his sin and also with his acceptance with God until he simply gave up, admitting he was a sinner who was striving to please God on his own merits. In so admitting his sinful striving Paul simultaneously embraced the righteousness that alone is found in Christ and which Christ provides for us. There are a pile of important theological words that end up in this sort of theory, like satisfaction and double imputation and alien righteousness and merit-seeking and total depravity, but our concern here is not with those. Instead, this (perhaps most) common of theories at the populist level sees Paul's conversion as the release of an inner struggle that leads, finally, to peace with God. While evidence is what matters, that is not our concern yet. What also matters is that many, if not most, Pauline scholars have not only called into question this reading of Gal 2 and Rom 7 but, even more, they have abandoned this way of reading Paul's life.[7] The struggle of the "I" in Rom 7:7–25, it is usually argued, does not fit well with the lack of struggle in either of Paul's clear autobiographical reflections, Gal 1:13–14, where Paul looks back with some pride at his zeal and his success in Torah (or Tradition) observance, and Phil 3:6, where Paul says "as to righteousness under the law" he was "blameless" (*amemptos*). In the

---

6. Unless otherwise noted, all biblical quotations are from NRSV.

7. A major pushback came from W. G. Kümmel, *Römer 7 und die Bekehrung des Paulus* (Leipzig: Hinrichs, 1929). Recent attempts to revive the older Lutheran reading of Paul can be found in R. H. Gundry, "The Moral Frustration of Paul Before His Conversion: Sexual Lust in Rom 7.7–25," in *Pauline Studies: Essays Presented to F. F. Bruce* (ed. D. A. Hagner, M. J. Harris; Grand Rapids: Eerdmans, 1980), 228–45. For a recent good sketch of the issues, see R. Jewett, *Romans: A Commentary* (Hermeneia; Minneapolis: Fortress, 2007), 441–5, who contends that the autobiographical reading cannot be dismissed. The "I" refers to Paul's pre-Christian Jewish stance, who for Jewett was a "zealot," but as now seen through the lens of his Christian theology. Perhaps the most readable critique of the whole approach can be found in K. Stendahl, *Paul Among Jews and Gentiles*, 78–96.

words of Stendahl, who thought Paul did not have that classic Lutheran "introspective conscience," Paul . . .

> Experiences no troubles, no problems, no qualms of conscience, no feelings of shortcomings. He is a star pupil . . . a very happy Jew.[8]

And Beverly Gaventa agrees, saying:

> His own statements do not indicate that Paul was tormented by guilt or unhappiness in his early life. . . . If Paul was aware of a prolonged period of searching and questioning, he gives the reader no indication of this struggle.[9]

Another theory has been bolder and cruder: Paul *changed religions* in moving from Judaism to Christianity. This view lingers on in spite of the gallant efforts and brilliant studies of scholars like George Foot Moore, K. Stendahl, E. P. Sanders, J. D. G. Dunn, and N. T. Wright, not to forget also Markus Bockmuehl, who have each in their own way impressed upon generations of students how embedded messianic Judaism (or Christianity, whatever you want to call it) was in the diverse Judaism of its day. Jesus the Jew was followed up by Paul the Jew (Rom 11:1; Acts 22:3). And when is it appropriate to begin calling the faith of those followers of Jesus "Christianity"? When was there the so-called "parting of the ways"? So, no matter how much ground has been gained in this direction, many simply have not heard the message. The trickle-down theory of education does not work. Judaism for many is something that existed until Jesus and then, with one big bang of a resurrection, it all changed and from Pentecost on Judaism was done with and everything was now Christian. What fascinates, then, is what happens to Paul's conversion if he never changed religions? Is it still a conversion? For some, once one admits that neither Jesus nor Paul started a new religion, the word "conversion" morphs into the word "call" or "commission."

But I have left this theory with a second dilemma without mentioning it. For some, once we settle on whether or not Paul remained a Jew and "within Judaism," which is its own set of issues, we can then conclude "yes" or "no." If he remained inside the walls of Judaism in his faith in Jesus as Messiah, then he did not convert. If he did not remain in those walls, then he was a convert. In some ways, this is the point of Stendahl's famous essay, and I quote him:

---

8. K. Stendahl, *Paul Among Jews and Gentiles*, 13.

9. B. Gaventa, *From Darkness to Light* (OBT 20; Philadelphia: Fortress, 1986), 36–37.

> The emphasis in the accounts is always on this assignment [of Paul to the Gentiles], not on the conversion. Rather than being "converted," Paul was called to the specific task—made clear to him by his experience of the risen Lord—of apostleship to the Gentiles, one hand-picked through Jesus Christ on behalf of the one God of Jews and Gentiles ... The mission is the point. It is a call to mission rather than a conversion.[10]

Stendahl classifies Paul as a fruit. No matter how much we are indebted these days to Stendahl, this set of words masks a problem, and one that I am convinced can be resolved in part and which is insufficiently examined. Namely, what is "conversion"? If conversion, as Stendahl says, means switching religions, then sure, Paul is not a convert. But what if "conversion" has a more nuanced voice? This will occupy the second part of our paper, but, before we get there, we need to examine two more theories of Paul's own biography.

A more nuanced understanding of the "from Judaism to Christianity" theory of Paul's spiritual revolution is found among those who think Paul's conversion was simply a conversion about Jesus.[11] He went from denying Jesus as Messiah to affirming Jesus as Messiah. No one, of course, denies the significance of Christ in Paul's own life. When Paul, in a piece of autobiographical reflection, sums up what happened on the Damascus Road, the substantive claim is that God "called" him and was pleased "to reveal his Son *in* me" (Gal 1:15-16). What happened revolves around Christ, whatever you call it. If Paul can say Jews find the cross of Christ a "stumbling block" (*skandalon*) in 1 Cor 1:23 and can say that anyone crucified is under a curse (Gal 3:13 from Deut 21:23), then we can infer that Paul thought the same about Jesus before his Damascus Road encounter (cf. Acts 9). What matters is that Paul, after the Damascus Road encounter, became one who preached "Christ crucified" (1 Cor 1:23), and in Rom 4:25 he ties crucifixion to resurrection to set out both forgiveness of sins and justification. So the "conversion," or whatever you call it, was a radical shift in his conviction of Jesus as Messiah.[12] But is it more? That is

---

10. K. Stendahl, *Paul Among Jews and Gentiles*, 7, 10-11. One of the more interesting observations by Stendahl is how Paul's name change (from Saul to Paul) occurs only after Paul has encountered the Romans (11; cf. Acts 13:9).

11. On this view, see H. G. Wood, "The Conversion of Paul: Its Nature, Antecedents and Consequences," *NTS* 1 (1954-1955): 276-82.

12. Another issue hangs like a footnote at this point: how much of Paul's Christology (and theology) derive from the Damascus Road encounter? See, for one study, Richard N. Longenecker, "Christology—A Realized Hope, A New Commitment, and a Developed Proclamation: Paul and Jesus" in *The Road from Damascus: The Impact of Paul's Conversion on His Life, Thought, and Ministry* (ed. R. N. Longenecker; Grand Rapids: Eerdmans, 1997), 18-42.

our question.[13] A christological shift would only be an intra-Judaism shift on Paul's part, and the question would arise whether or not such a shift within one faith can be called a conversion. This we will examine in our next section.

One more theory sticks within the Jewish world, and it contends that Gal 2:19–21 tells us Paul's own story:

> [19] For through the law I died to the law, so that I might live to God. I have been crucified with Christ [20] and it is no longer I who live, but it is Christ who lives in me. And the life I now live in the flesh I live by faith in the Son of God, who loved me and gave himself for me. [21] I do not nullify the grace of God; for if justification comes through the law, then Christ died for nothing.

Paul's own story of his own "conversion" is the story of shifting from Torah to gospel. Paul's shift was from *zeal* for Torah, which led to his persecuting of others (cf. Phil 3:6), to zeal for Christ or for the gospel of Christ. He moved from persecuting followers of Jesus to following Jesus, and that move entailed a shift in perception of the relationship of followers of Jesus and the Torah. I am not as confident as some are today about Paul's observant lifestyle, because I cannot see 1 Cor 9:19–23 reflecting a typical Jewish observant life style:

> [19] For though I am free with respect to all, I have made myself a slave to all, so that I might win more of them. [20] To the Jews I became as a Jew, in order to win Jews. To those under the law I became as one under the law (though I myself am not under the law) so that I might win those under the law. [21] To those outside the law I became as one outside the law (though I am not free from God's law but am under Christ's law) so that I might win those outside the law. [22] To the weak I became weak, so that I might win the weak. I have become all things to all people, that I might by all means save some. [23] I do it all for the sake of the gospel, so that I may share in its blessings.

But I have to say this: Paul's stance is not quite as clear to me now as it once was and it is conversations with my colleague, Joel Willitts (who often points me to Acts 21:24), that has made me rethink this question. What we need to observe, however we explain it, is that in some sense Paul shifted from his former adherence to the Pharisaic-shaped reading of Torah to an adherence to Christ and his Torah

---

13. Dunn, for his part, thinks that this theory does not go far enough. It was not, he says, the claim that Jesus was the Messiah that created ambiguity in Paul's world but that all Jews must believe in Jesus as Messiah that caused offense. See his "Paul's Conversion," 352–53.

and grace that have, at the very minimum, given him a new lens on Torah and Israel (and probably Judaism itself).

The story, as is the case always with Paul—especially once we let scholars say what they think—is not simple. Paul makes some amazingly positive statements about Torah, and it is the word "amazingly" that shows that we have perhaps misunderstood this Jewish follower of the Jewish Messiah. One of my favorites is that Paul says that "the just requirement of the Torah might be fulfilled in us who walk not according to the flesh but according to the Spirit" (Rom 8:4). And he can push one direction and another and when he comes down he is on the side of the Torah, even if that "but" clause surprises: "Circumcision is nothing, and uncircumcision is nothing; but obeying the commandments of God is everything" (1 Cor 7:19).[14] Like Jesus, he can reduce the Torah to love—but it is still the Torah that one is doing when one loves (cf. Mark 12:28–32; Gal 5:14; Rom 13:8–10). It will not do, then, to say Paul's conversion was from Torah/law to gospel/grace because there is room to maneuver, both within Judaism and within one's commitment to Torah, to say things as Paul did and, as we will see, they can also fit within a theory of conversion.

Perhaps Phil 3 tells us enough before we finish this section off. The text is rather straightforward for almost everyone, except we quickly learn that one person's "straight" is another person's "crooked." I quote this text now and make quick observations and we will be on to what I hope will be an observation that will help us resolve this debate.[15] We will return to this text later.

> Phil 3:2 Beware of the dogs, beware of the evil workers, beware of those who mutilate the flesh! 3 For it is we who are the circumcision, who worship in the Spirit of God and boast in Christ Jesus and have no confidence in the flesh— 4 even though I, too, have reason for confidence in the flesh. If anyone else has reason to be confident in the flesh, I have more: 5 circumcised on the eighth day, a member of the people of Israel, of the tribe of Benjamin, a Hebrew born of Hebrews; as to the law, a Pharisee; 6 as to zeal, a persecutor of the church; as to righteousness under the law, blameless. 7 Yet whatever gains I had, these I have come to regard as loss because of Christ. 8 More than that, I regard everything as loss because of the surpassing value of knowing Christ Jesus my Lord. For his sake I have

---

14. An interesting comment, this text is, on Gal 5:6 where instead of the commandments, Paul spoke of "faith working through love."

15. On Phil 3, see M. Bockmuehl, *The Epistle to the Philippians* (BNTC; Peabody, Mass.: Hendrickson, 1998); G. D. Fee, *Paul's Letter to the Philippians* (NICNT; Grand Rapids: Eerdmans, 1995); G. F. Hawthorne and R. P. Martin, *Philippians* (WBC 43; rev. ed.; Nashville: Thomas Nelson, 2004); J. Reumann, *Philippians* (AB 33B; New Haven: Yale University Press, 2008).

> suffered the loss of all things, and I regard them as rubbish, in order that I may gain Christ ⁹ and be found in him, not having a righteousness of my own that comes from the law, but one that comes through faith in Christ, the righteousness from God based on faith. ¹⁰ I want to know Christ and the power of his resurrection and the sharing of his sufferings by becoming like him in his death, ¹¹ if somehow I may attain the resurrection from the dead. ¹² Not that I have already obtained this or have already reached the goal; but I press on to make it my own, because Christ Jesus has made me his own. ¹³ Beloved, I do not consider that I have made it my own; but this one thing I do: forgetting what lies behind and straining forward to what lies ahead, ¹⁴ I press on toward the goal for the prize of the heavenly call of God in Christ Jesus. ¹⁵ Let those of us then who are mature be of the same mind; and if you think differently about anything, this too God will reveal to you. ¹⁶ Only let us hold fast to what we have attained.

This text proves to me that Paul was a Jew and, after believing in Jesus Christ, remained a Jew. He is still part of the "circumcision" (3:3) but worships in the Spirit and boasts in Christ and not in the flesh (3:3). In fact, for Paul "flesh" apparently means *Jewish* (or Hebrew or Israelite) flesh. His list includes his circumcision, membership in Israel, being a Benjaminite, a Hebrew, a Pharisee, a persecutor, and blameless in Torah observance. These all are counted as loss and rubbish for Paul, which just might make an old-fashioned Lutheran shout "Hallelujah!" until that same Lutheran reads on to see that Paul evidently does not give these things up—at least most of these things. Instead, Paul gives up only one thing: in Christ he has lost all these things but his focus is on a "*righteousness* . . . that comes through faith in Christ" and that does not come through the *Law* (3:8–10). Paul does not say he stopped being a Hebrew or an Israelite or that he reversed circumcision through epispasm or even that he was no longer a Pharisee. He stopped persecuting the church and he stopped having a righteousness of his own. He was persecuted and his righteousness came from Christ.

I am suggesting that we have found a partial answer to our question in this text, which is a midrash in some ways on both Gal 2:15–21 and Rom 7:7–25. But to get the fullness of this, we have to turn now to conversion theory itself.[16]

---

16. Other studies on Paul that have been sensitive to conversion theory include Beverly Gaventa, *From Darkness to Light*; Alan F. Segal, *Paul the Convert: The Apostolate and Apostasy of Saul the Pharisee* (New Haven, Conn.: Yale University Press, 1990). What distinguishes this study from those is the work of Lewis Rambo, whose consensus report placed the entire set of issues on a new shelf.

Conversion Theory: A Way Forward

Conversion has been examined by biblical scholars, by theologians, by sociologists, and by psychologists. Abstraction is the name of the game for sociologists and psychologists, not to mention bad prose and at times an overt hostility toward the biblical scholars and theologians. This is what makes Lewis Rambo's book so good—as I said in my book on conversion, "Rambo has the courage to grab a sacred bag [conversion] and examine its contents sociologically with such care that its contents remain sacred."[17] Biblical scholars and theologians, however, have been going at it for some time now on whether or not Paul is a "convert." I would like to propose that sociologists like Rambo have provided for us a paradigm for understanding three things: *what conversion is*, *its varied manifestations*, and *how one can detect a conversion*.

First, what is conversion? I will use two approaches. Lew Rambo says this:

> Conversion is what a group or person *says* it is. The process of conversion is a product of interactions among the convert's aspirations, needs, and orientations, the nature of the group into which she or he is being converted, and the particular social matrix in which these processes are taking place.[18]

Because religions are groups and not just self-made stuff, though we have got a few folks these days doing such a thing, conversion involves, as Rambo sees it, three elements: the individual or potential convert, the group into which one is converting, and the interaction of the two. If we convert this into theological language, conversion implies and only works within an *ecclesiology*. Now let us make this real: it is not just an ecclesiology, as if converts were moving into some theological box or into some ideological shelf of books. Conversion is ecclesiological at the most particular, concrete and local of levels. Conversion is what *a specific church* says it is. Since one is moving into a church, and since a church is in most cases a stable organization, conversion will mean taking on the ethics and ideas and practices and beliefs and relationships of a concrete, local church. Conversion, indeed, is what a group says it is. This is why there is an interactive phase in conversion: the individual *and the group* size one another up. Alan Segal has said this well:

---

17. Scott McKnight, *Turning to Jesus: The Sociology of Conversion in the Gospels* (Louisville: Westminster John Knox, 2002), 49 in reference to Lewis R. Rambo, *Understanding Religious Conversion* (New Haven, Conn.: Yale University Press, 1993).

18. Rambo, *Understanding Religious Conversion*, 7.

> [A convert's story] is always mediated through the values of the convert's new community, which defines what a conversion is and actually teaches the convert how to think of it.... Thus, [now moving into Paul himself] the accounts of Paul's and other ancient conversions, even the first-person accounts, are *retrospective retellings of events, greatly enhanced by group norms learned and appropriated in the years prior to the writing.*[19]

But there is also a profoundly existential and personal and individual side to conversion and James Fowler, another expert on conversion, expresses that side for us. In his classic *Stages of Faith*, Fowler defines conversion as follows:

> Conversion is *a significant recentering of one's previous conscious or unconscious images of value and power, and the conscious adoption of a new set of master stories in the commitment to reshape one's life in a new community of interpretation and action.*[20]

There is nothing like a sociologist's prose to make us wonder what he is on about. I am happy to announce that this definition, in another of Fowler's books, had a morning shave and gained a cleaner appearance. He puts it this way:

> Rather, by conversion I mean *an ongoing process*—with, of course, a series of important moments of perspective-altering convictions and illuminations—*through which people (or a group) gradually bring the lived story of their lives into congruence with the core story of the Christian faith.*[21]

Well, Fowler tried. Let me put this together now: conversion is the incorporation of a person into a new group, from which group the individual gains a new master story to govern life. I would like readers to hold on to this idea of a master story as I turn to another element of conversion and story that can help us understand what happened to the apostle Paul.

Conversion manifests itself in a variety of ways. Sociologists of conversion have observed that one can find at least five *kinds* of conversion. What this point will do is reveal that the old-fashioned question, "Did Paul change religions?" is an inadequate question to ask when it comes to Paul, if by that question one will determine whether or not Paul is a convert. Sociologists, to begin with, know that conversion involves

---

19. Segal, *Paul the Convert*, 29.

20. James W. Fowler, *Stages of Faith: The Psychology of Human Development and the Quest for Meaning* (San Francisco: HarperSanFrancisco, 1981), 282 (Fowler's emphasis).

21. James W. Fowler, *Becoming Adult, Becoming Christian: Adult Development and Christian Faith* (San Francisco: Jossey-Bass, 2000), 115 (Fowler's emphasis).

apostasy or, put differently, to join a new group one must leave one's old group. In a recent book I co-wrote with Hauna Ondrey, I was able to discern a "pattern of conversion" for those who actually abandoned their orthodox Christian faith. If all conversions are apostasies, I reasoned, then all apostasies are also conversions.[22] The question we would have to ask of Paul is if he left a group when he began following Jesus. Second, some "conversions" are *intensifications* of one's already-existing, but lightly held, faith. That is, the nominal Presbyterian goes to Geneva or Edinburgh and comes back fired up for the faith. Some call these "rededications" or "renewals" but if you listen carefully to those who go through such an experience, they talk like converts even though all they did was integrate the master story much more completely into their own identity and consciousness. I prefer to use this term for those who grow up in the faith but who only later individuate into that faith. Third, some converts have a conversion called *affiliation*. I use Rambo's own summary: "the movement of an individual or group from no or minimal religious commitment to full involvement with an institution or community of faith."[23] Affiliates are those who go from secularists, unsuspecting at times, to full-bore commitment in a religious group. Fourth, some conversions are *institutional transitions*: this describes the "change of an individual or group from one community to another within a major tradition."[24] One of my earliest studies of conversion involved what was to me a perplexing observation: former students of mine who were gung-ho evangelicals were becoming Roman Catholics.[25] Here we land on something vital for understanding Paul: sticking within Judaism and becoming messianic can be a form of conversion, an institutional transition. Finally, some converts change religions, and this is called *tradition transition*: the movement from one religious group to another. For my part, one of the more fascinating patterns I have seen in conversion stories is how modern-day, post Holocaust Jews become messianic followers of Jesus.[26]

There are lots of terms and definitions and categories here, but we have officially now landed on something about Paul: it is unfair to the evidence of conversion theory to say since Paul stayed within Judaism he was *not* a convert. Paul may or may not have changed religions, but that observation does not mean he was not a

---

22. Scott McKnight and Hauna Ondrey, *Finding Faith, Losing Faith: Stories of Conversion and Apostasy* (Waco, Tex.: Baylor University Press, 2008).

23. Rambo, *Understanding Religious Conversion*, 13.

24. Ibid.

25. McKnight and Ondrey, *Finding Faith, Losing Faith*, 183–227.

26. Ibid., 65–122.

convert. Which leads us now to what I think will part the waters for us, a third point we can draw from conversion theory.

How do you detect a conversion? When do you know it is a fruit or a vegetable? The answer to the former question is that a tell-tale sign of conversion is a *revised autobiography* that is expressed in one's "testimony" or one's "witness." The stories we tell ourselves, even if they are fundamentally mistaken and self-deceptive,[27] are told to make sense of our lives. Again Rambo states, "testimony is the narrative witness of a person's conversion, and it entails two interacting processes: language transformation and biographical reconstruction."[28] We go back to individuals and groups: as the convert tells her story, the group listens to see if the story is acceptable; as the group informs the convert what it expects, the individual learns to tell a story that fits the group's expectations. Rambo's observation puts all of this into a big bundle of clarity: "Although all of ordinary human life can be seen as a subtle process of reorganizing one's biography, in religious conversion there is often an implicit or explicit requirement to reinterpret one's life, to gain a new vision of its meaning, with new metaphors, new images, new stories."[29] Local churches have expectations and those expectations can backfire with their own because sometimes an individual will tell his story in a way that simply does not fit with that local church's preferred master story. Such folks often migrate to other churches or go through what is called an institutional transition. Sometimes a local church locks down its preferred story and prohibits variation, leading once again to some of their folks finding another church where their personal stories are accepted.

Now we can ask our question again, fruit or vegetable, "Was Paul a convert?" The answer can be found by asking if Paul revised his autobiography. Whether we take texts like Gal 2:15–21 and Rom 7:7–25 in a traditional Lutheran or Reformed manner, in a rhetorical strategy to express the Jewish experience under the Torah, or as a revised perspective on Paul's own past because of his experience with Christ, those texts indicate to one degree of intensity or another that Paul revised his own story and learned to tell his story as a movement from a life centered on Torah to a live centered on Christ, grace, and the gospel. If one believes the stories of Paul's "conversion" in the Book of Acts (9, 22, 26) are reliable, we have a profound example of "witness" or "testimony" in which Paul both revises his own story and in which he testifies to a movement from his life of zealous persecution to a life of gospel preach-

---

27. See now G. A. Ten Elshof, *I Told Me So* (Grand Rapids: Eerdmans, 2009).

28. Rambo, *Understanding Religious Conversion*, 137.

29. Ibid., 138.

ing. His master story, in other words, is a messianic story that moves away from his old story, and such a move is a sign of conversion. This emphasis on story-telling connects well with the conclusion of Beverly Gaventa in her book *From Darkness to Light*, where she argued Paul experienced a (cognitive) *transformation* instead of an "alternation" or "conversion." I do not agree with the taxonomy she establishes, mostly because of the newer work of Lewis Rambo, but her emphasis on Paul's experience as one of transformation complements our emphasis on the revision of Paul's own autobiography as a clear indication of the kind of experience Paul had.[30] This is where Alan Segal's study, *Paul the Convert*, lands more firmly for what we are examining in this paper:

> The basic metaphor is one of radical disjunction between past and present, punctuated by a remaking of a person's sense of meaning. A strict contrast between present life and past life is a significant aspect of the way converts describe their lives before and after conversion.[31]

It is all about how a person tells her story. But we are jumping ahead of ourselves here and need to get back to the evidence for Paul's retelling of his own story.

Because Gal 2 and Rom 7 receive other, less personal conversion types of interpretations and because some think the Lukan story of Paul's witness in Acts is more Lukan than Pauline, we are driven to ask if there are other passages where Paul tells his own story in such a way that revision is obvious. The answer is yes, and the two passages are Gal 1:13–16 and Phil 3:2–16.[32] I have already quoted Philippians so let us concentrate for a moment on Galatians and I will expand this in the next section. Our purpose here is only to show that Paul revised his autobiography. *How* he revised it is our next concern.

> [13] You have heard, no doubt, of my earlier life in Judaism. I was violently persecuting the church of God and was trying to destroy it. [14] I advanced in Judaism beyond many among my people of the same age, for I was far more zealous for the traditions of my ancestors. [15] But when God, who had set me apart before I was born and called me through his grace, was

---

30. See the whole study, Gaventa, *From Darkness to Light*. It is hard for me to think Paul has not rejected his past, in some way, when he calls such "rubbish" in Phil 3. Oddly enough, apostasy is a point Alan Segal makes about Paul in his movement into following Jesus; see his book *Paul the Convert*. My contention is that Rambo's studies provide for us a more nuanced understanding of conversion and give us a sharper profile of how to evaluate Paul's experience (as a conversion).

31 Segal, *Paul the Convert*, 29.

32. Eric Greaux pointed also to 1 Cor 15:9; Eph 3:2–6; and 1 Tim 1:13.

pleased [16] to reveal his Son to me, so that I might proclaim him among the Gentiles . . .

Paul has chapters in his life, the former being one called "Judaism" (v. 13) when he was a persecutor and destroyer of the church; it was also a time of advancement in Torah observance. But that all somehow and in some way came to crashing halt when Paul encountered Christ in a revelation by God that Jesus was indeed God's Son. The new chapter of Paul's life is characterized by "gospeling" Christ among the Gentiles.

Whether or not the exegetes and theologians want to call Paul a convert or not, sociologists and psychologists who detect conversions on the basis of how one tells one's own story have this to say: Paul's a vegetable. That does not quite sound right so I will say it this way: the pervasive presence in Paul's writing of a self-reflected revision of his own story, a story cut up into pre- and post-Jesus days, is a tell-tale sign of conversion. *Paul, I conclude, was a convert.*

On the basis of Paul's own autobiographical statements, what did Paul convert *from* and what did he convert *to*? The primary focus here will be on Gal 1:13–16 and Phil 3:1–14,[33] which I think can reasonably be seen as a "commentary" on, or at least a fuller statement of, Gal 1:13–16.[34]

Paul as Convert: From What to What?

Conversion theory reveals that generalities obtain less than particularities. That is, a convert from atheism to theism and then into an orthodox Christian framework, upon closer inspection, is much more likely to be a movement from a particular kind of atheism shaped by a particular past into a particular kind of theism, with its own connections and potentialities, into a particular kind of Christianity, let us say Roman Catholicism. These particularities will inevitably tell the realistic story of the convert instead of the broad-brush pattern.

The same obtains for the Apostle Paul. I quote Gal 1:13–14 again:

---

33. See also 2 Cor 11:22–23; Rom 11:1.

34. I hope by now the dichotomy between "call" and "conversion" is seen as a false one. To be sure, Paul's language in Gal 1:13–16 echoes texts like Jer 1:5–6; Isa 49:1–6 and the prophetic call, as Stendahl long ago observed, but there is more to the language than simply a call: there is a revised autobiography. On this, see again Dunn ("Paul's Conversion," 362–64), who emphasizes "call" more than I do though he sees both a call and a conversion at work.

> ¹³ You have heard, no doubt, of my earlier life in Judaism. I was violently persecuting the church of God and was trying to destroy it. ¹⁴ I advanced in Judaism beyond many among my people of the same age, for I was far more zealous for the traditions of my ancestors. ³⁵

Paul's former life was "in Judaism" and during that time he persecuted "the church of God,"³⁶ which ought to be connected to "Israel of God" in 6:16. Paul used violence³⁷ and his intent was to bring the "church of [his] God" down because it threatened the stability of what Paul called "Judaism" but which is to be understood, as we are about to see, as a form of Pharisaic Judaism. This word "Judaism" is first found in surviving literature in 2 Maccabees (2:21; 8:1; 14:38; cf. 2 Macc 4:13; 4 Macc 4:26).

> 2 Macc 2:21 . . . and the appearances that came from heaven to those who fought bravely for Judaism, so that though few in number they seized the whole land and pursued the barbarian hordes,
>
> 2 Macc 4:13 There was such an extreme of Hellenization and increase in the adoption of foreign ways because of the surpassing wickedness of Jason, who was ungodly and no true high priest . . .
>
> 2 Macc 8:1 Meanwhile Judas, who was also called Maccabeus, and his companions secretly entered the villages and summoned their kindred and enlisted those who had continued in the Jewish faith, and so they gathered about six thousand.
>
> 2 Macc 14:38 In former times, when there was no mingling with the Gentiles, he had been accused of Judaism, and he had most zealously risked body and life for Judaism.
>
> 4 Macc 4:26 . . . when, I say, his decrees were despised by the people, he himself tried through torture to compel everyone in the nation to eat defiling foods and to renounce Judaism.

Shades and nuances can be found in these texts, but most would agree the term refers to those who (perhaps) live in Judah (or the Land of Israel), who are Jews,

---

35. On Galatians, see R. N. Longenecker, *Galatians* (WBC 41; Dallas: Word, 1990); J. D. G. Dunn, *The Epistle to the Galatians* (BNTC; Peabody, Mass.: Hendrickson, 1993); J. L. Martyn, *Galatians* (AB 33A; New York: Doubleday, 1997). See also B. Gaventa, *From Darkness to Light*, 22–28.

36. However you explain this text, "church of God" contrasts with "Judaism"; see Longenecker, *Galatians*, 28; see the developed discussion in Martyn, *Galatians*, 161–63.

37. See Num 25:1–5, 6–15; Ps 106:31; Sir 45:23; 1 Macc 2:23–48.

and who are in "Judaism" because they are faithful to the Torah and to God's people Israel even if that means taking up arms.[38] One layer of suggestion is that it forms an antithesis with "Hellenism" and denotes those who would resist leading Jews in a Hellenistic direction.[39] Another layer is added if one takes into consideration Gal 2:11–14 and Peter's so-called "Judaizing" moves where, if we take that text as it is, "Judaizing" would be connected to the "marks" that separate Jews from Gentiles. But our question is slightly different: What does it mean, then, for *Paul* to say Paul's former life was in "Judaism"? Does this text suggest Paul left Judaism? Gal 1:13 give us information about this, with its use of the explanatory *hoti* (persecuting and gaining in reputation), but we can press for more details. We find them in Phil 3, where we gain the clarity of particularity. Paul saw his past with concrete nuances:

circumcised,

Israelite,

the tribe of Benjamin,

Then comes what Gordon Fee calls the "swing term" because it sums up the first three:[40]

a Hebrew (reader, speaker),[41] and

a Pharisee.

It is not without importance that Paul does not stop with his particular "denomination" within Israel, the Pharisees, who were one party among other options, including Sadducees, "Zealots," and Essenes (cf. Josephus, *Ant* 18.12–23; *B.J.* 2.120–165) alongside some who were no doubt more inclined toward the Hellenists, including such groups as the Herodians and Boethusians. Somewhere amidst this

---

38. J. L. Martyn goes against the grain in seeing Galatians speaking directly and repeatedly about Judaism as a religion (*Galatians*, 154).

39. See Dunn, "Paul's Conversion," 357–8; his fuller study is "Judaism in the Land of Israel in the First Century," in *Judaism in Late Antiquity. Part 2: Historical Syntheses* (ed. J. Neusner; Leiden: Brill, 1995), 229–61; Longenecker, *Galatians*, 27.

40. Fee, *Philippians*, 307.

41. On which, see Hengel, *Pre-Christian Paul*: "Neither in II Cor. 11.22 nor in Phil. 3.5 can Hebrew mean anything other than . . . a Palestinian Jew speaking the sacred language or Aramaic, or a Diaspora Jew, who in origin and education had extremely close connections with the mother country and who therefore also understood Hebrew" (25). But G. D. Fee disagrees; see *Philippians*, 307 n. 14, where he points to this view as emphasizing too much the Lukan perspective and suggests that Paul's first language would have been Greek. G. F. Hawthorne, R. P. Martin, suggest it could mean "a Hebrew born of Hebrew parents." See *Philippians*, 185. The emphasis in this case is on heritage instead of language.

swelter of options were folks that were later called "bandits," there were baptist movements as well as apocalyptists, and there must have been mutations and permutations in the Diaspora of each of these.[42] But Paul was an official member of the influential block of Pharisees, and this meant he took a stand for one of these groups, and is also clear he took a stand *against* the messianists. This is why he gives his form of Pharisaism another nuance: he was a "zealot" (lower case)[43] and he was also "blameless" as a zealotic, Pharisaic Israelite. He was good at it and he was proud of it—this is why in both Phil 3 and Gal 1 he speaks of his "gain" and his "advancing in Judaism beyond many among my people of the same age." There is here much discussion, not the least of which is how in the world the Christian Paul could speak of being "blameless" in Torah observance. And here our Reformation lenses are perhaps hurting us. In Paul's world one could be both blameless and not sinless because of the atonement system at work in Israel's laws. It is something like this that leads Paul to speak of himself as "blameless."[44]

If Martin Hengel is accurate in his conclusion that Paul spent his early, formative years in Jerusalem, and can support (if not prove) this from Acts 22:3 and 26:4, then we have one more dimension of particularity to add to Paul's words.[45] There would then be reason (though hardly compelling) to think that Paul was a leading light in the Greek-speaking synagogues of Jerusalem prior to his conversion, and it was perhaps in these that the issues arose and from which synagogues the (Hellenistically-inclined) messianists were driven to Damascus.[46] Dropping the suggestions now, we would be wise to say that Paul's past was that of a zealous, violent, Torah-observant Jew in the Pharisaic stream of the Jewish faith and practice. He persecuted messianic Jews, partly perhaps for their Torah-observance decisions and partly, if not more than partly, for their adherence to a crucified Messiah (Gal

---

42. The literature here is vast: among other works cited elsewhere in this paper, see also J. M. G. Barclay, *Jews in the Mediterranean Diaspora: From Alexander to Trajan (323 BCE – 117 CE)* (Edinburgh: T. & T. Clark, 1996); M. A. Elliott, *The Survivors of Israel: A Reconsideration of the Theology of Pre-Christian Judaism* (Grand Rapids: Eerdmans, 2000).

43. See the excellent observations in Bockmuehl, *Philippians*, 198–200.

44. On this one begins with E. P. Sanders, *Paul and Palestinian Judaism* (Philadelphia: Fortress, 1977).

45. See Hengel, *Pre-Christian Paul*, 18–39.

46. Following the suggestion of Hengel, *Pre-Christian Paul*, 66–86. But not all agree; see, e.g., Martyn, *Galatians*, 162.

3:10–14). He was driven by, in the words of Markus Bockmuehl, "a nationalist dedication to the purity of Israel."[47]

Is it this list of defining terms, then, that he left? Or which bits of that longish sentence/life did he leave? To begin with, neither in Gal 1 nor in Phil 3 does Paul say he left Judaism (or its particularities).[48] He only says "You have heard, no doubt, of my earlier life (*tēn emēn anastrophēn*) in Judaism."[49] This expression does not necessitate that he left Judaism; it only necessitates that Paul himself divides his life in chapters and one of them was his former life in Judaism. The new chapter in his life might be called "My Messianic and apostolic life in Judaism." As I said earlier, in Phil 3 Paul does not say he reversed circumcision, or that he ceased being an Israelite, or that he jumped out of his tribe of Benjamin. Perhaps he left Pharisaism. He clearly left his zealous persecution of the church and he abandoned that he was "blameless" under the Torah. I say "Perhaps he left Pharisaism" because I am stealing something from the Book of Acts. In Acts 23:6 Paul says something that, if we are serious about language, might not only make the hearts of the Sadducees, but also those of every Lutheran, sag.

> When Paul noticed that some were Sadducees and others were Pharisees,
> he called out in the council, "Brothers, I am a Pharisee, a son of Pharisees.
> I am on trial concerning the hope of the resurrection of the dead."

Paul did not say "I *was* a Pharisee" but "I *am*."[50] He was reared a Pharisee, he was a Pharisee, and he *remains* a Pharisee. One can perhaps explain this way as a very clever ploy, if entirely a lie, by Paul to divide the house at a critical rhetorical moment or, which is preferable, to say that Paul *remained a Pharisee after his Damascus Road encounter*, even that means he developed a messianic form of Pharisaism.[51]

---

47. Bockmuehl, *Philippians*, 200.

48. See here ibid., 194–98.

49. My colleague, Joel Willitts, pointed out to me the NLT's interpretive translation: "You know what I was like when I followed the Jewish religion".

50. *Egō Pharisaios eimi*. On Pharisaism, see J. Bowker, *Jesus and the Pharisees* (Cambridge: Cambridge University Press, 1973); J. Neusner, *The Rabbinic Traditions about the Pharisees Before 70* (3 vols; Atlanta: Scholars Press, 1999). Hengel, *Pre-Christian Paul*, in a way that pushes back against some of the more recent definitions, says: "It is well known that the Pharisees were a Palestinian lay holiness movement going back to the Hasidim of the Maccabean period, whose aim was above all the ritual sanctification of everyday life in Eretz Israel, as it was required of priests in the sanctuary" (30).

51. Klyne Snodgrass has suggested to me that Paul is a Pharisee when it comes to the matter of the resurrection. But, I would want to point to Acts 21:24 again.

In working down that list, then, Paul remains circumcised, Israelite, Benjaminite, Hebrew (speaking), and a Pharisee. It is precisely here, then, that I suggest that Paul draws his own line in the sand. And it is here that we must return to Galatians again. Paul was advancing in Judaism in his (Pharisaic-shaped) Torah observance and then the big moment arrived and he became a follower of Jesus. Galatians 2 is perhaps the first commentary on what happened to Paul when he encountered Jesus, and here I will swear off any discussions of the much-disputed issues involved, not the least of which are the meaning of "righteousness" and "faith in/of Christ." Galatians 2, in language I take to refer to the prototypical Jewish conversion-to-Jesus experience, says this:

> Gal. 2:15 We ourselves are Jews by birth and not Gentile sinners; 16 yet we know that a person is justified not by the works of the law but through faith in Jesus Christ. And we have come to believe in Christ Jesus, so that we might be justified by faith in Christ, and not by doing the works of the law, because no one will be justified by the works of the law. 17 But if, in our effort to be justified in Christ, we ourselves have been found to be sinners, is Christ then a servant of sin? Certainly not! 18 But if I build up again the very things that I once tore down, then I demonstrate that I am a transgressor. 19 For through the law I died to the law, so that I might live to God. I have been crucified with Christ; 20 and it is no longer I who live, but it is Christ who lives in me. And the life I now live in the flesh I live by faith in the Son of God, who loved me and gave himself for me. 21 I do not nullify the grace of God; for if justification comes through the law, then Christ died for nothing.

The first thing to be said of Paul's shift is something about Jesus. Paul became a believer in, and a follower of, Jesus Christ. Whether we go to the Book of Acts where Paul encountered Christ (Acts 9; 22; 26), to Gal 1:16, where God revealed his Son "in me," or to Phil 3, where Paul says it is all "because of Christ" (3:7), the turning point in Paul's life begins with Jesus Christ. Christology, then, is wrapped up in anything we say of Paul's conversion.[52]

The genius of Paul's move from church-persecuting zeal, wrapped up as it was in a Pharisaic rendering of Torah, was a movement from the works of the law or

---

52. This can be developed at length; see R. N. Longenecker, "Christology—A Realized Hope, A New Commitment, and a Developed Proclamation: Paul and Jesus," in *The Road from Damascus* (ed. R. N. Longenecker; Grand Rapids: Eerdmans, 1997), 18–42. Other themes are developed in this collection of studies: eschatology (I. H. Marshall), Gentile mission (T. L. Donaldson), justification (J. D. G. Dunn), reconciliation (S. Kim), covenant theology (R. N. Longenecker), Mosaic law (S. Westerholm), Holy Spirit (G. D. Fee), women (J. M. Gundry-Volf), and ethics (G. W. Hansen).

"righteousness based on works of the law" to "righteousness in Christ."[53] (Not to be forgotten here is that Paul also says this in Acts 13:39 in his gospel sermon at Pisidian Antioch.) Somehow, though, he says he remains an Israelite and a Pharisee (probably) and to some degree Torah-observant. According to Gal 2 Paul has "died to the Torah" because he has gone to the cross with Christ who is now alive in Paul himself. It is not a stretch to say that "Torah of Christ" in Gal 6:2 was Paul's messianic reading of Torah, and that he was now a Torah-of-Christ observant messianic Pharisee. Notice, though, what happens here: it is not the conversion experience itself that is Paul's watershed. The watershed is the cross (and resurrection) of Christ that came alive in Paul's own life on the Road to Damascus. What happened there happened first in some way on the cross when Jesus was crucified. The story of Paul is the story of salvation-history.

This is also what we learn from Phil 3. Paul's boast in just how good a Pharisee he was has become "loss" and "rubbish" (*skybala*) a word that would make all three sides of the Reformation blush. One of my students once translated it as "bull*geschichte*." But why did Paul consider it all rubbish now? Not because he has abandoned the Jewish dimensions of his former life in Judaism but because of union with Christ or, more particularly, of the "surpassing value of knowing Christ Jesus my Lord" (Phil 3:8).[54] It is as if he has suddenly been given an Apple iMac when all he knew was a Commodore 64. What he learns with that new computer called Jesus Christ is that genuine righteousness is found in him, and not in the works of the Torah. Righteousness "comes through faith in Christ" and this by "faith" (3:9). What he also still embraced from his past as a Pharisee was belief in the resurrection, but he now finds that he obtains that by dying with Christ (3:10). The ambivalence of his past and his present now come to full expression: "I press on to make it [the goal] my own because Christ Jesus has made me his own" (3:12). It is not, then, enough to say as does my own teacher, James Dunn, that Paul's conversion was from a zealous form of Judaism to a mission to the Gentiles.[55] Inherent to Paul's theology of salvation for Gentiles is a revision of his own biography along the lines of his own salvation, or justification, which comes not from the works of the Torah but through faith in Christ. It might be said that entailed in Paul's newly-discovered faith in Jesus as Israel's Messiah, where he found justification, is a Gentile mission, but it flows

---

53. See, e.g., M. Hengel, *Paul between Damascus and Antioch*, 98–101.

54. On the structure and logic of the passage, see Fee, *Philippians*, 311–15.

55. Dunn, "Paul's Conversion," esp. 362–64; cf. Hengel, *Paul Between Damascus and Antioch*, 91–98.

out of his discovery of justification. The essence of Paul's rewriting of his biography is first and foremost a new view of righteousness, and only then a new expansion of the people of God to include Gentiles. New perspective, fresh perspective, or old perspective—what we have got with Paul is a perspective on how righteousness is obtained in Christ and an accompanying perspective that righteousness is not obtained through works of the Torah. But this righteousness is for anyone who believes, Jew or Gentile. It is here that the new perspective's emphasis on Gentile inclusion, already a strong emphasis of Krister Stendahl, joins hands with what I am calling "conversion." At this point one could enter into the debates about how "righteousness" and "justification" are understood in the new perspective. In fact, the more tightly one connects "justification" to "Gentile inclusion" the less likely it is that "conversion" describes Paul, but it is precisely here that Phil 3 again speaks to our concern: if new perspective scholars have made a point of Paul's language emerging only where Gentile inclusion is at stake, they have spent most of their energies on Galatians and Romans. But Philippians brings up this "righteousness" talk *without Gentile inclusion* being at stake. More significantly, "righteousness" language comes up here in *Paul's revised autobiography*. Notice this expression: "not having a righteousness of my own that comes from the law, but one that comes through faith in Christ" (3:9).

Accordingly, in both Galatians and Philippians we have Paul's own description of his past as a life of Torah-observance in Judaism, and the drift of his own story is not that he *abandoned* Judaism so much as that he *found* Christ (and the Torah of Christ) *as a Jew*. More particularly, this church-persecuting Pharisee shifted to a church-loving Pharisee. More particularly, and here we find what I think is the gravity of Paul's own narration of his story, Paul moved from a "works of the Torah" righteousness to a "Christ" righteousness (cf. 1 Cor 1:30–31). If he can remain a Pharisee in Christ, that is fine with me.

I set out above the varieties of conversion sociologists like Lewis Rambo have described. In line with that classification, I conclude that Paul's conversion was an "institutional transition." Paul moved from one kind of Judaism to another, but even this "other" Judaism was like new wine in old wineskins and would soon burst the boundaries. Paul was a convert; but his kind of conversion was within a religion and not from one religion to another.

Pastors and preachers and spiritual directors can feast on this approach to Paul's conversion. Instead of asking all Christians to have the same story or to tell the same story, we all need to appreciate the manifold workings of God in the lives of diverse individuals. Paul's story is not my story or anyone else's story, though his similarity with fellow Jews of that day is noteworthy. Instead, as a first century Jew Paul encountered Jesus as the Jewish Messiah. Gentile Christians do not encounter the "Messiah" in quite the same way, so their encounter with the Messiah creates a different story. Those stories, too, need to be told as the work of God in conversion. But what we all need to see is the potent importance of story as the form we learn to express our faith and that witness and testimony form for the church a rock-solid basis upon which we can learn to hear the gospel story.

RESPONSE TO MCKNIGHT

Eric James Gréaux Sr.[1]

I would like to highlight two of Scot's assertions and perhaps seek clarification. I recently considered titling my response "Someone Told Me Paul was a Fruit." I quickly changed my mind because such terminology may be considered offensive. But it does remind us of the clever metaphor that Scot has given to us.

I say fruit because I remember those days in graduate school sitting around the seminar table with Dan Via arguing this issue after having read Krister Stendahl's, "The Apostle Paul and the Introspective Conscience of the West." Most of my colleagues bought into the argument, viz., that Paul was a fruit, i.e., called rather than converted on the Damascus Road.

On the other hand, Scot has ably demonstrated that the Apostle Paul was a convert, i.e., a vegetable—a vegetable from Ohio.

So here is my first question: Are you wedded to convert only? Because of my studies with Greg Beale and Richard Hays, my ears have been trained to hear echoes of the Old Testament in the New. Galatians 1 is one of those places where I can't remain deaf to the reverberations from Isaiah and Jeremiah:

> But when he who had set me apart before I was born, and had called me through his grace, was pleased to reveal his Son to me . . . (Gal 1:15–16a).[2]

> The Lord called me from the womb (Isa 49:1).

> Now the word of the Lord came to me saying, "Before I formed you in the womb I knew you. And before you were born I consecrated you. I appointed you a prophet to the nations" (Jer 1:5).

If we were to expand our corpus of inquiry to include Luke's accounts in Acts, we could also note the parallels to Ezekiel's call vision (Ezek 1:27—2:3).

---

1. I would like to thank Klyne Snodgrass for the invitation to participate in the Symposium, and thank Scot McKnight for his many fine contributions to New Testament Studies. I often find myself in his debt, especially in Petrine studies.

2. Unless otherwise noted, all biblical quotations are from NRSV.

In each of these texts the prophet is being *called* to preach to God's people. I think Paul may be echoing this language deliberately to demonstrate his own perception of prophetic calling. So would you be willing to make some allowances to say conversion *and* calling? I don't like the alternatives either/or.

Second, I loved your use of revised autobiography as a "tell-tale sign of conversion." The Black church assigns great significance to testimony for determining the genuineness of one's initial conversion as well as to the ongoing process of Christian growth, i.e., sanctification. Accordingly, there are some other places where Paul gives his testimony. To continue your metaphor, would you allow us to pick some tomatoes from over here? I think it is the same field. I have in mind three texts:

> I am the least of the apostles, unfit to be called an apostle, because I persecuted the church of God. But (*de*) by the grace of God I am what I am, and his grace toward me was not in vain (1 Cor 15:9–10).

> Among these we all once lived in the passions of our flesh, following the desires of our flesh following the desires of body and mind, and so we were by nature children of wrath, like the rest of mankind. But (*de*) God, who is rich in mercy, out of the great love with which he loved us, even when we were dead through our trespasses, made us alive together with Christ (by grace you have been saved) . . . (Eph 2:3–6).

> I formerly blasphemed and persecuted and insulted him (i.e., Christ Jesus our Lord); but (*alla*) I received mercy because I had acted ignorantly in unbelief (1 Tim 1:13).

Obviously I am assuming the Pauline authorship of the latter two texts. Each of them has the character of a revised autobiography: Chapter 1—Judaism; Chapter 2—Gospeling. The dividing line is an eschatological adversative conjunction (but) that refers to his conversion (*de* in Gal 1, 1 Cor 15, and Eph 2; *alla* in Phil 3 and 1 Tim 1). In each of these texts, Paul describes his condition before and after his encounter with Jesus Christ. The major difference between Gal 1/Phil 3 and 1 Cor 15/ Eph 2/1 Tim 1 is the absence of passionate arguments regarding works-of-the-law-righteousness vis-à-vis Christ-righteousness.

ROMANS 7 AND CONVERSION IN THE PROTESTANT TRADITION

Stephen J. Chester

Christian conversion is not a static category. Although there are profound continuities across time and space, conversion itself develops. The same elements appear again and again, but the relationship between them changes in different historical, social, and ecclesial contexts.[1] One arena in which such developments in the category of conversion can be discerned is exegesis. The history of interpretation of certain texts reveals shifts in the exegetical conclusions reached by interpreters that can be related to evolving concepts of conversion. The texts themselves certainly mold how interpreters understand conversion, but, where texts raise difficult exegetical questions or controversies, the concepts of conversion held by interpreters play a part in determining which conclusions they find most plausible. Romans 7 is one such text. It enjoys a deserved reputation as difficult and controversial, and generates classic exegetical disputes. The usual historical-critical procedure is to organize an analysis of the text around these disagreements. Does Paul's use of first person pronouns throughout 7:7–25 indicate that he is here autobiographical or does he in fact take on one or more different personae? Following his shift to present tense verbs in 7:14, does Paul speak of pre-Christian existence or do 7:14–25 describe the struggles of the Christian life? Rather than focus on these questions directly, this paper will instead chart the relationship between the answers given to them and interpreters' concepts of conversion. It will conclude with an assessment of the significance of this relationship for contemporary discussion of Rom 7 and of conversion. The focus of this paper will be Protestant interpretations of Rom 7, but the influence of key patristic readings of the text on all later interpretations is so pervasive that it is necessary to begin our exploration with them.

---

1. Alan Kreider, *The Change of Conversion and the Origin of Christendom* (Harrisburg, Pa.: Trinity, 1999) chronicles these changes in the first six centuries of the history of Christianity.

Conversion and Patristic Interpretations of Romans 7

The two most influential interpreters of Rom 7 among the Fathers are undoubtedly Origen (c.185–254) and Augustine (354–430), who pioneer very different approaches to Rom 7. For Origen,[2] the "I" of Rom 7 is no single individual but several. Paul speaks as himself in 7:7–13 and at 7:14a when declaring the Mosaic law spiritual, but does not do so again except for the exclamation of thanks at 7:25a. And just as Paul speaks under different personae, so also he speaks of different kinds of law. Since Paul, circumcised on the eighth day, had never lived without the Mosaic law, the reference in 7:9 to life lived apart from the Law must refer instead to natural law, which individuals properly grasp only on attaining adulthood. Later, in the conflict described in 7:21–23, Origen finds at least four laws at work: "the law of the mind is pulling the *egō* toward the law of God, while the law of the members is pulling the *egō* towards the laws (plural!) of sin."[3] He also finds two very different ways to conceive of the Mosaic law itself. Pursued in a fleshly way as within Judaism it is a killing letter, but when in 8:2 Paul speaks of the law of the Spirit of life he is there speaking of the Mosaic law pursued appropriately.[4] The whole chapter is a rhetorical panorama of the human struggle with sin rather than a description of the experience of any single individual at one stage in their struggle. What holds together this panorama is conversion. In 7:14b onwards Paul takes on the persona of a weak Christian whose will agrees with the Law of God but is not yet strong enough to translate this into reality and deeds: "the weakness in those who receive the beginnings of a conversion is of such a nature that when anyone wants to do all at once everything that is good, the accomplishment of this may not immediately follow the will."[5] The very existence of a struggle with sin is evidence that conversion has begun, but also that it is as yet not complete. In contrast, when Origen reads Rom 8 it is evident that Paul speaks of those, like the apostle himself, "who no longer are partly in the flesh and partly in

---

2. Origen wrote his commentary on Romans around 246 in Caesarea. Only fragments survive in Greek and the text now available is that of the abridged Latin translation of Rufinus, produced in Italy around 406–7. See PL 14. For an English text, see Origen, *Commentary on the Epistle to the Romans* (trans. Thomas P. Scheck; 2 vols, Fathers of the Church vols. 103 and 104; Washington D.C.: Catholic University of America Press, 2002).

3. Mark Reasoner, *Romans in Full Circle: A History of Interpretation* (Louisville: Westminster John Knox, 2005), 69.

4. Origen *Comm. Rom.* 6.12.2 (Scheck 2:48)

5. Origen *Comm. Rom.* 6.9.7 (Scheck 2:39).

the Spirit, but who are completely in Christ."⁶ Here Paul describes the condition of the fully converted. Evident in this exegesis is a concept of conversion that embraces the whole of the Christian life and not simply its beginning. For Origen, progress in conversion is a matter of slowly breaking sinful habits and replacing them with good ones. This cannot happen without the aid of the Holy Spirit, but it also requires application and effort from those converted, "who at first sin only a little, then later even less, and ultimately, if they are able to attain it, who no longer sin at all."⁷

Although he is by far the most explicit, Origen was not the only Father to connect Paul's argument in Rom 7 with conversion. John Chrysostom (347–407) differs from Origen in many respects, most notably in treating the Law spoken of in 7:7–13 as the Mosaic law and in regarding 7:14–25 as simply a description of human existence under that law. There is not Origen's panorama of personae and laws, and nor is there Origen's weak-willed convert in 7:14–25. Nevertheless, it is obvious to Chrysostom that Rom 8 speaks of the outcome of conversion. The requirement to fulfill the righteous demands of the Law (8:4) prompts the thought that "the Font will not suffice to save us, unless after coming from it, we display a life worthy of the gift."⁸ A worthy life is possible because the Spirit has put a stop to the internal war described by Rom 7, "slaying sin, and making the contest light to us and crowning us at the outstart, and then drawing us to the struggle with abundant help."⁹ The effectiveness of the Spirit's work is demonstrated by the proliferation among Christians of virgins and martyrs, social types virtually unknown before the advent of the gospel.¹⁰ Thus, as with Origen, Paul's meaning is discerned partly on the basis of presuppositions that reflect Chrysostom's concept of conversion. Origen was also to be more directly influential in the details of others' interpretations. In the exposition of 7:7–25 by Jerome (347–420) there is little "which is not paralleled in Rufinus' translation (of Origen)."¹¹ In the commentary of Pelagius (c. 354–420/40) on Romans, most of the details of his interpretation mirror those of Origen, although he

6. Origen *Comm. Rom.* 6.11.2 (Scheck 2:45).

7. Origen *Comm. Rom.* 6.11.2 (Scheck, 2:46).

8. *NPNF*¹ 11, 433. The text is Chrysostom's Homily XIII on Rom 7:14 (427–39).

9. *NPNF*¹ 11, 431.

10. *NPNF*¹ 11, 420 from Chrysostom's Homily XII on Rom 6:19: "Among the ancients, if any were found practicing virginity, it was quite astonishing. But now the thing is scattered over every part of the world. And death in those times some few men did with difficulty despise, but now in villages and cities there are hosts of martyrs without number, consisting not of men only, but even of women."

11. Caroline Hammond Bammel, "Philocalia XI, Jerome, Epistle 121, and Origen's Exposition of Romans VII," *JTS* 32 (1981), 53 (50–81).

is characteristically careful to insist that the formation of sinful habits arises through human choices freely made. The person sold as a slave under sin (7:14) "sold himself as a slave to sin."[12] His major departures from Origen are that Rom 7 describes not a weak-willed convert but a more straightforwardly "carnal" person, albeit one who is at least aware of sin and struggles with it, and that the Law of which Paul speaks in 7:7–13 is the Mosaic law. Yet, once again, Rom 8 describes the fruits of conversion, the culmination of the second section of Romans, beginning at 5:1, which considers "the transition from the 'death' of sin to the 'life' of righteousness."[13] In common with all the interpretations so far considered, the expectations of the practical righteousness which results from conversion are great; expectations which the internal struggle described in Rom 7 cannot possibly meet or fit.

Pelagius' interpretation was, of course, to become permanently linked with the opposition to it expressed by Augustine. Yet as is well known, Rom 7 is a text about which Augustine changed his mind. The younger Augustine held an interpretation not all that distant from Pelagius's own. While Augustine is already careful not to allow that human deeds contribute to salvation, he insists that human faith does so. "God justly elects those whom He foreknows will respond freely in faith to his call. God's call is the necessary precondition of man's salvation, but God issues this call on the basis of his foreknowledge of man's free decision."[14] In a context where the principal threat was the determinism of the Manichees, this defense of God's justice and of human freedom seemed essential if the holiness and goodness of the Mosaic law, on which Paul insists in 7:14, was also to be maintained. The younger Augustine is further like Pelagius in assuming that Paul speaks of the Mosaic law in 7:7–13. What makes Augustine's position distinctive is the strong framework which guides his interpretation of Rom 3–8 in general and Rom 7 in particular:

> Therefore, let us distinguish these four stages of man: prior to the law; under the law; under grace; and in peace . . . Prior to the law we do not struggle, because not only do we lust and sin, but we even assent to sin. Under the law we struggle but we are overcome. We admit that we do evil, and by that admission, that we do not really want to do it, but because we

---

12. Theodore De Bruyn, *Pelagius' Commentary on St. Paul's Epistle to the Romans* (Oxford: Clarendon, 1993), 101–5 (103).

13. De Bruyn, 35.

14. Paula Fredriksen Landes, *Augustine on Romans: Propositions from the Epistle to the Romans, Unfinished Commentary on the Epistle to the Romans* (Chico, Calif.: Scholars Press, 1982), xi. This quotation is from Fredriksen's description of the younger Augustine's position. These two texts on Romans date from the 390s.

still lack grace we are overwhelmed . . . Then comes grace, which pardons earlier sins and aids the struggling one, adds charity to justice and takes away fear. When this happens, even though certain fleshly desires fight against our spirit while we are in this life, to lead us into sin, nonetheless our spirit resists them because it is fixed in the grace and love of God, and ceases to sin . . . They will not cease save at the resurrection of the body, when we will have merited that transformation promised to us. Then there will be perfect peace, when we have been established in the fourth stage. Perfect peace, since nothing will resist us who do not resist God.[15]

Augustine connects this framework seamlessly to details of Paul's text. The reference to being alive apart from the Law (7:9) speaks of the period prior to the Law when there is little consciousness of a struggle with sin. Other aspects of 7:7–13, and the whole of 7:14–23, speak of life under the Law when there is a struggle with sin in which sin triumphs. Here Paul necessarily "put himself in the place of someone who is under the law, whose words he speaks in his own person."[16] Only in 7:24–25 does Paul offer the first hints of life under grace and possible victory over sin: "Though his carnal desires still exist, by not consenting to sin he does not serve them who, constituted under grace, serves the law of God with his mind even though with his flesh he serves the law of sin."[17] These hints then come to fruition in Rom 8, which describes life under grace. Sinful desires remain and will not be fully vanquished before the peace of the resurrection, but successfully resisting them and ceasing to sin is now an attainable goal. As in Origen's interpretation, the Mosaic law here ceases to be a killing letter but rather brings life, for "the fullness of the law is the love which *has been poured into our hearts through the Holy Spirit who has been given to us.*"[18]

---

15. Augustine, "Proposition 18" (Fredriksen Landes, 5–7).

16. Augustine, *Responses to Miscellaneous Questions: The Works of St. Augustine I/12* (trans. B. Ramsey; New York: New City, 2008), 175. This quotation comes from "Miscellany of Questions in Response to Simplician," 1.1.

17. Augustine, "Proposition 46" (Fredriksen Landes, 19). Many later commentators perceive tension between Paul's cry of despair and exclamation of thanks for deliverance in 7:24–25a and his statement in 7:25b that in the flesh he is still a slave to the law of sin. Paul praises God for deliverance but then remains as yet undelivered. Augustine and other Latin commentators of the era were able to alleviate this tension more readily because they took as original a textual variant now acknowledged as secondary. In their text of 7:24–25a, Paul's answer to his own question was not to say "Thanks be to God through Jesus Christ our Lord" but rather "The grace of God through Jesus Christ our Lord"; not *Deo gratias* but *gratia Dei*.

18. Augustine, "Miscellany of Questions in Response to Simplician," 1.17 (Ramsey, 184, his emphasis).

The four stages of humanity identified in the younger Augustine's interpretation are both salvation-historical and personal; they represent the progress towards God both of the human race and of the individual. Once again, it is clear that only Rom 8 with its greater confidence of victory over sin can satisfy the presuppositions and aspirations of the interpreter about and for conversion. The rejection of this assumption by the later Augustine is therefore a change of great magnitude, although it is not so much that his four stages of humanity are abandoned as that their correlation with Paul's text is adjusted. In his later view, fully presented in a series of sermons preached in Carthage in 419,[19] Augustine presents only 7:7–13 as chronicling existence prior to the Law and under the Law. Now, with its relentless struggle between sin and God's Law, 7:14–23 is identified with the life of the Christian under grace. The cry, "Who will rescue me from this body of death?" (7:24)[20] is no longer simply a cry for the deliverance of conversion, but rather also a cry for the deliverance of the bodily resurrection and the attainment of peace that is the goal of conversion.[21] Conversion retains its prominent place in Augustine's interpretation, but now it begins at 7:14 with the Christian's acknowledgement of the holiness of the Law and full recognition of personal sin. This represents a step forward worthy of conversion, for Augustine can say of the person under the Law that "the reason you haven't been victorious is that you have been presumptuously self-reliant."[22] In contrast, the believer calls on the Lord for help,[23] and recognizes that Paul speaks here in a different way of the same struggle between flesh and Spirit as he describes in Gal 5:17.[24] Augustine is still extremely careful to distinguish his position from that of the Manichees, making it clear that the struggle is an internal one. Desire is not an alien force: "It's our debility, it's our vice. It won't be detached from us and exist somewhere else, but it will be cured and not exist anywhere at all."[25] Yet, crucially, what distinguishes the Christian from the person under the Law

---

19. Augustine, *Sermons: The Works of St. Augustine III/5* (trans. E. Hill; New York: New City, 1992). The relevant sermons are nos. 151–56, although Sermon 154A, which interprets Rom 7:15, is not from the Carthage series and is of uncertain date. For the Latin text of the Carthage series, see PL 38:814–59. For the Latin text of sermon 154A, see PLS 2:667–70.

20. Unless otherwise stated, all biblical quotations are from NRSV.

21. Thomas F. Martin, *Rhetoric and Exegesis in Augustine's Interpretation of Rom 7:24–25A* (Lampeter: Edwin Mellen, 2001), 146–51, 203–9.

22. Augustine, Sermon 153.7 (Hill, 61).

23. Augustine, Sermon 154A.3 (Hill, 80).

24. Augustine, Sermon 151.2 (Hill, 41).

25. Augustine, Sermon 151.3 (Hill, 42).

is that, aided by the Spirit, the former experiences sinful desires but does not consent to them or act upon them.[26] This is the personal experience and victory of Paul who now summons Christians to the same battle.

Charting Augustine's change of position and the reasons for it has fascinated scholars. The beginning of the transformation can be found in 396. In that year, Augustine answered the questions of his friend Simplicianus about Rom 7 using his earlier interpretation, but in the same work his treatment of Rom 9:10-13 rejects the idea that God elects only those whose faith is foreknown. Instead, divine grace is utterly gratuitous and beyond human discernment, as demonstrated by the conversion of Paul himself, overwhelmed by grace in the very act of persecuting believers.[27] In time, this new perspective led Augustine to regard Pelagius' interpretation of Romans as dangerous heresy which compromised the priority of divine grace. Augustine rejected Pelagius's insistence that sin is a matter of bad habits freely chosen and that baptism removes even this hindrance to the essentially intact human capacity to choose the good and to reject evil. For Augustine, this kind of freedom is not where the Christian life begins, but rather its goal. The tragedy of sin lies precisely in its capacity to disable our freedom of choice and the Christian life is therefore a process of healing.[28] With these new assumptions in place, Augustine came to conform his interpretation of Rom 7 to his interpretation of Rom 9. It now seemed entirely credible that 7:14-23 might speak of the struggle of the Christian life.

It has often been noted that this change began in 396, only shortly after Augustine became a bishop at Hippo in the previous year. His previous reading of Paul was formed in the ascetic and quasi-monastic atmosphere of Augustine's community of "servants of God" on his family estates at Thagaste, but his new interpretation of Paul reflected the far less elite atmosphere of Hippo.[29] What Augustine encountered in his work as a bishop was large numbers of Catholic laity whose lifestyle fell short

---

26. On this important distinction, see Eugene TeSelle, "Exploring the Inner Conflict: Augustine's Sermons on Romans 7 and 8," in *Engaging Augustine on Romans: Self, Context and Theology in Interpretation* (ed. Daniel Patte and E. TeSelle; Harrisburg, Pa.: Trinity, 2002), 111-46.

27. E. TeSelle, "Exploring the Inner Conflict," 111-12. Paula Fredriksen, "Beyond the body/soul dichotomy: Augustine on Paul against the Manichees and the Pelagians," *Recherches Augstiniennes* 23 (1988), 87-113 (102-03) also suggests that the example of Paul's conversion was important for Augustine.

28. On the Pelagian controversy and what was at stake, see Peter Brown, *Augustine of Hippo: A Biography* (2nd edition; London: Faber & Faber, 2000), 367-77.

29. William S. Babcock, "Augustine and Tyconius: A Study in the Latin Appropriation of Paul," *Studia Patristica* XVII.3 (ed. Elizabeth A. Livingstone; 1982), 1209-15.

of the demands of Pelagius and his followers. What divided the two sides in the controversy was at least in part whether such distinctly average Christians counted as the true church and were truly recipients of divine grace:

> For the Pelagians still thought of the Christian church as if it were a small group in a pagan world. They were concerned to give a good example: the 'sacrifice of praise', that is such an intimate matter for Augustine, means for the Pelagian that praise of pagan human opinion that would be gained by the Christian church as an institution made up of perfect men . . . Augustine described just the sort of man that he had found a place for in the Catholic church: a man with a few good works to his name, who slept with his wife, *faute de mieux*, and often just for the pleasure of it; touchy on points of honor, given to vendettas; not a landgrabber, but capable of fighting to keep hold of his own property, though only in a bishop's court; and, for all that, a good Christian in Augustine's sense, "looking on himself as a disgrace, and giving the glory to God."[30]

In his new interpretation of Rom 7, Augustine is able to offer a picture of the Christian life applicable to such laity and their pastoral needs. His sermons speak of and to them and their struggles with the challenges of sin. In effect, Augustine has constructed a paradigm of conversion that reflects the post-constantinian church and Rom 7 is one of its principal biblical foundations. One of the fundamental differences between the later Augustine and previous patristic interpreters of Rom 7, including himself, is a different set of assumptions about what counts as conversion.

Early Protestant Interpretations of Romans 7

More than a thousand years later, early Protestant interpretations of Rom 7 display significant continuity with patristic interpretations, but there are also important new developments. Yet, strikingly, although there are trends, answers to the classic questions of the identity of the "I" and of whether 7:14–23 applies to life under law or to life under grace do not harden along confessional boundaries. A majority of early Protestant commentators take 7:14–23 to refer to the Christian life, but not all do so, and only a minority of Roman Catholic commentators believed that these verses describe life under the Law.[31] Although there is nothing among Protestant

---

30. Brown, *Augustine of Hippo*, 348–49. Brown quotes from *c. Epp. Pel. (Against Two Letters by the Pelagians)* III, v, 14.

31. See the discussion in David C. Steinmetz, "Calvin and the Divided Self of Romans 7," in *Calvin in Context* (ed. D.C. Steinmetz; Oxford: Oxford University Press, 1995), 110–21. In the medieval pe-

commentators that resembles Origen's wide cast of personae, there are those such as Martin Bucer (1491–1551) and Alexander Alesius (1500–65) who think that Paul is not straightforwardly autobiographical in 7:14–23: "Paul is perhaps exaggerating his sin on order to represent his (Christian) people."[32] There are also even those, such as Bucer and Wolfgang Musculus (1497–1563), who think with Origen that 7:14–23 describes a weaker Christian, someone only on the journey towards the kind of maturity in Christ described in Rom 8: "Romans 7 is about the post-conversion Paul but one who is on the way to a fuller belief in Christ and reception of his Spirit; thus the Romans 7 'Paul' is one who is more like a saint of the Old Testament or like pre-Pentecost Peter."[33] Where confessional boundaries do become decisive for interpretation is in relation to anthropological questions about the nature of human sin which relate strongly to concepts of conversion.

Here we may begin with Martin Luther (1483–1546), whose interpretation is in other respects idiosyncratic. For not only does Luther see 7:14–23 as speaking of the Christian life, but also 7:7–13.[34] Although Luther betrays no interest in the nature of the experience for Paul as an individual, it seems that there is but one moment of awakening when the commandment came (7:9) which began a struggle with sin that persists for a lifetime. Conversion is for the young Luther both that moment and perseverance in lifelong struggle with sin.[35] Yet despite his unusual position on 7:7–13, and the non-publication of his *Lectures on Romans* (1515–1516), which therefore exercised no direct influence upon contemporaries, until the twentieth century, Luther develops two exegetical positions concerning the nature of sin that were to become characteristic of Protestant interpretation. The first concerns Paul's statement that sin once lay dead apart from the Law (7:8). While he does not discount the opinion of "blessed Augustine" that Paul refers to childhood experience

---

riod the dominant trend was to follow the younger Augustine, but Thomas Aquinas was a notable exception. Steinmetz notes three sixteenth century interpreters (two Protestant and one Catholic) who regard 7:14–23 as concerning life under the Law, but twelve interpreters (including four Catholics) who regard 7:14–23 as concerning life under grace.

32. Mark Elliott, "Romans 7 in the Reformation Century," in *Reformation Readings of Romans* (ed. Kathey Ehrensberger and R. Ward Holder; New York: T. & T. Clark, 2008), 171–88 (182).

33. Elliott, "Romans 7 in the Reformation Century," 180.

34. *LW* 25:327 = *WA* 56:339, 5–7: "From this passage on (7:7) to the end of the chapter the apostle is speaking in his own person and as a spiritual man and by no means merely in the person of a carnal man." I know of no other interpreter who does this.

35. Marilyn Harran, *The Concept of 'Conversio' in the Early Exegetical and Reform Writings of Martin Luther* (Ann Arbor, Mich.: University Microfilms International, 1979), 216–17.

before both the attainment of reason and the breaking forth of desire in adolescence, Luther also offers his own rather different view. This is that sin lying dead apart from the Law refers to those who burn with great zeal for the Law but who are unable to recognize their own sin. Luther seems to have in mind particularly those who covet the religious life and feel that nothing else will please God, failing to see that God has called them to other things and that "whatever is coveted besides God, even if one covets it for the sake of God, becomes a sin."[36] The coming of the Law and the awakening of sin is thus implicitly their deliverance from this illusion. For the first time they know their own sin and their true position before God. Before they thought they were under the Law but were in fact without it. What is not clear is where and when in the experience of the individual Luther locates this deliverance from illusion and how it relates to conversion.

Luther's second significant exegetical position is his insistence on the holistic nature of human sin and on the nature of sin as a power. By speaking of dying to the Law (7:6), Paul indicates "that man rather than sin is taken away, for sin remains as a kind of relic, and man is purged from sin rather than the opposite. But the human mind says the contrary, that sin is taken away while man remains and that man is cleansed."[37] Only those separated from sin by God can do anything other than serve sin. The sin which remains as a relic has its characteristic sphere of operations in Paul's life but it cannot be held only to refer to one part of him:

> The apostle does not wish to be understood as saying that the flesh and the spirit are two separate entities, as it were, but one whole, just as a wound and the flesh are one ... The flesh is itself an infirmity or wound of the whole man who by grace is beginning to be healed in both mind and spirit. For who imagines that in a sick man there are these two opposing entities? For it is the same body which seeks health and yet is compelled to do those things which belong to its weakness.[38]

The significance of these two points becomes clear when they are incorporated into exegetical positions that take only 7:14–23 to speak of the Christian life and not also 7:7–13. Protestant interpreters come to apply to Paul in a more directly biographical fashion Luther's idea that sin lying dead apart from the Law (7:8) refers to those who burn with great zeal for the Law but who are unable to recognize their

---

36. *LW* 25:337 = *WA* 56:348, 26–27.
37. *LW* 25:322 = *WA* 56:334, 15–18.
38. *LW* 25:339–41 = *WA* 56:350, 22 – 352, 9.

own sin. Paul's time alive apart from the Law was his time as a Pharisee when he believed in his own righteousness. Thus John Calvin (1509-64) can say of Paul that:

> As he says elsewhere, a veil was interposed to prevent the Jews from seeing the light of life in the law (II Cor 3.14). So too, in his own case, as long as his eyes were veiled while he lacked the Spirit of Christ, he was satisfied with the outward mask (*larva*) of righteousness. He refers, therefore, to the law as absent because, although it was before his eyes, it did not impress on him a serious sense of the judgment of the Lord . . . Paul now refers to the law as *coming* on the other hand, when it has begun to be truly understood. It therefore 'awoke' sin from the dead, because it showed Paul how great was the depravity which abounded in the innermost part of his heart, and at the same time it put him to death.[39]

That what Paul speaks of as life apart from the Law was in fact his time of blind zeal for the Law as a Pharisee was also argued in various forms by Oecolampadius (1482-1531), Melanchthon (1497-1560), Bullinger (1504-75), Brenz (1499-1570), Ochino (1487-1564) and Alesius.[40] What is new here is not the idea that the arrival of the Law makes sin known and makes the offence of sin even graver since it is now the violation of stated commandments, for this is commonplace in patristic interpretations. The new elements are the identification of life apart from the Law with life as a law observant Jew and the identification of life after the coming of the Law with the conviction of sin and conviction of the impossibility of fulfilling the Law's commands. When the description of the struggles of the regenerate in 7:14-23 is added, there are thus three possible human conditions or types of person. As Melanchthon puts it: "One is the carnal who live secure . . . The second category is those who are oppressed by fears and torments of conscience . . . The third category consists of those who are raised up in the midst of their terrors by the voice of the Gospel."[41] The possibility seems clearly implicit here of not just three conditions or types of person, but also of a three-stage sequence of conversion for the individual. If it is true of Paul's argument, as Calvin expresses its intention, that "his purpose was to begin with a universal proposition, and afterwards to explain the subject by his own example," then one might expect the suggestion that there were three such

---

39. John Calvin, *The Epistles of Paul to the Romans and Thessalonians* (trans. R. Mackenzie; Grand Rapids: Eerdmans, 1961), 144 = CR 49, 125-26.

40. See Elliott, "Romans 7 in the Reformation Century" for details.

41. Philip Melanchthon, *Commentary on Romans* (trans. F. Kramer; St Louis, Mo.: Concordia, 1992), 157 = CR 15, 648.

stages in Paul's experience. Yet this does *not* appear, reflecting uncertainty in early Protestant theology as to whether the conviction of sin brought by the Law arrives only at the moment of conversion itself or if it comes earlier and opens a period of preparation for conversion.[42] While interested in Paul's experiences in so far as they helped to explain the theology of his argument, early Protestant commentators display little interest in dwelling on those experiences for their own sake or in drawing experiential implications for others. It is the theological categories that provide the focus.

The significance of Luther's second point, that sin within the believer in 7:14–23 concerns the whole person, can be seen by contrasting Protestant insistence on this with a rather different Roman Catholic perspective. For those Roman Catholic commentators who take 7:14–23 as speaking of the Christian life, the desires of the flesh are not sinful unless they are given assent by the believer. In this they closely follow the older Augustine. The Christian may not be able perfectly to do God's will, but is nevertheless not in a state of mortal sin. The struggle between the spirit and the flesh is therefore a contest between different parts of a person in which sin disrupts the healthy hierarchies between soul and body, and between reason/the will and the other faculties of the soul, so that the lower parts refuse to obey the higher as they ought to do.[43] As Erasmus paraphrases Paul:

> Now when reason calls in one way, desire in another, the worse in me gains control, the better is conquered. For the inclination to sin is so deeply fixed in the flesh, and the habit of committing wrong so powerful (as if now a part of my nature), that like some struggling and unwilling captive I am dragged into sin.[44]

On the Protestant side, in a decisive departure from the later Augustine, it is insisted that concupiscence itself is truly sin and that part of its very nature is that

---

42. Norman Pettit, *The Heart Prepared: Grace and Conversion in Puritan Spiritual Life* (New Haven, Conn.: Yale University Press, 1966), 45 traces three distinct Reformed positions on this question held by Peter Martyr, Calvin and Bullinger respectively: "that grace comes only as an effectual call, with no preparatory disposition of the heart; that grace, while entirely a matter of seizure, may nevertheless involve preparation through divine constraint of the heart; and that grace follows the heart's response to God's offer of the covenant promises in preparatory repentance."

43. Steinmetz, "Calvin and the Divided Self of Romans 7," 112–13.

44. D. Erasmus, *Paraphrases on Romans and Galatians* (R. D. Sider ed.; Toronto: University of Toronto Press, 1974), 44. See also J. Colet, *An Exposition of St. Paul's Epistle to the Romans* (trans. J. H. Lupton; London: Bell and Daldy, 1873; repr., Eugene, Ore.: Wipf & Stock, 2007), 20–25, who vigorously presents the same position in his 1497 Oxford lectures.

it may be involuntary and not only a matter of the consent of the will. This leads in turn to the understanding that the conflict of the spirit and the flesh is a matter of the orientation of the entire person towards God. The spirit is everything within a person that has been renewed by God; the flesh is everything that remains un-renewed. "Flesh is not a faculty but the *totus homo* in opposition and rebellion against God."[45] Thus Paul's contrast in 7:21–23 between the inner person and the members of the body is not one between body and soul. For Calvin, Paul is instead drawing a metaphor in which the superiority of the spirit to the flesh is merely compared to that of the soul over the body:

> The *inward man*, therefore, does not mean simply the soul, but the spiritual part of the soul which has been regenerated by God. *Members* means the other remaining part. As the soul is the more excellent and the body the inferior part of man, so the spirit is superior to the flesh. The spirit takes the place of the soul in man, but the flesh, which is the corrupt and polluted soul, that of the body.[46]

Similar positions are adopted by, among others, Melanchthon, Bullinger and Beza (1519–1605). What is at stake here is, of course, rival conceptions of justification and hence of conversion. In the Roman Catholic view, grace is understood as something that God does within a person. It is infused, and God accepts the sinner because the righteousness of Christ has wrought a renewal within the person. Christ in his righteousness enters into a person and, with their co-operation, produces a righteousness that is inherent to them. There is an objective judgment based on what the human has become: "life is to be conceived of as a *via* for our transformation . . . 'In the end' the human should be able to stand before God on account of his merits. That merit is gained through working with God's grace, in which the human remains rooted."[47] If the concupiscence spoken of in Rom 7 were sin in its full sense then there would be little hope for the growth of justifying righteousness, hence the importance of the distinction between mortal and venial sin. In contrast, Protestant interpreters regard justification as a divine declaration at the outset of the Christian life which in no way depends upon what human beings do or become: "Christians are already righteous because of the righteousness of Christ and need no longer fear

---

45. D. C. Steinmetz, "Calvin and the Patristic Exegesis of Paul," in *The Bible in the Sixteenth Century* (ed. D. C. Steinmetz; Durham, N.C.: Duke University Press, 1990), 100–118 (115).

46. Calvin, *Epistles of Paul to the Romans and Thessalonians*, 153 = CR 49, 133–4.

47. Daphne Hampson, *Christian Contradictions: The Structures of Lutheran and Catholic Thought* (Cambridge: Cambridge University Press, 2001), 83–84.

God's judgment."[48] Renewal will follow, and several early Protestant conceptions of justification intimately connect God's justifying declaration with renewal,[49] but renewal is never a cause or basis of justification. The concupiscence spoken of in Rom 7 can be sin in its full sense without threatening the justification of the believer.

Romans 7 among Puritans, Pietists, and Methodists

In Puritan interpretations of Rom 7, the insistence that concupiscence is truly sin and the framework of understanding of justification within which it sits were assumed and uncontroversial. So too was the conviction that Paul speaks in 7:14–23 of the life of the believer, and the opinion that Paul's reference to being alive apart from the Law (7:9) concerns his time as a zealous Pharisee when he was not fully conscious of his own sin. Yet despite these essential continuities, there are new features. In particular, a new level of introspection is apparent, focusing on the conscience and its condition, with a profound interest in the experiential implications of Paul's argument. Thus, for example, when commenting on Rom 7:9, the English preacher John Flavel (1627–91) speaks conventionally enough of Paul as formerly "full of vain hope, false joy, and presumptuous confidence; a very brisk and jovial man," but when the commandment came "the apprehensions he then had of his condition struck home to the heart and damped all his carnal mirth."[50] The new dimension compared to Protestant readings of the sixteenth century is Flavel's concern then to list and describe the seven ways in which Satan keeps quiet the consciences of men in their delusions. Further, he regards a deluded slumbering conscience as possible not just for those who do not know or reject the gospel of Christ, but also for those who regard themselves as Christians. Flavel says of the unregenerate that they have "a sensitive joy in things carnal," and "a delusive joy in things spiritual":

> They rejoice in corn, wine, and oil, in their estates and children, in the pleasant fruitions of the creature; yea and they rejoice also in Christ and the promises, in heaven and in glory: with all which they have the kind of communion as a man hath in a dream with a full feast and curious music; and just so their joy will vanish when they awake.[51]

---

48. Steinmetz, "Calvin and the Divided Self of Romans 7," 115.

49. Not least among those who do so is Luther himself. See Stephen J. Chester, "It is No Longer I Who Live: Justification by Faith and Participation in Christ in Martin Luther's Exegesis of Galatians," *NTS* 55 (2009), 315–37.

50. John Flavel, "The Method of Grace in the Gospel Redemption," *The Works of John Flavel* Vol. II (London: 1820; repr., Banner of Truth, 1968), 288.

51. Ibid., 290.

The possibility of satanic counterfeits of conversion and new birth is a real one: "It is very frequently seen that even carnal and unrenewed hearts have their meltings and transports, as well as spiritual hearts."[52] Although it concerns 7:23 and therefore the life of the believer, similar introspective features appear in another Puritan sermon by Roger Drake (1608–69). Drake observes that the unregenerate may sometimes experience a limited consciousness of sin because of social customs, natural disposition and the remains within them of the image of God. Yet this is different from the struggle with sin experienced by believers and spoken of in Rom 7. It therefore becomes crucial to know that one is indeed regenerate and truly engaged in that struggle. Drake entitles his sermon "What Difference Is There between the Conflict in Natural and Spiritual Persons?" He identifies seven differences between the two types of conflict before proposing eight strategies by which his hearers might ensure that they sided with the Spirit.[53] The particular burden imposed upon believers by the struggle with sin is that it "makes them drive heavily, because they doubt whether they be Israelites or Egyptians."[54]

Despite significant differences in context and developments in theology, the same exegetical features can be seen among New England theologians in the eighteenth and early nineteenth centuries. The desire of which Paul speaks in Rom 7 truly is sin and in 7:14–23 he speaks of his experience as a Christian. Paul is discussing here the same experience as the struggle of the Spirit and the flesh in Gal 5:17. The crucial question in application is whether the conviction of sin experienced by the believer is genuine. Jonathan Edwards (1703–58), who himself struggled as a young man with a lack of such conviction,[55] asked his congregation to "Inquire whether your supposed grace has that influence as to render those things wherein you have failed to holy practice to be loathsome, grievous and humbling to you."[56] One of his examples of true contrition and appropriate self-loathing is Paul's cry of wretchedness in Rom 7:24. That such an experience of conviction of sin is essential to true

---

52. Ibid., 303.

53. James Nichols, ed., *Puritan Sermons 1659–1689 Volume I: The Morning Exercises at Cripplegate or Several Cases of Conscience Practically Resolved* (London 1661; repr., Wheaton, Ill.: R.O. Roberts, 1981), 284–92.

54. Nichols, ed., *Puritan Sermons 1659–1689 Volume I*, 287.

55. See George Marsden, *Jonathan Edwards: A Biography* (New Haven, Conn.: Yale University Press, 2003), 25–43.

56. Jonathan Edwards, "Charity and its Fruits," in *Ethical Writings* (ed. Paul Ramsey; New Haven, Conn.: Yale University Press, 1989), 310. One of Edwards' major works, "Religious Affections" is devoted to distinguishing between religious affections truly the result of grace and those that are not.

conversion is insisted upon by Edwards' protégé Samuel Hopkins (1721–1803). In a sermon on Rom 7:7, Hopkins pictures the multitudes who

> hope and expect to be saved by Christ; they speak much of the grace of the gospel, and the wonderful mercy of God to sinners; but they at the same time are ignorant of the divine law, and never were reconciled to it as holy, just, and good; so never saw sin in its true odiousness and ill desert. Let such rise as high as they will in their admiration of gospel grace and, though they are affected even to raptures, they are wholly ignorant of the true grace of God.[57]

Such characteristic Puritan concern with whether the experience of the individual indicates that he or she truly numbers among the elect might be expected to have consequences for relating Rom 7 to conversion. It might at last produce an emphasis on the conviction of sin resulting from the coming of the Law (7:9) as opening a period of preparation for conversion. Here would be an opportunity to distinguish true conviction of sin from its counterfeits. Such emphasis on preparation is certainly present in Puritan theology generally, a strong theology of covenant and infant baptism enabling this to be reconciled with commitment to the doctrine of predestination:

> The children, as the seed of the covenant, were to be given the benefit of the doubt until such time as they experienced or failed to experience conversion. And when it was further assumed that a child might even possess grace without being conscious of it, this allowed for an introspective element in Reformed theology which went hand in hand with the rigors of predestination.[58]

Nevertheless, the notion of a period of preparation for conversion does not appear in relation to interpretations of Rom 7. Although Flavel does urge those among his hearers with no or only slight experience of the power of the word to apply themselves and to plead with God for a sense of conviction,[59] he does not identify this with Paul's argument. Instead the conviction of sin produced by the coming of the Law in 7:9 is identified with Paul's experience on the road to Damascus, with the

---

57. Samuel Hopkins, "On the Necessity of the Knowledge of the Law of God, in order to the Knowledge of Sin," Bruce Kuklick (ed.), *The Works of Samuel Hopkins* Vol. III (ed. Bruce Kuklick; Boston: 1854; repr., New York: Garland, 1987), 519–42 (530).

58. Pettit, *The Heart Prepared*, 12.

59. Nichols ed., *Puritan Sermons 1659–1689* Volume I, 301–4.

moment of conversion itself.[60] The same is true much later in New England, where Nathanael Emmons (1745-1840) argued that before his conversion Paul believed himself blameless under the Law (Phil 3:5), but Rom 7:9-11 describes the conviction of sin that came upon him at his conversion.[61] The reason is the recognition, based on texts like Acts 9, that Paul's experience of grace had been sudden and overwhelming. In urging the validity of a more gradual process of conversion in which human preparation played a significant part, the Puritans found their biblical resources not in Paul but in the prophetic texts of the Old Testament calling people back to their covenant obligations, or in the example of such as Lydia (Acts 16:13-15), who was already a worshipper of God before her heart was opened to receive Paul's message. Although introspective concerns abound in their interpretations of Rom 7, Puritan interpreters do not assume that Paul himself experienced a significant period of struggle with the Law and conviction of sin before his conversion and, while regarding such an experience as essential for others, they do not base such an expectation upon this particular text.

The Puritan pattern of identifying the coming of the Law in 7:7-9 with conviction of sin, and of regarding such conviction as essential to conversion, continued throughout the Evangelical Revival of the eighteenth century. John Wesley (1703-91) and Count Zinzendorf (1700-60) and the Moravians were to break with each other in 1739 over precisely this issue, Wesley insisting on the necessity of the Law bringing conviction of sin before an experience of grace. Ways were even found to make Paul's experience fit the pattern. When preaching at Glasgow in 1741, George Whitefield (1714-1770) made the story of Paul's conversion in Acts 9 a paradigm of evangelical conversion: "Saul's vision on the Damascus Road was his awakening of conscience; his period of three days darkness was his evangelical humiliation; his recovery of sight under Ananias' prayers was his New Birth."[62] However, despite these very significant continuities with the Puritan past, a new interpretation of Rom 7 was to develop among the Wesleyans in a move dependent upon the exegesis of German Pietism. Through his own experience of conversion, August Hermann Francke (1663-1727) had come to insist on a period of penitential struggle (*Busskampf*) as an essential prelude to a breakthrough to consolation and grace (*Durchbruch*). He

---

60. Nichols ed., *Puritan Sermons 1659-1689* Volume I, 293-94.

61. Nathanael Emmons, "The True Character of Good Men Delineated," in *The Works of Nathanael Emmons Vol. 5* (ed. Jacob Ide; Boston: Crocker & Brewster, 1842), 196-208 (196).

62. Bruce C. Hindmarsh, *The Evangelical Conversion Narrative: Spiritual Autobiography in Early Modern England* (Oxford: Oxford University Press, 2005), 143.

applied this to Rom 7, regarding 7:14–23 and not merely 7:9–11 as descriptive of this experience:

> In contrast to Luther and Lutheran Orthodoxy, Francke asserted an effectively new determination of Christian existence and placed this exegetically in his interpretation of Romans 7, where the apostle would describe the condition of a Christian person, who is not yet reborn but is being found in the process of conversion.[63]

This interpretation is then also advocated by the great Pietist biblical commentator, Johann Albrecht Bengel (1687–1752), who suggests that Rom 7 describes "the whole process of a man, in his transition from his state under the Law to his state under grace, thinking, striving, and struggling forth."[64] Paul does not speak in Rom 7 of his own character but "*all along from ver. 7 . . . under the figure of a man, who is engaged in this contest.*"[65] The cry of wretchedness in 7:24 is "the last thing in the struggle . . . *the very moment of mystical death.*"[66] In this interpretation, Bengel is followed very closely by Wesley in his own exegetical notes on the New Testament, who openly acknowledges his debts to the German scholar.[67] The evangelist also makes striking use of the interpretation in a sermon of 1746 entitled *The Spirit of Bondage and Adoption*. The text is Rom 8:15, with the cry "Abba Father" taken as that of those who have broken through to liberty and life under grace. Yet much of the sermon interacts in detail with Rom 7 as a description of a person under the Law:

> How lively a portraiture is this of one "under the law!" one who feels the burden he cannot shake off; who pants after liberty, power, and love, but is in fear and bondage still! Until the time that God answers the wretched man, crying out, "Who shall deliver me" from this bondage of sin, from this body of death?—"The grace of God, through Jesus Christ thy Lord."[68]

---

63. Markus Matthias, "August Hermann Francke," in *The Pietist Theologians* (ed. Carter Lindberg; Oxford: Blackwell, 2005), 100–114 (107).

64. Johann A. Bengel, *Gnomon of the New Testament Vol. 3* (trans. A.R. Fausset; Edinburgh: T&T Clark, 1859), 91–92.

65. Bengel, *Gnomon*, 92 (his emphasis).

66. Bengel, *Gnomon*, 95–96 (his emphasis).

67. John Wesley, *Explanatory Notes upon the New Testament* (London: 1754; repr., London: Epworth, 1976), 543–6. See the Preface (7) for Wesley's acknowledgement of Bengel's influence.

68. John Wesley, *The Works of John Wesley Volume I, Sermons I, 1–33* (ed. Albert C. Outler; Nashville: Abingdon, 1984), 248–66 (260).

If Bengel is the primary influence on Wesley here, there is no doubt that the younger Augustine comes a close second. The entire sermon is framed by Augustine's stages of man, the first three of which are termed by Wesley the "natural man," one "under the law," and one "under grace."[69] Just as Augustine himself was able to retain this exegetical framework despite his switch to a different understanding of the detail of Rom 7, so Wesley is able to employ it effectively in a radically different context in the service of Protestant understandings of conversion and of human sinfulness rather different from Augustine's own.

The appeal for Wesley of this Pietist interpretation of Rom 7 is that it sits comfortably with his views on sanctification, which emphasized the power given to justified and regenerate believers not to commit sin. Wesley was determined not to slight the Holy Spirit by attributing too little to its transformation of the believer. Although by no means resolving the dilemma of how to champion this view effectively and persuasively without going so far as to teach Christian perfection, reading the whole of Rom 7:7–23 as a description of one under law did remove one of the principal exegetical barriers to this task. Somewhat suggestively given that Wesley was famously to separate from Whitefield in 1741 over the issue of predestination, many of the details of this new Wesleyan interpretation of Rom 7 had in fact been anticipated by Jacobus Arminius (1560–1609). In a lengthy tract on Rom 7 Arminius had also employed Augustine's anthropological categories, suggested that the person described in the chapter is one in the process of moving from impiety and infidelity to regeneration and grace, and insisted of 7:14–23 that "such a contest cannot be ascribed to the Holy Spirit without an enormous disgrace to Him."[70] Arminius notes that the later Augustine took 7:14–23 to describe the struggle of the believer but does so on the basis of the distinction between experiencing desire itself and giving consent to it. Only if consent is given is sin truly committed. This may be an erroneous view of sin but it does not slight the Holy Spirit like Protestant interpretations which correctly assert that desire itself is sin but then declare the Spirit ineffective against it. In Arminius's view the only understanding of Rom 7 consistent with Protestant anthropology is that the whole of 7:7–23 describes a person under law, convicted of sin but not yet delivered from it by conversion.

---

69. Outler notes, *The Works of John Wesley Volume 1*, 248, that Augustine's interpretive framework was mediated to Wesley through Thomas Boston, *Human Nature in its Fourfold State* (Edinburgh: 1720).

70. "Dissertation on the True and Genuine Sense of the Seventh Chapter of the Epistle to the Romans," in *The Works of James Arminius Volume 2* (trans. J. and W. Nichols; 1828; repr., Grand Rapids: Baker, 1996), 471–683 (657). The dissertation was first published in 1613.

Thus, just as Augustine's change of mind over Rom 7 was connected with his acceptance of predestination, the emergence of a new and different interpretation of Rom 7 within Protestantism comes among those who question predestination. The two sets of relationships between theological convictions and exegetical conclusions provide mirror images of each other. So too do the two sets of relationships with conversion as a social reality. For Augustine had changed his interpretation of Rom 7 in the context of the post-constantinian church, where the emergence of Christendom was foreshadowed by the inclusion for the first time of the vast majority of the population. In contrast, the Evangelical Revival emerged just as Christendom was waning:

> The evangelical conversion narrative flourished, then, when Christendom, or Christian civil society, had eroded far enough to allow for toleration, dissent, experimentation, and the manifestation of nominal and sincere forms of adherence to faith, but not so far as to erode a traditional sense of Christian moral norms and basic theological and cosmological assumptions. It was precisely in the seventeenth and eighteenth centuries that the emerging modern identity could cross paths with the fading Christian moral hegemony. Evangelical conversion narrative appeared on the trailing edge of Christendom and the leading edge of modernity.[71]

Further, just as Augustine's interpretation of Rom 7 helped to make room in the church for distinctly average Christians, so Methodist preaching sought to challenge them. Early Methodist converts record its impact:

> They remarked that they were surprised to learn that "going to church and sacrament" and "doing no harm" did not fulfill their religious obligations. This is why we find the recurring trope of "Pharisee" as a description of their state before they encountered this shattering message ... Wesley stressed that both the brazenly sinful and those with "a little outward religion" were alike but "baptized heathens."[72]

To read and preach Rom 7 as the narrative of a struggle towards conversion is to offer grace to all and is to make Rom 8 the description of a Christian life available to all, but it is also to exclude those nominal Christians who will not or cannot accept that message or share that experience.

---

71. Hindmarsh, *The Evangelical Conversion Narrative*, 340.

72. Ibid., 137.

Romans 7 in the Historical-Critical Era

In the nineteenth century, the rise of historical-critical scholarship produced a different focus in the interpretation of Rom 7. There is quite simply a greater concern with the historical and the relationship between the content of Rom 7 and Paul's biography. This can be seen even among those who would otherwise count as traditional interpreters not particularly molded by new methods. Robert Haldane (1764–1842) stands exegetically in complete agreement with earlier Puritan readings. Paul's time without the Law is his time as a Pharisee when he did not know his own sin and from 7:14 onwards he describes Christian experience. Yet while Haldane is clear that these experiences apply to his readers' lives, entirely absent is the earlier Puritan concern with distinguishing between true and counterfeit conviction of sin in conversion and true and counterfeit struggle with sin in the Christian life. The focus is instead Paul's experience and Rom 7 is straightforwardly autobiographical. In 7:14–25, Paul "speaks in the first person about forty times, without the smallest intimation that he is referring to anyone else, or to himself at any former period."[73] Similarly conservative in his exegetical conclusions and with more of a doctrinal than a historical concern, Charles Hodge (1797–1878) nevertheless also insisted that Paul describes his own experience.[74]

The dominant opinion in the nineteenth century, which rejected the view that in 7:14–23 Paul speaks of the Christian life, was no less focused on Paul's experience. The apostle speaks of a struggle that he actually experienced before his conversion. Schweitzer reports the widespread assumption of mid-nineteenth century scholarship that Rom 7 is "written from the point of view of the pre-Christian consciousness of the Apostle. He had experienced this agony of soul, and it was by this that the Jewish religious attitude had been broken down in him."[75] This assumption crossed confessional boundaries. The Pietist commentator August Tholuck (1799–1877) follows Bengel closely in his interpretation of Rom 7 except precisely for Bengel's key assertion that Paul here speaks in the person of another. Tholuck believes that Paul speaks from personal experience.[76] The Reformed commentator F. L. Godet (1812–

---

73. Robert Haldane, *Exposition of the Epistle to the Romans Vol. 2* (1837; repr., Evansville, Ind.: Sovereign Grace, 1955), 302.

74. Charles Hodge, *Commentary on the Epistle to the Romans* (1864; repr., Grand Rapids: Eerdmans, 1980), 239–45.

75. Albert Schweitzer, *Paul and his Interpreters* (London: A&C Black, 1912), 39. The comment comes in a chapter entitled "From Baur to Holtzmann."

76. August Tholuck, *Exposition of St. Paul's Epistle to the Romans* (Philadelphia: Sorin & Ball, 1844), 214–15, 235.

1900) departs from the whole of his confessional tradition in regarding 7:14–25 as concerning the pre-Christian Paul. Like many others, he rejects as historically inadmissible the idea that Paul's reference to life without the Law (7:9) pertains to his time as a Pharisee. "Could Paul really say of himself, that, as a Pharisee, he *was without law*? . . . Certainly if these words refer to his conversion, some indication or other would not be wanting to designate this transition to a new faith."[77] Paul must be speaking rather of his childhood as without the Law.

Others are even more explicit in suggesting that 7:14–25 recounts a period of struggle experienced by Paul as a preparation for his conversion on the Damascus road. H. A. W. Meyer (1800–73) explicitly compares Paul's struggle with the Law to the *Anfechtungen* experienced by Luther before his Reformation breakthrough.[78] W. Sanday (1843–1920) and A. C. Headlam (1862–1947) initially express some hesitancy in relating everything in Rom 7 to Paul's personal experiences but do regard it as nevertheless strongly reflected. They say of 7:14–25 that:

> Without putting an exact date to the struggle which follows we shall probably not be wrong in referring the main features of it especially to the period before his conversion. It was then that the powerlessness of the Law to do anything but aggravate sin was brought home to him . . . The apparent suddenness of St. Paul's conversion was due to the tenacity with which he held onto his Jewish faith and his reluctance to yield to conclusions which were merely negative.[79]

H. Weinel (1874–1936) produced a life of Paul in which he made the whole of Rom 7:7–25 the preliminary struggle to Paul's conversion: "In this conflict Saul lived, as Pharisee and persecutor. Heavier and heavier did the curse of the law become to him, the more he studied it and the more exactly he tried to keep the commandment."[80] Paul's experience on the Damascus road is the answer he received to his cry of wretchedness in 7:24. An essentially similar view of the passage was propagated long into the twentieth century by C. H. Dodd (1884–1973): "We may therefore take verses 22, 23, and 25b as describing the state of a man who has

---

77. Frederic L. Godet, *Commentary on Romans* (1883; repr., Grand Rapids: Kregel, 1977), 275.

78. Heinrich A.W. Meyer, *Critical and Exegetical Handbook to the Epistle to the Romans* (New York: Funk & Wagnall, 1884), 266.

79. William Sanday and Arthur C. Headlam, *Romans* (ICC; Edinburgh: T. & T. Clark, 1895), 186–87.

80. Heinrich Weinel, *St. Paul: The Man and his Work* (New York: G.P. Putnam's Sons, 1906), 74–75.

reached desperation in the moral conflict—describing . . . Paul's own state when he set out for Damascus."[81] The need to provide a historical explanation for Paul's conversion other than as a sudden eruption of divine grace is apparent in this focus on struggle with the Law as psychological preparation. So too is the unmistakable shift of interest promoted by historical-critical methods. The text is no longer interpreted primarily to discover its implications for the lives, and especially the conversions, of its readers, but instead primarily for what it can tell us of Paul. It is his conversion rather than that of the readers that has taken center stage. Insofar as their conversion is in view at all it is implicit, the attitude of interpreters towards it depending upon whether they evaluate Paul's pre-conversion struggle with the Law positively or negatively.

Romans 7 and Conversion in the Twentieth Century

It is widely held that the landmark moment in twentieth century study of Rom 7 is the publication in 1929 of W.G. Kümmel's monograph on the chapter.[82] Yet that status is conferred not because the author's interpretation of Rom 7 gained pre-eminence. Kümmel (1905–95) argues that the "I" in Rom 7 is not in any sense autobiographical and the first person is a rhetorical device used in order to depict more vividly the situation of humanity under the Law as seen from a Christian perspective. There is little sign in subsequent scholarship of consensus around this position but instead considerable diversity. Indeed, the prominence of Kümmel's interpretation initially owed something to its immediate acceptance and promotion by Rudolf Bultmann, who employed it in the service of his own interpretation of Rom 7. Yet Bultmann's interpretation is itself now widely rejected.[83] Kümmel's significance rests rather on his success in utterly destroying the credibility of a previously dominant interpretation. In order to clear the ground for his own interpretation, Kümmel demonstrates, on the basis of Paul's claim to blamelessness under the Law in Phil 3:6, that Rom 7 simply cannot refer to a pre-conversion struggle with the Law in which Paul experienced a bad conscience due to his inability to perform the Law.[84] Despite very

---

81. Charles H. Dodd, *The Epistle of Paul to the Romans* (London: Hodder & Stoughton, 1932), 115.

82. Werner G. Kümmel, *Römer 7 und die Bekehrung des Paulus* (Leipzig: Hinrichs, 1929).

83. Rudolf Bultmann, "Romans 7 and the Anthropology of Paul," *Existence and Faith: The Shorter Writings of Rudolf Bultmann* (New York: Meridian, 1960), 147–57. Bultmann wrote this essay in 1932.

84. Kümmel, *Römer 7*, 111–17.

occasional attempts to dispute this conclusion,[85] its acceptance is near universal. Yet, as Jewett observes, the argument from Phil 3:6 "does not really sustain Kümmel's conclusion that all autobiographical theories should be abandoned. As with his subsidiary argument that nowhere else does Paul speak of a life 'apart from the Law' (7:9), these details could be co-ordinated with some other version of autobiographical self-reference."[86]

Among those commentators who wish to retain at least an element of autobiography, there are some prominent commentators, most notably C. K. Barrett (b. 1917), C. E. B. Cranfield (b. 1915) and James Dunn (b. 1939), who continue to advocate the view that in 7:14–25 Paul discusses his life as a Christian.[87] However, the most popular contemporary view is that Paul is here reflecting on his own experience under the Law but doing so from his current Christian perspective.[88] As N. T. Wright (b. 1948) expresses it, Paul provides "a Christian theological analysis of what was in fact the case, and indeed what is still the case for those who live 'under the law,' not a description of how it felt or feels."[89] This position had been suggested in the nineteenth century by F. C. Baur (1792–1860) but it had not gained widespread support.[90] Baur says of the struggle Paul describes that:

> Man cannot emerge from this state of division and distraction so long as he is under the law, and the law itself is there, just to create in him the full consciousness of the division. But as soon as he becomes conscious of the enormity of the division, and begins to long for deliverance from it, he has in reality got past it, and the lower negative standpoint is now looked back upon and judged by a standard which only the superior standpoint has given . . . We have therefore a right to say that no one ever so felt so

85. E.g., J. M. Espy, "Paul's Robust Conscience Re-examined," *NTS* 31 (1985), 161–88.

86. Robert Jewett, *Romans* (Minneapolis: Fortress, 2007), 441.

87. Charles K. Barrett, *The Epistle to the Romans* (London: A. & C. Black, 2nd edition, 1991), 130–44; Charles E.B. Cranfield, *Romans Volume 1* (Edinburgh: T. & T. Clark, 1975), 340–70; James D.G. Dunn, *Romans 1-8* (Dallas: Word, 1988), 374–412.

88. See, among many others, Jewett, *Romans*, 440–73; Käsemann, *Commentary on Romans* (Grand Rapids: Eerdmans, 1980), 191–212; Douglas Moo, *The Epistle to the Romans* (Grand Rapids: Eerdmans, 1996), 423–67; Thomas Schreiner, *Romans* (Grand Rapids: Baker, 1998), 357–94.

89. Nicholas T. Wright, "Romans" in *The New Interpreter's Bible Volume 12* (ed. L. Keck et al; Nashville: Abingdon, 2002), 393–770 (553). Wright emphasizes that although Paul is reflecting on what was true of him he does so in order to describe the position of Israel under Torah.

90. An exception is James Denney (1856–1917), who comments that "No one could have written the passage but a Christian: it is the experience of the unregenerate, we may say, but seen through regenerate eyes, interpreted in a regenerate mind." "St. Paul's Epistle to the Romans," William R. Nichol (ed.), *The Expositor's Greek Testament Volume Two* (Grand Rapids: Eerdmans, 1897), 639.

> truly this disunion of man with himself—this division which prevails at the standpoint of the law—as the apostle who, when he felt it, had already overcome it . . . Only in presentiment of the state of grace can one feel rightly what is wanting in the state of law.[91]

Among more recent interpreters advocating a similar view there are various opinions as to whether and to what degree Paul intends his own experience to be understood as typical of that of Judaism or, indeed, of humanity as a whole, and this is reflected in differing conclusions as to whether or not 7:7–11 are modeled upon the figure of Adam and whether or not Paul is referring throughout to the Mosaic law.[92] However, all agree that it is in retrospect that Paul discerns that sin worked death in him through the good law (7:13) and that he had been sold under sin (7:14). In most cases this position is argued in relation to historical-critical questions and the relationship to conversion left undeveloped except for the important conclusion that Paul himself did not suffer from a pre-conversion guilty conscience.

However, there are some implicit consequences for perspectives on conversion. These derive from Baur's observation that the person who recognizes the division and wishes to be delivered from it has in fact already been freed from it. Not only does Paul not experience a pre-conversion struggle with conscience, but it will be difficult on this view of Rom 7 to use the text to sustain the position that a period of struggle with conviction of sin is an essential prelude to, or first step in, conversion. That Paul's post-conversion assessment of his earlier life is so radically different from that which he made at the time does suggest that he now regards as sin that which he would previously have accepted as ethical behavior, but that this change in perspective is the consequence of conversion rather than its initial phase. Conversion brings conviction of sin but only as it simultaneously delivers the convert into the newness of life described in Rom 8. Reading Rom 7 as Paul's Christian perspective on his pre-conversion life thus seems to accord with wider studies of conversion in the New Testament from scholars in the Evangelical tradition who urge the abandonment of rigid expectations as to patterns of conversion experience.[93]

---

91. Ferdinand C. Baur, *Paul the Apostle of Jesus Christ: His Life and Works, His Epistles and Teachings: Two Volumes in One* (1873; repr., Peabody, Mass.: Hendrickson, 2003), Vol. 2, 146–7.

92. Thus, for example, Käsemann (*Romans*, 196) insists that in 7:7–11, "there is nothing in the passage that does not fit Adam, and everything fits Adam alone," whereas Moo (*Romans*, 423–31) argues that Paul focuses exclusively on the giving of the Law at Sinai.

93. Richard Peace, *Conversion in the New Testament: Paul and the Twelve* (Grand Rapids: Eerdmans, 1999); Scot McKnight, *Turning to Jesus: The Sociology of Conversion in the Gospels* (Louisville: Westminster John Knox, 2002).

Romans 7 and Theological Critics of Conversion

The twentieth century did not only see greater flexibility in expectations concerning the shape of conversion experiences from theological traditions that continued to place great emphasis upon them. It also saw reflection upon Rom 7 containing criticism of Protestant conceptions of the place of conversion in the Christian life. One such critique is found in the existential interpretation of Rom 7 offered by Rudolf Bultmann (1884–1976). Beginning from Kümmel's conclusions that the "I" of Rom 7 is a rhetorical device used in a general discussion of the position of humanity under the Law, Bultmann argues for a particular view of Paul's anthropology and of his portrayal of sin. The problem Paul describes is not that of a person's good intentions being overwhelmed by desire, but rather the misguided desire to become righteous through obedience to the Law:

> His fundamental approach is not that the way of the law is wrong, because by reason of transgressions, it fails to reach its goal (that is the position, say of IV Ezra), but rather than the direction of this way is perverse and, to be sure, because it intends to lead to 'one's own righteousness' (Rom 10:3; Phil 3:9). It is not evil works or transgressions of the law that first make the Jews objectionable to God; rather the intention to become righteous before him by fulfilling the law is their real sin, which is merely manifested by transgressions.[94]

Much subsequent reaction has focused on the important issue of what Bultmann here implies about Judaism. Although Bultmann's position contains considerable continuity with early Protestant polemics against works-righteousness, at another level he also significantly alters the nature of the critique. It is no longer that zeal for the Law is used by sin to blind its proponents to their own sinfulness and to lead them falsely to believe in the reality of their own righteousness. It is not the unrecognized transgressions that are the problem but rather, as Bultmann says so clearly, the zeal itself. His position has often been perceived as anti-Jewish, and also as difficult to reconcile with Paul's insistence on the nature of the Law as "holy and righteous and good" (7:12), a description which suggests that Paul would regard full obedience to the Law as a good thing if it were possible. There is further an absence of any sense of striving after righteousness in 7:14–23. However, also noteworthy is what Bultmann says and implies about conversion. Conviction of sin still matters, but no longer is it the conviction of sins committed. Instead it is the giving up of

---

94. Bultmann, "Romans 7 and the Anthropology of Paul," 149.

"the false will to be oneself."[95] Human beings find authentic existence by abandoning this attempt at self-righteousness and surrendering to the claim of God: "What is portrayed in vss. 7–13 is not 'the psychological process of the emergence in man of individual sins' (Lietzmann), but rather the process that is at the basis of existence under the law and that lies beyond subjectivity and psychic experience."[96] Whatever conversion understood in existential terms might look like in practice, it is clearly not for Bultmann a matter of the kind of experience pre-supposed in the Puritan, Pietist, and Methodist traditions.

A similar conclusion holds true for Karl Barth (1886–1968). In the first edition (1919) of his commentary on Romans,[97] Barth chose his discussion of Rom 7 in which to attack Pietism on the grounds that true faith is a calling away from preoccupation with self, whereas Pietism's focus on individual experience and individual salvation promotes such concern.[98] Precisely in its concern with conversion experience, Barth sees Pietism as all too complicit with the individualism of modernity in general and theological liberalism in particular. When Barth revised his commentary for the second edition (1922), this specific polemic disappeared and the rejection of worldliness inherent in Pietist values and behavior is appreciated, but the polemic is replaced by a general critique of religion no less serious in its implications. Religion

> tries to pass off what is not visually perceptible (new creation) and impossible as a human possibility, making it visually perceptible. This becomes a way 'to elevate myself above other people' . . . Religion . . . asserts a position where the religious person sees himself as an exception to sinful human possibilities, claiming a perceivable nearness to God.[99]

The implication is that, through conversion experience, Pietism understands faith as a visible, pious possession. Barth thus attacks the view that new birth is real only when it is experienced. In an essentially theological treatment, Barth does relatively little to anchor his case in exegetical argument but he does make it clear that he regards Rom 7 as about human existence and not as describing a historical

---

95. Ibid., 156.

96. Ibid., 156–57.

97. Karl Barth, *Der Römerbrief* (Bern: Bäschlin, 1919).

98. For a fuller account, see Eberhard Busch, *Karl Barth and the Pietists: The Young Karl Barth's Critique of Pietism and its Response* (trans. D. W. Bloesch; Downer's Grove, Ill.: Inter Varsity, 2004), 9–68.

99. Busch, *Karl Barth and the Pietists*, 84.

progression: "There is no question of contrasting a particular epoch in the life of a single individual, or of a group, or indeed of all mankind, with some other epoch, past or future. The passage refers to that timeless age in which all men belong."[100] Indeed, "Paul describes his past, present, and future existence."[101] Barth thus takes the existential nature of his approach a step further even than Bultmann and, in doing so, avoids a specific critique of Judaism, which is instead included in his more general comments on religion. Barth identifies law with religion and by this means preserves the tension in Paul's argument between the holiness of the Law and its use by sin to work death:

> We do not escape from sin by removing ourselves from religion and taking up with some other and superior thing—if indeed that were possible. Religion is the supreme possibility of all human possibilities; and consequently grace, the good tree, can never be a possibility above, or within, or by the side of, the possibility of religion. Grace is man's divine possibility, and, as such, lies beyond all human possibility.[102]

In his later *Church Dogmatics*, Barth offers a more exegetical treatment of Rom 7. He regards it as describing the beginning of justification in the midst of sin. It is a deliberately backwards step in Paul's argument, powerfully reminding his readers that justification is entirely a divine act, created out of its opposite: "The chapter does not interrupt the great sequence of Rom 3–8, but with its apparently backward movement it brings it to its climax."[103] This larger pattern is mirrored in the ending of Rom 7 where Paul's cry in 7:24–25a, with its apparent rescue, is followed by a statement of enslavement in the flesh to the law of sin in 7:25b, before the sudden emergence into liberty in 8:1. Far from joining other exegetes in finding this climax puzzling and contradictory, for Barth it serves to make Paul's point clearly and forcefully:

> Every morning and every evening his situation is one of departure in the very midst of sin. And only as he sees this, only as he acknowledges that

---

100. K. Barth, *The Epistle to the Romans* (trans. E. C. Hoskyns; Oxford: Oxford University Press, 1933), 249.

101. Ibid., 270.

102. Ibid., 242. Barth's critique of religion is taken up and used exegetically by E. Käsemann (*Perspectives on Paul* [London: SCM, 1971], 70–78), but Käsemann has subsequently been attacked as anti-Jewish because he treats piety as entirely negative, forgetting Barth's reservation that it remains the supreme human possibility.

103. K. Barth, *Church Dogmatics IV.1: The Doctrine of Reconciliation* (trans. G. W. Bromiley; Edinburgh: T. & T. Clark, 1956), 581.

this is his situation even as a Christian and an apostle, only as he looks away from himself, dare he take the leap forward: 'There is therefore now no condemnation to them which are in Christ Jesus' (Rom 8:1). From this point the leap can and must be hazarded, in this most realistic and therefore genuinely spiritual self-knowledge. But it can be hazarded only from this point. The function of vv.7–25 is therefore to retard. They show clearly the point of departure from which the way leads forward. In this way they safeguard the mystery of justification as the transition from wrong to right, from death to life. They prevent us from representing this transition as anything but an event and this event as anything but a miraculous act of God.[104]

Barth thus provides a reading of Rom 7 that is an extended meditation upon what it means to be *simul iustus et peccator*. Conversion is prized as a divine miracle, but it is not a once for all event that can be left behind at the outset of the Christian life. Rather believers have to live constantly in repentance and conversion. Further, the kind of awareness of sin displayed by Paul in Romans cannot be understood from within the human possibilities of religion but comes from outside as a result of grace. An experience of the conviction of sin is the result of conversion not its essential prelude or first step. For Barth, salvation is not just a mere possibility until human beings appropriate it in the experience of conversion or in any other way. Rather, conversion is always a matter of divine revelation becoming real for us because God has reached out to us. The objective reality of God's work for us in Christ as sinners is to be emphasized in conversion, not a subjective experience on which to base a false assurance that we have escaped from among the ranks of sinners: "There is no sinless Christian. If thou chancest upon such a man, he is no Christian, but an anti-Christ."[105]

Romans 7 and Anti-theological Critics of Conversion

If Bultmann and Barth interpret Rom 7 in ways that critique Protestant conceptions of conversion they do so in the name of theology, offering theological interpretations of their own. There are other recent interpreters who offer anti-theological readings of Rom 7, for whom almost all the acts of interpretation described in this paper are cases of simple misreading of Paul's text. The key figure here is Krister Stendahl (1921–2008) who, while not opposed to theological application of exegeti-

104. Barth, *Church Dogmatics IV.1*, 583–4.
105. Barth, *Epistle to the Romans*, 263.

cal conclusions, insisted that the task of interpretation is initially purely descriptive. In relation to historical texts like Paul's epistles, "what it meant" must be kept rigorously distinct from "what it means."[106] He says of Romans, "My first admonition to those who read it is to forget everything they ever knew about it."[107] Stendahl argues that from Augustine onwards Paul's concern with justification has been wrongly interpreted in relation to issues of conscience and guilt. Paul's cry of wretchedness in 7:24 is provoked by weakness in the face of the cosmic power of sin, not by guilt as a result of personal transgressions. Within Protestantism this reading into the text of elements that are absent is mediated through the experience of Martin Luther: "The Pauline awareness of sin has been interpreted in light of Luther's struggles with his conscience."[108] Stendahl follows Kümmel in arguing that Phil 3:6 makes impossible the idea that Paul struggled with inability to obey the Law prior to his conversion. Justification in Romans is not Paul's answer to a guilty conscience but rather an expression of his theology of mission, used to argue for the status of his Gentile converts after the model of Abraham.[109]

In relation to Rom 7 itself this leads Stendahl to argue that 7:7–12 is simply a midrash on the account of the Fall in Genesis and that deep concern with the identity of the "I" is a mistake, stemming from the influence of Augustine.[110] In relation to 7:13–25, it must be recognized that Paul only engages in anthropological observation in order to promote:

> a very special argument about the holiness and goodness of the Law. The possibility of a distinction between the good Law and the bad Sin is based on the rather trivial observation that every man knows that there is a difference between what he ought to do and what he does ... Unfortunately—or fortunately—Paul happened to express this supporting argument so well that what to him and his contemporaries was a common sense observation appeared to later interpreters to be a most penetrating insight into the nature of sin.[111]

---

106. Krister Stendahl, "Biblical Theology: A Program," in *Meanings: The Bible as Document and Guide* (Philadelphia: Fortress, 1984), 11–44.

107. Krister Stendahl, *Final Account: Paul's Letter to the Romans* (Minneapolis: Fortress, 1995), 9.

108. Krister Stendahl, "Paul and the Introspective Conscience of the West," *Harvard Theological Review* 56.3 (1963), 199–215 (200).

109. Stendahl, *Final Account*, 4.

110. Ibid., 28.

111. Stendahl, "Paul and the Introspective Conscience of the West," 212–13.

If Rom 7 concerns conversion it is for Stendahl only as part of Paul's wider demonstration that in converting to become followers of Jesus, Gentiles do not first have to become converts to Judaism.

Stendahl's work was to provide inspiration for subsequent interpreters who wished to push wider and deeper his thesis that the history of interpretation is largely a history of misinterpretation. Stanley Stowers (b.1949) regards traditional interpretations of Romans from Augustine onwards as molded by the assumption that intense spiritual struggle is normative. Within such wider interpretations, Rom 7 is the key to understanding humanity as lost in the abyss of sin. On this basis, the letter is read in overly individualized and psychologized ways, a consequence of which has been characteristically introspective traditions of conversion.[112] Through attention to ancient philosophical, literary, and rhetorical contexts and conventions, Stowers proposes instead to re-read Romans as if it had never become Christian Scripture.[113] "Paul's letters reveal a kind of Christianity that existed before Christianity became a religion of an intrinsically sick human nature and its cure."[114] The only theological readings that are helpful in this process of re-reading are pre-Augustinian patristic readings, such as that of Origen, which, while lacking in understanding of Paul's social world, do display some sensitivity to ancient style and rhetoric.[115]

For Stowers, Paul writes against the background of the concern of ancient philosophy with the goal of self-mastery (*enkrateia*), which requires the overcoming of the lack of self-control (*akrasia*) engendered by passions and desires. In contrast to Jewish writers who promote the Mosaic law as the best path to self-mastery, Paul urges instead the imitation of Christ and his faithful death. He is writing to persuade a Gentile audience attracted towards Judaism as a school for self-mastery that here lies a better way. Kümmel is correct that the "I" of Rom 7 is not autobiographical and does not include Paul. The apostle is here engaged instead in a depiction of a Gentile struggling with the issue of self-mastery.[116] Using close allusion to the example of Euripides' *Medea*, who knows that to kill her children is not rational but whose judgment is overcome by the passion of anger, Paul offers a virtuoso example of the

---

112. Stanley K. Stowers, *A Re-reading of Romans: Justice, Jews and Gentiles* (New Haven, Conn.: Yale University Press, 1994), 259–60

113. Ibid., 1–6.

114. Ibid., 329.

115. Ibid., 269.

116. Ibid., 258–84.

rhetorical technique of speech-in-character (*prosopopoiia*). He uses it to demonstrate that the Law is not a successful antidote to desire:

> Romans 7 divides the person between a true self identified with the mind or rationality and a lower or false self identified with the body or the flesh. According to Paul, the passions and desire reside in the flesh or the body and its parts (Gal 5:16, 24; Rom 6:12–13, cf. 1:26–27; 7:5, 18, 22; 8:3). The mind rationally apprehends and wills to do the law (7:22), but since it has been corrupted by the turn to idolatry (1:21–22, 28), the desires of the flesh overcome it. Only a mind renewed by infusion with God's Spirit can enable the gentile to resist the flesh and act according to God's law (8:5–8).[117]

In turn, Stowers's thesis is extended further in a recent monograph by Emma Wasserman (b.1975). The plight that Rom 7 addresses is not simply a failure to achieve self-mastery in the face of passions and desires. Rather, Paul draws on specifically Platonic traditions which speak of the death of the soul as the result of extreme immorality. Desire so overwhelms reason as to kill it and to leave the self unable to do anything that it knows as good. It is this specific condition of overwhelming passions that Rom 7 addresses and not universal human sinfulness. It is "a particularly Gentile plight, one that is ascribed to a particular group, for particular reasons, and for a particular period of time."[118] This reading is placed in contrast to a western tradition that "running from Augustine to Martin Luther to John Calvin made Rom 7 central to its understanding of sin and in so doing ascribed a condition of total depravity to all humans and moral conflict even to the Christian."[119] Paul is wrongly understood to depict an intense inner struggle with sin as the normative human condition. The key error here lies in the identification of sin as an enslaving apocalyptic power. "By understanding sin as an invading cosmic agent, such theories can project onto the cosmos the Augustinian-Lutheran axiom that the human being is incapable of goodness in itself."[120] Wasserman argues instead that the apparent personification of sin as an agent in Rom 7 is a representation of the passions. In common with the other anti-theological interpretations described, it is denied that

---

117. Ibid., 279–80.

118. Emma Wasserman, *The Death of the Soul in Romans 7: Sin, Death, and the Law in Light of Hellenistic Moral Psychology* (Tübingen: Mohr (Siebeck), 2008), 148.

119. Ibid., 1.

120. Ibid., 147.

Rom 7 contains an analysis of the human condition that can be interpreted so as to provide a framework for understanding the experience of Christian conversion.

Conclusions

Our survey demonstrates that a complex text like Rom 7 produces a great variety of interpretations. Even interpreters who substantially agree with each other will have differences in detail, and there are always some interpreters who defy even general categorization. Nevertheless, it is possible to identify broad groups or constellations of interpretations. In this paper I have sought to show that a fruitful way to approach such a classification is through consideration of the relationship between interpretations and their authors' convictions and expectations about Christian conversion. As the latter have changed and developed, so too have interpretations of Rom 7. In the history of Protestant interpretation of Rom 7 we find the following six broad categories:

1. Romans 7:14–23 is identified with Paul's Christian life and its struggles and therefore it is 7:7–13 that speaks of conversion. In Protestant accounts, particularly pre-critical ones, this serves to establish conviction of sin through the Law as essential to conversion. However, the relationship of this conviction to the stages of conversion experience is complex. There is a lack of clarity on the question in early Protestant interpretations. Most Puritan interpreters are in fact clear that this conviction brings a period of struggle that prepares for conversion, but their textual basis is not Rom 7. Paul here speaks of himself and his experience was of sudden grace.

2. Romans 7:7–23 is read in its entirety as an account of pre-Christian existence as experienced by those described. In very different forms this position is characteristic both of the Pietist and Wesleyan traditions and of nineteenth century historical-critical scholarship. In the former Paul speaks of others and in the latter he speaks autobiographically, but, in either case, if applied to the praxis of conversion, this approach establishes the expectation that conviction of sin through the Law will bring a period of inner struggle prior to conversion. Only Rom 8 can be identified with Christian existence.

3. Romans 7:14–23 describes the situation of those who are genuinely converted but who, although in Christ, are not yet fully in Christ. They do not

enjoy the fullness of Christian existence spoken of in Rom 8. Paul is therefore not primarily discussing himself. Advocated principally by Origen, there are also some Protestant commentators who hold this view.[121]

4. Romans 7:7–23 is read in its entirety as Paul's retrospective account of his pre-Christian existence. It records his current estimate of his former life, not his actual experience of it at the time and, for many interpreters, Paul regards what he says of himself as typical of others, either of Jews or of humanity as a whole. It is Rom 8 that speaks of his Christian existence. The crucial distinction from the second approach in relation to conversion is that here conviction of sin through the Law is no longer a pre-requisite. This is the most widespread position of the late twentieth and early twenty-first centuries.

5. From within the Protestant tradition early twentieth century thinkers such as Barth and Bultmann offer existential interpretations of Rom 7 that, while still concerned with conversion, criticize in their different ways the rooting of that concern in a subjective conversion experience.

6. Other more recent interpreters offer radical critiques of traditional interpretations of Rom 7. They are anti-theological in the sense that they deny that there is anything in Rom 7, especially in its discussion of sin and the human plight, which can legitimately be applied to provide a framework for understanding Christian conversion in contexts subsequent to Paul's own.

Such a classification of interpretations raises a whole host of questions concerning the relationship between the plausibility of interpretations and the historical contexts in which they were formulated. For example, why do seventeenth century Protestant interpretations of Rom 7, which retain the basic theological and exegetical frameworks of earlier Protestant interpretations, become so much more radically introspective in tone? Or, why is it so obvious to nineteenth century interpreters that Paul here speaks in a straightforwardly autobiographical fashion when it is not so to interpreters in either previous or subsequent eras? Along with these questions about context comes a profound hermeneutical issue. Will interpretations dominant today come to seem just as implausible to future generations of scholars as those of some

---

121. This approach does persist today. See John Stott, *The Message of Romans* (Leicester: Inter Varsity, 1994), 205–11.

previous eras appear now? There are solid exegetical reasons for the current popularity of the view that Paul speaks retrospectively, describing his pre-conversion life but doing so from his present Christian perspective.[122] In spite of the complexity of discussion surrounding Rom 7, three major factors emerge very clearly:

1. The persistent use of the first person, and the intense expression of dependence upon Christ in 7:24–25a, suggests that Paul here speaks of himself, even if what is true of him is also true of others.

2. The tension between this account and Paul's claim to blamelessness under the Law in Phil 3:6 suggests that he does not here speak as he would have done as a Pharisee but rather as it seems to him looking back.

3. The absence of any mention of the Holy Spirit in the conflict described in 7:14–23 suggests that he does not here speak of the Christian life.

Nevertheless, it is possible to propose contextual reasons as to why this appears the most plausible interpretation to a majority of contemporary interpreters. This interpretation can accommodate recent revisions of historical perspective on early Judaism with which would not easily fit a conscious struggle with inability to keep the Law. That Paul should retrospectively evaluate as sinful behavior that he once regarded as ethical fits well with a western social context in which ethical assessment of actions is for many no longer governed by traditional Christian norms. In such a context, conversion to Christianity will often entail the re-categorization by the convert as sinful of actions previously regarded as morally acceptable. We are left to ponder whether the exegetical arguments would appear as compelling in a different context. And if the plausibility of exegetical and historical arguments is itself in part historically conditioned, what other theological criteria might we also draw on in order distinguish between appropriate interpretations and poor ones?

There are also important issues raised by the sequence of interpretations. History notoriously declines to move in straight lines, and subsequent interpretations are often overlaid upon existing ones rather than replacing them. Yet it is striking in the classification provided above that the second three approaches all belong primarily to the last century of interpretation. They also all, in varying degrees, react against the impulse, dominant in many Protestant interpretations, to identify conviction of sin as the central theological contribution of Rom 7 and to apply that conviction

---

122. See Stephen J. Chester, *Conversion at Corinth: Perspectives on Conversion in Paul's Theology and the Corinthian Church* (London: T. & T. Clark, 2003), 183–95.

to the praxis of conversion by identifying it with introspective struggle. For those belonging to Protestant traditions in which conversion remains a central theological category this raises the issue of precisely how Rom 7 might be used in the proclamation of the Christian gospel. If it does not speak about conversion in this way, how does it do so? Are anti-theological interpreters correct that to use Rom 7 as part of the biblical basis for understanding conversion, particularly in relation to sin, is an error?

At one level, the historical shortcomings of the anti-theological interpretations reviewed are so significant that it is not difficult to disrupt their critique. Stendhal is simply wrong to imply that Paul is read by so many as centrally concerned with sin and guilt because Luther's struggles with his conscience are projected back onto Paul. We do not find this in Luther, and not even in other Protestant interpretations before the nineteenth century.[123] Stowers's thesis that in Rom 7 Paul uses the rhetorical technique of speech-in-character is innovative in relation to recent historical criticism, but something very similar appears in Bengel and Wesley in the service of precisely the kind of interpretation of Rom 7 that Stowers wishes to discredit. Despite the fact that he perceives Augustine as largely responsible for a subsequent history of misinterpretation, Stowers' own account of an inner conflict in which the rational mind is overwhelmed by the desires of the flesh unless aided by the infusion of the Holy Spirit sounds remarkably Augustinian. Wasserman correctly identifies a shared sense of the *seriousness* of sin as an important element of continuity between Augustine and early Protestant interpreters, but entirely ignores the fact that their understanding of the *nature* of sin in the Christian life is radically different from each other. To dispute the notion of sin as an apocalyptic power simply does not impact the interpretations of each in the same way. Perhaps most tellingly of all, it is simply not possible to discover pre-Augustinian purity in the interpretation of Rom 7. Origen interprets the text as concerning conversion and an inner struggle with sin, and as being of universal application, even in the midst of a commentary characterized overall by concern with Paul's reflections on the address of the gospel to Jews and Gentiles.[124] Whatever the virtues or failings of *how* they do it, the many

---

123. Stephen J. Chester, "Paul and the Introspective Conscience of Martin Luther," *Biblical Interpretation* 14.5 (2006), 508–36.

124. In a history of interpretation of Romans in which Origen is the theological hero, M. Reasoner, *Romans in Full Circle*, 69 breaks into his descriptive account of interpretations of Rom 7 in order to pull Origen back on message and to offer an interpretation couched in Jew/Gentile categories.

interpreters who read Rom 7 as concerned with these themes are responding to features of the text not engaging in exegetical fantasy.

Yet, despite these historical shortcomings, the contention of recent anti-theological interpreters that there are exegetical failings in the history of Protestant interpretation of Rom 7 is indisputable. Paul discusses themes relevant to the conversion of the individual in a way that can also be applied to salvation history and in the service of an argument designed to defend the goodness of the Law. Although given more attention than can be reflected in a survey focusing on the theme of conversion, there is undoubtedly a deficit in the attention paid in Protestant interpretations to salvation history and to Paul's wider rhetorical purposes. There is also a great deal that can accurately be characterized as introspective. In the period from the seventeenth to the nineteenth centuries it is the dominant shared characteristic in Protestant interpretations that consistently identify conversion with a particular religious experience in which subsequent assurance of salvation is linked to a preceding experience of conviction of sin. It is this that not only anti-theological interpretations wish to dispute, but also the theological critiques of Barth and Bultmann and even, albeit less explicitly, historical-critical interpretations that regard Rom 7 as Paul's retrospective reflections on his life as a Pharisee. While we may share in this reaction against introspection and regard flexibility in expectations about patterns of conversion as a positive development, larger questions are thereby raised. Is conversion primarily to be understood as a religious experience? Or is the objective nature of Christ's redemptive work instead to be emphasized? Even if subjective experience is granted a smaller place overall in our understanding of conversion, what does Rom 7 have to tell us about it? Previous generations of Protestant interpreters were much clearer than is currently the case about the significance of Rom 7 for conversion. The history of Protestant interpretation of Rom 7 thus sets before our generation of interpreters a challenge: how do we forge interpretations of Rom 7 that are exegetically and theologically credible and yet still have something definite enough to say to be usable in the praxis of Christian conversion?

RESPONSE TO CHESTER

Mary Veeneman

I want to start out by saying that I found Stephen Chester's paper to be fascinating. It shows a connection between theology and exegesis, and suggests that the two can never be fully separated, despite the hopes of Protestants. Of course this is not hopeless, because church history has shown us numerous times that the Word can and does invade and transform our theological ideas.[1]

As I approached my own reading of the paper, I wondered how I might respond to it given that I am not a New Testament scholar, but am rather a theologian, and given that I agree with the major claims of the paper. While I read though, the paper's discussion raised an additional question that I want to pursue.

While Chester's paper focuses primarily on Protestant interpretations of Rom 7 and Protestant conceptions of conversion, I wondered if Catholic readings of Rom 7 would reflect or echo Catholic ideas about conversion. While it is well beyond the scope of this response to put together the amount of resources that are in the original paper, I did consult the *Catechism of the Catholic Church* on conversion and also looked at the work of Jesuit biblical scholar, Joseph Fitzmyer. My initial questions circled around "individual vs. communal" understandings of conversion, but what I found has more bearing on questions about the character of the conversion process.

The *Catechism* has a number of important statements about conversion, but it makes a couple of key points. While asserting that Jesus' call to conversion is central to the Christian understanding of the kingdom of God, the *Catechism* locates the first and fundamental conversion not in a moment of immediate response to Christian preaching and not in a moment of immediate response to an interior experience of God, but rather in baptism. The *Catechism* states, "Baptism is the principal place for the first and fundamental conversion. It is by faith in the gospel and by baptism that one renounces evil and gains salvation, that is, the forgiveness of all sins and the gift of new life."[2]

---

1. I am grateful to Scot McKnight for pointing this out to me.
2. *Catechism of the Catholic Church*, Chapter Two, Article Four, Section III.

One of the implications of this statement is that in the Catholic context, conversion is something fundamentally communal. Baptism in the Catholic context is usually in the form of infant baptism, though adults who convert to Catholicism from outside of Christianity would receive baptism at that time. Because the vast majority of Catholics are baptized as infants, there are others involved in that first moment of conversion, namely the parents who present their child for baptism and profess faith on behalf of the child, and the godparents who promise to assist in the spiritual formation of the child.

The first conversion is not the only conversion, according to the *Catechism*. Rather, the call to conversion is always present for Christians. "This second conversion" is the task of the whole church, and is not something that human beings can accomplish alone. Rather, this conversion is, "the movement of a 'contrite heart' drawn and moved by grace to respond to the merciful love of God who loved us first."[3]

Thus this second part of conversion is communal insofar as it is discussed as a task for the entire church. The discussion of the movement of the contrite heart towards God as a response to grace makes clear that there is an individual component as well. I am not claiming that Catholicism fails to recognize or see the importance of individual conversion and personal faith, since we clearly see evidence for that in the *Catechism*. I am also not implying that Protestantism, or better, various versions of Protestantism fail to recognize a communal component to conversion. Probably the more significant observation to make here is that there are two steps to conversion: a first conversion that comes in baptism, and a second conversion that is an ongoing, lifelong process.

The question still remains, though, of how Rom 7 is treated by Catholic biblical interpreters? While there are a number of scholars I could have consulted, Joseph Fitzmyer is one important voice who may be helpful in this discussion due to his extensive work on Romans. Fitzmyer seems to interpret Rom 7:7–25 as Paul speaking generally about the Law. He writes that vv.14–25 seek to give a positive account of the Law and that it is for this reason that the passage is in the present tense. Paul in this passage is describing the experience of the self faced with the Law. This is depicted as a conflict within the self between the flesh and the spiritual law of God. Because the self is intrinsically on both sides of this conflict, it is torn. In v. 24, we

---

3. Ibid.

find an expression of frustration over this situation before v. 25 offers "thanks for the hope of liberation that has come through Christ Jesus."[4]

I think ultimately, Fitzmyer's reading raises more questions than it answers. It is clear that he does not read this passage as one where Paul speaks autobiographically and so this is not a passage in which Paul is talking about himself prior to his conversion/call. It seems that for Fitzmyer this is a more general description of one's struggle with sin and one's hope in Christ, which would likely place this in the category of the long process of justification after the initial conversion that *could* be described as the second conversion, the movement of the contrite heart towards God. As a result, I am left with more questions, and this is perhaps because the conceptions of conversion within Catholicism and Protestantism are different enough that it may be hard to pose Chester's question to Catholic readings of both conversion and Rom 7. I certainly think that the larger point about the relationship between our theological positions and our exegetical conclusions is a critical one and think we could find other examples of this playing out in both the Catholic and Protestant traditions.

---

4. Joseph A. Fitzmyer, *Romans* (AB 33; San Francisco: Doubleday, 1993).

AMBROSE, PAUL, AND THE CONVERSION OF THE JEWS[1]

J. Warren Smith

Paul in Rom 9:2–3 begins his discussion of Israel with words of lamentation, "I have great sorrow and unceasing anguish in my heart. For I could wish that I myself were accursed and cut off from Christ for the sake of my brethren, my kinsmen by race."[2] The cause of Paul's distress was that many of his fellow Jews had not believed in Christ. Without faith in Christ, he writes, their zeal for God is unenlightened and they do not submit to the righteousness of God (10:2, 4). Although he sees the hardening of Israel as part of God's plan for the salvation of the Gentiles, nevertheless, the Jews who have not believed in Christ have a paradoxical status: "As regards the gospel they are enemies of God, for [the Gentiles'] sake; but as regards election they are beloved for the sake of their forefathers" (11:28). Ultimately, Paul holds that this contradiction will be overcome and the Jews will receive God's mercy and be "grafted back into their own olive tree" (11:24). Paul's opening lament finds consolation in the hope of Israel's restoration. The questions this raises for the Church of the Gentiles are legion. How does Israel's paradoxical status inform the way we Gentiles view the righteousness of faith by which we are incorporated into the people of God? What, in other words, does Israel's failure to "submit to the righteousness of God" mean for our understanding of the character of faith in Christ that is the heart of our conversion? How does the hope of Israel's restoration affect our understanding of the mission of the Church? What is the role of the Church in the conversion of the Jews?

One fourth century theologian who may prove a helpful conversation partner in our reflection upon these questions is Ambrose of Milan (339–97). Ambrose sadly has an infamous reputation for his anti-Jewish rhetoric in his *Commentary on the Gospel of Luke* and for his threat to excommunicate the emperor Theodosius if he

---

1. I am grateful to my New Testament colleague at Duke, Douglas Campbell, for reading a draft of this paper and to George Kalantzis of Wheaton College for his gracious reply to the paper—a reply that expanded and enriched our conversation.

2. Unless otherwise noted, all biblical quotations are from RSV.

compelled a bishop in the eastern provinces to rebuild the synagogue at Callinicum that members of his congregation burned down (388/9). For these I will offer no *apologia*. Even more shameful is the thought that neither Ambrose's rhetoric nor his action in the Callinicum affair represents the lowest of forms of Christians' uncharitable treatment of the Jews. Yet at times, the proclaimed gospel reveals a truth greater than the virtue of the preacher and exposes his or her failings. Ambrose's homilies on the patriarch Joseph are one such case. Here Ambrose interprets the story of Joseph and his brothers as figure of the relationship between Christ and the Jews. In doing so, I will argue, he finds a model to explain the character of the life of faith to catechumens. Moreover, the Joseph saga enabled him to work out Paul's account in Romans of the paradoxical status of the Jews and the hope of their conversion.

Conversio in Ambrose

Before turning to Ambrose's treatment of Joseph and his brothers, I need to say something about conversion in Ambrose's writings. Ambrose rarely uses the noun *conversio*. There is little evidence that he employs it in a technical sense referring to "a conversion." Instead, he tends to use *conversio* to mean a "turning," religious or not. Ambrose is in fact more apt to use a form of the verb *converso* suggesting that he is more concerned with the *action* of turning than he is *when* or *how* the turning occurred. It would be, therefore, anachronistic to speak of Ambrose's theory of conversion. This is equally true of the writers of the New Testament. Yet as historians, biblical scholars, theologians, and sociologists, our interest is in how the phenomenon we call conversion is described in our ancient sources. In other words, we are interested in how they understood and narrated the religious "turning" of the person toward God. In this paper, I will argue that Ambrose depicts conversion to Christianity as coming in the sacramental "turning" that occurred in Milanese baptism. Contrary to Krister Stendahl's distinction between "calling" and "conversion," Ambrose depicts the *conversio* at baptism as the culmination of the calling of God to which the neophyte responded when she enrolled in the catechumenate. He narrates the catechumen's journey to baptism in his catechetical homilies by depicting the patriarchs and matriarchs as exemplars of the Christian life as well as types of the catechumens themselves. In his opening homilies of his six week catechesis, Ambrose begins with God's calling of Abraham "Go from the land of your fathers and go to a land I will show you" (Gen 12:1). Abraham's departure from the land of Ur in order to follow God to the promised land represents for the catechumens both their Lenten journey to baptism and their journey as baptized members of the church who are sojourners in the world and whose hope lies with their citizenship (*conversatio*) in heaven.[3]

The catechumen's response to God's call, like that of Abraham, entails a leave-taking. It is a departure from the world in the sense of breaking the soul's attachments to the worldly pleasures or passions that include both sensual pleasures and abstract pleasures, such as honors and prestige. This separation of the soul from the material and immaterial delights of the world is, for Ambrose, a process that stretches beyond the six weeks of catechesis and baptism to the whole length of one's life. Yet it is in baptism that the formal entry on the journey to the promised land begins and it does so with the sacramental *conversio* of baptism. The catechumen is led backwards into the baptistery so that she is facing west. After the bishop asks the catechumen if she renounces the world and its luxuries, at her reply "I do renounce" she is turned from the west to the east toward the baptismal font in the middle of the baptistery. This *conversio* is simultaneously a turning from the world and a turning to Christ.[4] The turning to Christ is completed when the catechumen becomes united with Christ in the waters of the font through her profession of faith in the triune God and faith in Christ's justifying death. With the *conversio* of renunciation and confession, the catechumen passes from a state of fault into a state of grace. The *conversio* is fundamentally an expression of faith renewed by the Spirit both prior to and in baptism which Ambrose calls the sacrament of illumination. Through her faith the neophyte is justified or made righteous because her faith bears a likeness to Christ's *fides* and *devotio* to the Father.[5] Even as Christ's faith and devotion led to his crucifixion and resurrection so the neophyte's faith leads to her sacramental death and resurrection.

The entry into the Christian life through sacramental *conversio*, in Ambrose's mind, is possible only through the work of the Word and the Spirit. In the incarnation, the Word who fashioned creation according to the Father's will renewed

---

3. The reorientation of the Christian's life that Ambrose describes as "leaving earthly conversations and worldly pleasures" (*exire conversatione terrena*) entails a change, "not only in location but in the self" by giving up worldly custom (*mos*) and action. Thus the *conversio* of baptism is closely associated with the entry into *conversatio in caelis* (*De Abraham* I.2.4). Also see *Abraham* II.1.2, II.7.41, II.8.54; *Isaac* 7.63; *Iacob* I.8.39, II.9.38; *Ioseph* 12.73.

4. Because of the war between the flesh and the spirit (Rom 7:23), the catechumen, like Abraham, turns to Christ since there is no other guide among men who enables one to overcome this inner conflict (*Abraham* II.6.27).

5. For a discussion of Ambrose's view of the relationship between baptism and justification by faith, see J. Warren Smith, "Justification and Merit before the Pelagian Controversy: The Case of Ambrose of Milan," *Pro Ecclesia* 16.2 (2007): 195–217.

the image among Adam's race by refashioning human nature in Mary's womb and perfecting it at the resurrection. As firstborn from the dead Christ is the prototype of resurrected humanity. Christ, the new Adam, inaugurates the new creation in which humanity participates through baptism.[6] This participation is possible through the Spirit's gift of grace that allows the neophyte to renounce the world, confess the Triune God, and believe in the justifying grace of Christ's cross. Ambrose equates the neophyte's conversion with the reception of the Lord's passion.[7] Thus the Spirit's gift of faith allows the baptized to receive the pardoning benefits of Christ's passion and to imitate Christ's example of faithfulness to the Father. Through the confession of faith and the pledge of devotion to God, the neophyte merits the pardon of justification and heavenly citizenship in Christ. Yet, the neophyte's salvation is grounded primarily upon Christ's righteousness and only secondarily on the disposition of faith. Thus her salvation is not based upon the righteousness of her own works. It is in the context of catechetical preparation for this sacramental turning that Ambrose's presents his account of the conversion of Israel.

The Joseph Saga for Catechumens

Ambrose's treatise, *De Ioseph*, is an edited collection of sermons that Ambrose preached during Lenten catechesis.[8] After enrolling among the *competentes*, who desired to be baptized during the Easter vigil, the catechumens entered a period of daily instruction by Ambrose throughout Lent. In the five weeks preceding Holy Week, Ambrose's homilies focused on Proverbs and the lives of Israel's patriarchs

---

6. For a discussion of the christological and pneumatological foundation of Ambrose's theology of baptism, see chapter 6 of J. Warren Smith, *Christian Grace and Pagan Virtue: The Theological Foundation of Ambrose's Ethics* (Oxford: Oxford University Press, forthcoming).

7. *De Abraham* I.5.39. Ambrose treats Abraham and Sarah's reception of the three visitors with the catechumen's conversion at baptism. Sarah represents the church whose kneading three measures of flower corresponds with Mary's proclamation of Christ's resurrection. Abraham's selection of the calf and dispatching a young servant to prepare the meal is a figure of the catechumen's reception of Jesus' passion. The calf Ambrose associates with the sacrificial offering for sin and thus with Christ's passion. The reception of Christ's passion in faith Ambrose sees as leading to the conversion Jesus spoke of in Matt 18:3 "unless you be converted and become as this child, you shall not enter into the Kingdom of Heaven."

8. See Ambrose *De mysteriis* 1.1; also Marcia L. Colish, *Ambrose's Patriarchs: Ethics for the Common Man* (Notre Dame, Ind.: University of Notre Dame Press, 2005), 13–29; Craig Alan Satterlee, *Ambrose of Milan's Method of Mystagogical Preaching* (Collegeville, Minn.: Liturgical Press, 2001), 150–51; and J. Warren Smith, *Christian Grace and Pagan Virtue: The Theological Foundation for Ambrose's Ethics* (Oxford: Oxford University Press, forthcoming).

in Genesis. In these catechetical homilies, Ambrose presented the patriarchs as exemplars of Christian virtue whose lives would provide models of the Christian life into which the catechumens were entering. The moral instruction sought to help the *competentes* to order their lives according to virtue so that they might be ready to be baptized and to illustrate the character of life in the Christian community in which they would become members through baptism. During Holy Week, Ambrose doubled the number of lectures instructing them in the Creed, the *traditio symboli*. After their baptism, the neophytes' instruction would be completed with a series of post baptismal homilies that interpreted the elements of baptismal initiation, now that they had passed through the holy mysteries, the *sacramenta*.

The patriarchs, for Ambrose, are types of both the catechumen and of Christ. They can serve as role models of the Christian life into which the catechumen is preparing to enter because they possess certain virtues that prefigure the perfection of virtue embodied in Christ. Of all Israel's fore-parents, Joseph is, for Ambrose, the supreme type of Christ. Joseph models the virtues of self-control and chastity in resisting the sexual advances of Potiphar's wife. He also exhibits the virtue of faith in his grasping the prophetic character of his dreams.[9] As Pharaoh's prime minister, Joseph's stockpiling of grain for the years of famine and his distribution of the grain, even to his brothers, provides Ambrose's catechumens, especially those in the imperial service in Milan, an example of prudent and just administration of affairs of state. That is the meaning of the Joseph saga at its moral level.

Even more important for the catechumens is mystical meaning. Joseph's compassionate treatment of the brothers who wronged him is a type of Christ's gracious treatment of sinful humanity, particularly the Jews.[10] The details of the Genesis narrative lend themselves easily to comparison with the narrative of the gospel. Joseph is the most beloved son of Jacob just as Jesus is the beloved Son of God the Father. Based on a christological reading of Ps 148:3 "Praise him, sun and moon; praise him all you stars and light," Ambrose argues that Joseph's dream of the sun, moon, and eleven stars bowing down to him (Gen 37:9) denotes Joseph as a type of Christ. Joseph's brothers, who resent Joseph and his seemingly pretentious interpretations of the dreams about their bowing down to him, are the Jews. His family's censure of Joseph for the arrogance of his interpretation is like the Jews' refusal to acknowledge

---

9. *De Ioseph* 2.7. Ambrose is able to treat the patriarchs as exemplars of Christian faith because they possess some prophetic knowledge that apprehends the coming of Christ and his passion and resurrection. Thus their belief in the resurrection is akin to Christian faith.

10. *De Ioseph* 1.3.

Christ's divinity and to worship him.[11] Jacob's sending Joseph to his brothers to check on the sheep prefigures the Father's sending Christ in the Incarnation to the lost sheep of Israel. "Therefore, Joseph was sent by his father to his brothers, or rather by that Father 'who has not spared his own Son but has delivered him for us all,' by that Father of whom it is written, 'God, sending his Son in the likeness of sinful flesh.'"[12] From the beginning, Ambrose stresses the Father's sending the Son out of love for the lost sheep of Israel. They are lost in that they, like Adam, have withdrawn from God's presence and hidden themselves from the face of God. So Christ must seek them out.[13] The name "Joseph" which Ambrose asserts means "divine grace" and "expression of the Highest God" confirms the relation between Joseph and Jesus.[14] Jacob during the blessing of his sons tells Joseph that upon him "the blessing prevailed over the blessings of the enduring mountain" (Gen 49:26). Joseph's blessing corresponds to Christ's unparalleled merit and grace. Even as Joseph repaid his brothers' enmity with grace such that "they are both excused from their guilt and made holy by the gift of revelation" so too with the Jews "[Christ's] grace destroyed guilt; guilt did not diminish grace" but became the source of happiness.[15]

One exegetical problem that Ambrose encounters in the Genesis narrative is that Jacob chastises Joseph for suggesting that all his family, like the sun, moon, and stars in his dream, will bow down before him. How can Jacob be a type of the Father who sends Christ and yet can rebuke Joseph? Ambrose acknowledges the problem, but then explains that Jacob's rebuke of Joseph's presumption reflects his love for his other sons, "In him [i.e. Jacob], paternal love did not go astray, but rather is depicted

---

11. Ambrose explains the Jews' refusal to acknowledge Christ's divinity as precisely because he was born among them and is their brother according to the flesh. *De Ioseph* 3.8. Although Ambrose does not appeal directly to Jesus' rejection in Nazareth (Luke 4:16–30), the reaction of the people of Nazareth "Is not this Joseph's son?" represents the mindset of all Jews who do not confess Jesus to be the Christ and God.

12. *De Ioseph* 3.9.

13. "And it was right that [Joseph] wandered about, for he was seeking those [i.e. his brothers] that were going astray ... Indeed, Jesus also, when he was wearied from his journey, sat at the well. He was wearied, for He was not finding the people of God whom He was seeking; they had gone out from the face of the Lord. The man who follows sin goes out from Christ; the sinner goes out, the just man enters in," (*De Ioseph* 3.10). Here Ambrose elides Jesus' image of the sinners whom he seeks to save as "the lost sheep of Israel" from Matt 15:24 with John's image of Christ who is the good shepherd who is the door of the sheep fold through whom the sheep must pass to enter the fold (John 10:7). While Ambrose clearly overlooks John 10:10 that describes the sheep as going in and out and finding pasture, his focus is on the prior point that those in the sheepfold are those who believe in Christ.

14. *De Ioseph* 3.13.

15. *De Ioseph* 3:13.

as affection for a people that was going astray."[16] Thus Jacob's love for his other sons is a type of the Father's love for the lost sheep of Israel to whom he sends the only begotten Son.

Joseph's dream, though initially being the source of Joseph's alienation from his brothers, points to his brother's ultimate deliverance from famine when they will bow down to Joseph and receive the life-giving grain. For Ambrose, the dream's prophetic meaning is twofold, pointing both to the reconciliation of Joseph with his brothers who sold him into slavery and to the redemption of Israel by Christ. Commenting on Jacob's blessing of Judah, "The sons of your father shall bow down to you," (Gen 49:8), Ambrose says, "Surely this is appropriate to Christ alone, for whom it was in store that He should be worshipped by His brothers [i.e. the Jews] and awaited by the nations, and that he should wash His tunic in wine by the passion of His own body, because He did not stain the flesh with any sin."[17]

Israel's Unbelief

Although Joseph's prophetic dream reveals the climax of the divine economy, namely that the Jews will eventually bow the knee before Christ and so be saved; nevertheless, their initial rejection of Jesus results in their alienation from God. Ambrose's comparison of the brothers' selling Joseph illustrates the foolishness and depravity of Israel's reaction to Christ. Even as Joseph was sold to the Ishmaelite for twenty gold pieces, Judas sold Christ for thirty pieces of silver. Judas's betrayal of Jesus for a paltry sum epitomizes the Jews' rejection of Christ. For, Ambrose rhetorically asks, who is sold but the One who by virtue of his equality with God is of infinite value?[18] The result of Israel's rejection of Christ is that the Jews are, for the present, cut off from God and salvation. Jacob's rending his garments at the return of his sons with Joseph's bloodied coat foreshadows the rending of the temple curtain at the moment of Jesus' death. Indeed, Jacob wept not for just for Joseph whom he believed dead, but also "as a prophet he mourned the destruction of the Jews." Jacob's prophetic lamentation for Israel parallels Jesus' weeping over Jerusalem (Luke 19:41–2) and Paul's lamentation in Rom 9:2–3. Ambrose plays with the image of the tearing of the curtain in two,

---

16. *De Ioseph* 3.8.
17. *De Ioseph* 3.13.
18. *De Ioseph* 3.14.

> The curtain of the temple was also torn, so that it might be made clear by such signs that the mysteries had been profaned, the people had been stripped of the garments of salvation, and that the kingdom had been divided and was to be destroyed, because every divided kingdom will easily be destroyed. And it really was divided, when that which was Christ's began at that time to be the devil's. For those who separated the Son from the Father could not remain undivided.[19]

The rending of the curtain was literally the profanation of the Holy of Holies made with hands. It is also symbolic of the profanation of the temple not made with hands, that is, the body of Christ. Moreover, the splitting of the temple veil symbolizes the splitting and resulting destruction of the "kingdom." Ambrose is not clear exactly what he means by "the kingdom had been divided." One possible interpretation is that the kingdom refers to Israel that is now divided between Jews who confess Christ and Jews who do not. The former are the church and the latter the synagogue. The former belong to Christ, the latter to the devil. The former by their confession of faith are clothed with the garment of salvation at baptism while the latter by their unbelief are stripped of the garment of salvation. Ambrose's logic is simple. The rejection of the Son is tantamount to the rejection of the Father. Therefore, the Jews' refusal to believe that Jesus is the Christ, the Son of God, and their complicity in his death has cut them off from God the Father and thus from salvation as well.

Ambrose's statement, "For those who separated the Son from the Father could not remain undivided," expresses his theological understanding of the "Jews." Although there was a synagogue in Milan during Ambrose's governorship and his episcopacy, Ambrose's presentation of the Jews in his homilies and treatises do not reflect any personal contact with the Jewish community.[20] Rather when he speaks of the "Jews," as when he speaks of the "Arians," the term labels the group as "other" based on theological differences. The term "Jews" is a cipher for two theological errors. The first—the error mentioned here in *Joseph*—is the separation of the Son from the Father. In this the Jews are not alone but share company with the Arians, Sabellians, Apollinarians, and other heretics. In his treatise *On the Sacrament of Our Lord's Incarnation*, Ambrose discusses God's rejection of Cain's offering and his acceptance of Abel's gift. Cain's error is paradigmatic for all heretics; he "failed to divide rightly."[21] In order for a sacrifice to be acceptable it must be a spiritual sacrifice, i.e.

---

19. *De Ioseph* 3.18.

20. Ambrose, *Epistula* 74.8.

21. The explanation of God's displeasure with Cain's gift, Ambrose locates in Gen 4:3 and 4:7, "If you offer rightly, but do not divide rightly, you have sinned." *De sacramento Domini incarnationis* 1.2.

an outward sacrifice expressing the inner disposition of faith.[22] Ambrose's main concern is for Eunomians and Sabellians. For although they celebrate the sacraments of the Catholic Church, because they do not have a right faith—a correct understanding of the God at work in the sacrament—they do not "divide rightly" and so have sinned and their sacrifice is not acceptable to God.[23] By charging the Eunomians and Sabellians with having not "divided rightly" Ambrose means that they have failed to distinguish rightly between the Son and the Father. Sabellius conflated the Father and Son[24] whereas Eunomius divided the Father and Son, not at the level of person, but at the level of essence.[25] The Jews make the same error as the Eunomians, ". . . if a Jew, who separates the Son of the Virgin Mary from God the Father, makes an offering, it is said to him, 'If you offer rightly, but do not divide rightly, you have sinned.'"[26] By not recognizing the divinity of Christ, the Jews have failed to grasp the eternal and essential relationship of the Father and Son.

The second theological error of which the Jews are guilty is related to their not "dividing rightly"; it is that they are carnal, not spiritual, in their thinking. For Ambrose, Jews and Christians have decidedly different ways of thinking. Conjoining Paul's language of the "inner man" from Rom 7:22 with baptismal imagery from Col 3:9–10, "You have put off the old man with its practices and have put on the new man, which is being renewed in knowledge according to the image of him who is his creator," Ambrose treats "inner man" as a synonym for the "new man" born in the waters of baptism.[27] The term "inner man" refers to the mindset of the baptized who, having the gift of faith, are turned from the external things to the internal things of the Spirit and the gospel. Because the Christian in faith embraces the gospel, which is the perfection of the Law, she apprehends the spirit of the Law and so is freed from

---

22. *De incarnationis* 1.3.

23. "Abel also knew how to divide . . . teaching that the gifts of the earth, which had degenerated in the sinner, will not please God, but those in which the grace of the divine mystery shone forth," *De incarnationis* 1.4.

24. *De incarnationis* 2.8.

25. *De incarnationis* 2.7.

26. *De incarnationis* 2.6. Ambrose expands upon this point later, "For certain others are either Arian Jews or Jewish Arians, for just as the former separate the Son from the Father, so the latter also separate the Spirit of God from the Father and the Son of God," *De incarnationis* 2.9.

27. *Expo Luc* V.23. This discussion of purity of the inner man who has put off the works of the old man comes in the context of Ambrose's analysis of the call of Levi and his leaving his former life as a tax collector to follow Christ (Luke 5:27–32) which follows the discussion of the healing of the leaper and the paralytic. Thus Ambrose sees in these pericopes the baptismal themes of healing and of transformed lifestyle.

bondage to its letter. Ambrose illustrates the contrast between the Christian and Jew in his discussion of Jesus' parable of the Fig Tree (Luke 13:6–9). The barren fig tree is a type of the Jews who have ceased to bear good fruit because they are focused on external things (e.g., the letter and works of the Law) due to their "strictness and pride." But then Ambrose reminds the reader of the hope for Jews that is implicit in the parable. God, like the gardener, shows forbearance with his fruitless tree, the Jews. Consequently, God sends the apostles to till the soil around the fig tree. Through their reception of the gospel, the hardened hearts of the Jews shall be dug up, as by the gardener's trowel. Like the gardener's application of dung, the power of God contained in the apostles' proclamation of the gospel enables the Jews to bear good fruit.[28] Not surprisingly, Ambrose describes the repentance of the Jews—when their hardened hearts and pride are dug up—in the same language he uses to depict the conversion of the Gentiles from paganism. "If they [the Jews] were to die and as it were, perish to this world, so that they were reborn to the inner man through the grace of baptism, they would assuredly be fruitful. But the unbelief of stubborn men rendered the synagogue useless, and, therefore, it is ordered to be cut down as barren."[29] The Jew, by his strict adherence to the ritual demands of the Mosaic law, is concerned with externals, the things of the outer man. Ironically, the Jew who is focused upon the outward works of the Law is placed in the same category as the hedonistic pagan who is focused upon the external pleasures of the body.

The Jews' orientation to the Law in its outward form produces a self-righteousness that is antithetical to the righteousness founded upon grace. This pride is resistant to faith in Christ and a righteousness founded upon his grace. In order to understand the Jewish predicament, we need a sense of Ambrose's view of the human condition after the Fall. In Eden, humanity possessed a natural form of faith, a disposition that recognized the authority of God and God's natural law. With the Fall,

---

28. "Thus through the exercise of spiritual understanding and the disposition of humility, that good husband thinks that even the Jews will be fruitful for the gospel of Christ . . . by its [i.e., the church's] grace, through the sanctification in baptism the peoples of the Jews and the gentiles [can] possess the fruit of their own merit," *Expo Luc* VII.169.

29. Ambrose issues a warning to Christians that because they are people who enjoy the power of the gospel and have been born anew in the grace of baptism they are under greater judgment if they do not bear fruit. "I think that all, and especially we, should be wary of saying this about the Jews, lest devoid of merit we occupy the fertile place of the Church," *Expo Luc* VII.171. Although language of "cutting down" when applied to a synagogue sounds like rhetoric intent upon inciting his congregation to perpetrate violence against the local synagogue or members of the Jewish community (as happened to the synagogue at Callinicum in Dec. 388), this is not Ambrose's intention. It is merely Jesus' language in Luke that Ambrose is quoting.

humanity lost the natural disposition of faith.[30] Sin, which Ambrose often depicts as intemperate behavior or as the "sacrilegious hunger" of gluttony, has so turned the mind from the things of God to the pleasures of the flesh (e.g., luxury, ambition, wealth) that we have forgotten the precepts of God. The trusting submissiveness of faith was replaced with a form of corrupt *concupiscentia* that hardens the mind to God.[31] Because stony-hearted humanity resisted God's authority and continued in sin, God gave Israel the Law on Sinai that exposes sin but is powerless either to forgive sin or to free us from bondage to sin. That is, the Law does not overcome the hardness of heart that is the result of concupiscence; consequently, the knowledge of the moral good provided by the Law does not allow one to fulfill the Law.[32] For the Law can be fulfilled only when performed out of love for God. Love that fulfills the Law is the fruit of faith in Christ's grace that is given in baptism. In his interpretation of John the Baptist's words, "God could raise up sons to Abraham from these stones," Ambrose depicts the stones as a figure of the hardened heart of the Gentiles.

> Indeed God prepared to soften the hardness of our minds and from stumbling blocks erect husbands of religion . . . Therefore, faith (*fides*) is prophesied to be poured out (*infundenda*) into the stony hearts (*saxosis pectoribus*) of the Gentiles and the oracle promised that through faith (*per fidem*) there will be sons of Abraham in whom through hardness of mind (*per duritiam mentis*) the stony, insensitive, and irrational practice of nature had set fast (*inoleuerat*).[33]

Faith must be poured into (*infundere*) the stony and unbelieving hearts of Gentiles so that *per fidem* they might be made sons of Abraham.[34] The "bedewing" of the soul in baptism is the work of the Holy Spirit. In his explication of Luke's ac-

---

30. In Ambrose's interpretation of Jesus' parable of the Good Samaritan, he draws a parallel between the effects of the Devil's temptation of Adam and the temptation of Christians. "These [thieves] first steal the garments of spiritual grace which we have received and are thus wont to inflict wounds, for if we preserve inviolate the garments which we have donned, we cannot feel the robbers' blows. Therefore, beware lest you are stripped as Adam was first stripped of the heavenly command, defrauded of protection, divested of the garment of faith, and thus received a mortal wound, whereby the whole human race would have fallen if that Samaritan, on his journey, had not tended his grievous injuries," *Expo Luc*VII.73. The logic of the parallel is that when Adam sinned he and Eve lost "garments of spiritual grace" that include knowledge of the God's law and the "garment of faith."

31. *De Iacob* I.1.2.

32. *De Iacob* I.3.14.

33. *Expo Luc* II,75; CCSL 14, p.64.

34. *Expo Luc* II.75; SC 45 p.105; PL15, 1661 B–D.

count of Jesus with the disciples upon the Mount of Transfiguration, Ambrose used the image of the cloud to describe the work of the Spirit.

> 'While he thus spoke there came a cloud, and overshadowed them.' That is the overshadowing of the Divine Spirit, which is not dark with emotions of men, but unveils secrets... when the voice of God is heard saying 'This is my beloved Son,'... You see that the perfect faith of not only beginners but also the perfect, nay, even of Heavenly Beings, is to know the Son of God. But since we said these things already above, know that the cloud was not a black mist of the cloudy moisture of smoking mountains and compressed air which covers the heaven with terror and darkness, but a luminous cloud which does not soak us with rainwater or the downpour of storm, but from which dew sprinkles the minds of men with faith sent by the voice of Almighty God.[35]

The faith that the Spirit imparts to the heart is the knowledge of Christ as the Son of God—the faith that the catechumen declares in the public confession at her baptism. Ambrose speaks of the dew of faith as having two chief consequences for the soul. First, faith, like dew that moistens the hard ground, softens the heart that we might receive the seeds of the Divine word. Second, the dew of faith cools the fiery and intemperate passions of the soul that the mind might no longer be fixed upon the things of the flesh but seek the wisdom of God. The bedewing of the soul with faith is, for Ambrose, the Holy Spirit's regenerative work that restores fallen human nature to the Paradise of the Heavenly Jerusalem. Whereas the gift of faith in Christ counters the pride and passion of sinful concupiscence, unbelief renders the soul arid or resistant to God.[36] Therefore, although the Jews have the Law, because they do not have faith in Christ who is the fountain of living water, their religion is arid legalism.[37] In *Joseph*, Ambrose, playing with the image of the Ishmaelites buy-

---

35. *Expo Luc* VII, 19–20 in Ambrose of Milan, *Exposition of the Holy Gospel according to Saint Luke; With Fragments on the Prophecy of Isaias* (trans. Theodosia Tomkinson; Etna, Calif.: Center for Traditionalist Orthodox Studies, 1998), 250.

36. Warning against the trial that the persecution will bring to test the fruit of our baptism, Ambrose writes "through the multitude of offenses, the dew of the holy fountain (*sacri fontis*) will dry up in us ... for unbelief renders [the soul] arid, but faith bedews (*rorare*)." *Expo Luc* X. 38; PL 15, 1905D. Tomkinson translates *sacri fontis* as "of the Holy Spirit." While in Ambrose's conception of baptism the Holy Spirit is the one who makes the waters of baptism efficacious, there is nothing in the passage which specifically mentions the Holy Spirit as the one that bedews the soul.

37. Ambrose explains that the dry pit into which Joseph's brothers threw him is a sign of Israel's dryness. Based on Christ's conversation with the woman at the well (John 4:1–15), Ambrose implicitly reads the Jews' rejection of Jesus as the apostasy that Jeremiah's prophetic words (2:13) foretold, "my

ing Joseph, says that Christ must be bought with incense "with which the altars of a devoted heart are ablaze" and the *resina* which denotes both cement and balm. *Resina* that heals sins and binds together broken parts of the soul is faith. He goes on to explain that because the synagogue lacks faith the balm "has passed to the Church . . . so that the balm might heal the sins of the nations."[38] Later Ambrose illustrates the gracious nature of the salvation Christ offers by observing that, although Joseph's brothers brought money with which to pay for the grain, Joseph gave them the grain and returned their money to them. The mystical significance of the passage, Ambrose explains, is that "Christ is not bought with money but with grace; your payment is faith and with it are bought God's mysteries."[39] In other words, faith gains the catechumen access to the *sacramenta* of baptism and Eucharist. It is by faith in Christ's atoning death that the catechumen will gain forgiveness of her sins and have her soul healed of its disordered division between the rational soul and the passions of unholy concupiscence. Ambrose's logic is that through faith conferred by the Spirit in baptism the Christian is able to receive forgiveness of sin that the Law cannot give. Consequently, she is able to participate in the sanctified humanity of the new creation that is able to resist the impulses of sinful concupiscence and instead burn with a greater love for God. Peter's commanding Aeneas the paralytic to get up and walk (Acts 9:34) and raising the dead woman to life (Acts 9:40) illustrates the healing balm of faith. Later describing Joseph's distribution of the grain during the famine, Ambrose explains that Christ, like Joseph, "taking pity on the hungers of the world . . . opened his granaries and sold, while asking not monetary payments, but the price of faith and the recompense of devotion. He sold, moreover, not to a few men in Judea, but sold to all men so that he might be believed by all people."[40] Thus Ambrose adapts the logic of Paul's argument that faith is taken from the Jews and passed to Gentiles so that all nations may be drawn to Christ. However, given the Jews' pride that hinders their acceptance of Christ, Ambrose faces the perplexing question, "How will Israel come to faith in Christ by which she may be restored to the covenant?" He finds the answer in the conversion and ministry of Paul.

---

people have committed two evils, they have forsaken me, the fountain of living waters, and hewed out cisterns for themselves, broken cisterns, that can hold no water." *De Ioseph* 3:16.

38. *De Ioseph* 3.17.

39. *De Ioseph* 8.45.

40. *De Ioseph* 7.41.

Paul and the Mission to the Jews

In Joseph's brother, Benjamin, whom Jacob keeps home with him due to Benjamin's infirmity, Ambrose finds a figure of St. Paul. Not only was Paul from the tribe of Benjamin, but Paul, like Benjamin, experienced an infirmity, blindness which proved to be "an infirmity unto salvation."[41] Moreover, even as Benjamin was the youngest of Joseph's sons, Paul was "least of the apostles."[42] When Paul sets off on his mission, he is like Benjamin bearing incense and cement to buy grain, which represent faith. By his proclamation, Paul applied "a spiritual cement [that] fastened together living stones" and honey that "destroyed the festering infection and drained off the tainted fluid with the sting of its argument, for it sought rather to cauterize the sick vitals of the heart than to cut them."[43] The incense is a sign of Paul's prayers. Here Ambrose describes Paul's preaching and prayer in the very way he earlier spoke of faith that both heals and restores unity to the conflicted and disordered soul. The "living stones" likely refer to the souls that receive the cement/balm of faith. As is typical of Ambrose's oratory that piles allusion on top of allusion, here the "living stones" refer not to the soul alone but to the church that is united in faith. The stones represent the hardness of Gentile souls that are without belief. But Paul's preaching of faith bedews the hardened souls and so fashions "living stones" that are united to form the church. Thus the church consists of the sons and daughters of Abraham that John the Baptist said God would raise up out of stones.[44]

The turning point in Ambrose's exegesis comes when he explains Joseph's reception of his brothers when they return with Benjamin whereas "when they came without Benjamin, he did not even recognize them but turned away from them."[45] The difference, Ambrose explains, is that the second time Joseph receives his brothers out of love for Benjamin. So too, the Jews "advance by the merit of Paul, whom the Lord loved more than the other brothers, as being a younger brother begotten

---

41. *De Ioseph* 8.44.

42. Although Ambrose does not quote 1 Corinthians 15:8–9 directly, it is implicit in his comparison of the older brothers who were first sent to Egypt and so are figures of the original apostles. "The patriarchs had gone at first without Benjamin, and the Apostles without Paul. Each came, not as the first, but was summoned by those who came first, and by his [i.e. Benjamin and Paul] arrival he made the goods of those who were first more plenteous," *De Ioseph* 8.45.

43. *De Ioseph* 9.46.

44. *Expo Luc* II.75

45. Joseph's rejection of his brothers is based on Gen. 42:7, "and he spoke harshly to them."*De Ioseph* 9.47.

from the same mother."⁴⁶ Although the Jews, like the other brothers, have a common parent, Paul has a distinctive relationship with Christ prefigured in Joseph's relationship with Benjamin. Who the "same mother" is that Paul and Christ share is not made explicit; however, the bond between them, represented by the common mother, may be Paul's faith. For, Ambrose proceeds to say, "Let the Jews turn to him whom they have denied to be their Lord. Even though he was crucified from their synagogue, yet he loves them more as born of the *same parent*, if only they come to know, even late, the author of their salvation."⁴⁷ Christ loves the Jews because they are his brothers in spite of their complicity in his death. But his love for them will become even greater, as it is for Paul, if they recognize him as Lord and savior, as Paul did.

So how does Paul bring his fellow Jews to their brother Christ through faith? Paul is able to play the role of mediator between Christ and the Jews because of the character of his conversion. It is not the Damascus Road experience *per se* that is important as much as it is the change in Paul's life from being a Pharisee and a persecutor of the Church to the servant of Christ. That is, there is a shift from self-righteousness under the Law to righteousness or justice through faith. Paul the Pharisee is the Jew of Jews who justified himself by his adherence to the Law. So too, the Jewish people prefer to justify themselves according to works of the Law rather than be justified by grace. The passage in the Joseph saga that Ambrose focuses on here is the brothers' return to Egypt after having discovered that someone put the money with which they intended to buy the grain into their sacks. Afraid of being accused of robbery, they are reluctant to enter Joseph's house but preferred to justify themselves to the steward at the gate (Gen 43:19–22). The brothers fearfully arguing in their own defense at the gate are, for Ambrose, a fitting type of Israel under the Law because "They still hesitate to enter in and prefer to be justified from their works, for they desire to prove a case rather than to receive grace, and so they are refuted at the gates."⁴⁸ Self-justification, however, is futile because the Jews, like the brothers who are guilty of selling Joseph into slavery, are guilty of rejecting and handing Christ over to be crucified. Yet they are conscious of their guilt and so, like Joseph's brothers who refuse to enter Joseph's house, refuse Christ's offer of forgiveness and salvation.⁴⁹ Ambrose's argument seems to be internally contradictory. How

46. *De Ioseph* 9.47.

47. *De Ioseph* 9.47

48. *De Ioseph* 9.48.

49. Immediately after having said that Christ loves the Jews as his brothers even though they killed

can the Jews be proudly self-justifying and at the same time alienated from Christ because they are conscious of their own guilt? Yet his insight is that the burden of guilt can be so great that one finds recourse in denial and self-justification. The guilty are often the loudest in declaring their innocence. (We have only to think of the rhetoric of holocaust deniers or Southern defenders of slavery in the nineteenth century.) It is the paradox that the Law brings knowledge of sin and yet even under the condemnation of the Law self-righteousness remains.

This too was Paul's story. He believed himself righteous under the Law and yet was guilty of persecuting Christ and his Church. Ambrose speaks of Paul's condition before coming to faith as "blindness." Yet the blindness in question is not the condition that befell him on the road to Damascus, but a more fundamental form of spiritual blindness, unbelief. Ambrose writes, "Paul's faith hastened the coming of noon. Before Paul was blind; afterwards he began to see the light of justice, because if anyone opens his way to the Lord and hopes in him, the Lord will also bring forth his justice as the light and his judgment as the noon."[50] Faith opens the eyes to receive the "light of justice" which Ambrose equates with the presence of Christ.[51] When in faith we enter the presence of God we experience the two-fold aspect of Christ's justice: judgment and grace. Although Paul rightly stands condemned before Christ's just judgment, he nonetheless receives the grace of Christ's justice which is forgiveness of sin through his assumption of our debt of sin. In faith Paul ceases to be proud and stiff-necked and so is pardoned by Christ. Ambrose writes, ". . . when the Gospel is brought to completion, Christ embraces Paul in the arms of his mercy, as it were, so as to lift him up into heaven once the latter has shown submission by inner belief as if by bending his neck."[52] Thus Paul becomes an illustration for the Jews of Christ's mercy that forgives even those who, like Joseph's brothers, persecuted their brother,

---

him, Ambrose says of the Jews and their role in Christ's death "But being aware of their own offenses, they do not believe that Christ is so very merciful as to forgive their sin and pardon their wrongdoing. And thus their future line of conduct was prefigured in the patriarchs. They were invited to grace, were summoned to the banquet of the table of salvation, and suspected that a false accusation was being readied against them and an ambush was being laid," *De Ioseph* 9.47.

50. *De Ioseph* 10.52. The identification of "faith" with "noon" refers to Gen 43:25 that explains that Joseph greeted his brothers at noon.

51. Ambrose's intertextual reading of the Old Testament leads him to understand Joseph's appearance at noon as the time of judgment and justice in Ps 36:6 (*Vul*) "*Et educet quasi lumen iustitiam tuam, et iudicium tuum tanquam meridiem*" (He will bring forth your vindication as the light, and your right as the noonday, Ps 37:6 RSV). Moreover his identification of the "light of justice" with Christ's presence is supported by God's appearance to Abraham at noon (Gen. 18:1).

52. *De Ioseph* 12.73.

Christ. In Jesus' mercy toward Paul, the Jews have hope that they too will receive Christ's forgiveness. This hope overcomes the hardness and guilt that keeps the Jews estranged from Christ.

Paul is able draw his fellow Jews to Christ because in Paul, a persecutor of Christ like themselves, they are able to see and believe the mercy of Christ. Paul's washing his face and the return of his sight symbolizes the washing of baptism which Ambrose calls the "sacrament of illumination." Ambrose makes the cryptic comment that "Christ washed his own face when Paul was baptized, so that through him the Lord Jesus might be seen by many men."[53] In what sense can Christ wash his own face in the baptism of Paul? Thinking of Paul's claim in Gal 2:19–20 "It is no longer I who live, but Christ who live in me," Ambrose likely means that when Paul put to death the old man in baptism and was raised with Christ, Christ lived in him and so was visible to the world through him. Specifically, it is through Paul's faith that the Jews come to know the justice of Christ. Although the Law is impotent to grant forgiveness, its instruction prepared Paul for faith, "the word of heavenly instruction already shone in Paul's body, since he was instructed in the Law."[54] Yet, like the cup that Joseph hid in the grain sacks of which the brothers were ignorant, the justice of Christ that was contained in the Law was nevertheless hidden and remained unknown to Paul until he came to faith. "When the sack was opened, the money shone forth, and when the scales fell, in a way like fastenings on the sack, Paul saw straightaway. His bond was unbelief; the loosening of it became faith."[55] At this point in Ambrose's narrative, the cup or money in the sacks has served as a figure for Christ, the works of the Law, and the Law itself. In this passage, Ambrose brings their meanings together. The opening of the sack, like the opening of Paul's eyes represents his coming to faith and the discovery of Christ's justice. Having faith in Christ, the "veil set over the hearts of the Jews" (2 Cor 3:13–18) becomes lifted and Paul is able to see how Christ is contained in the Jewish Scriptures. With the lifting of the veil through faith, Paul, like Moses after beholding God's glory, is transformed into the image of Christ.

Although the conversion of Paul is to illustrate to the Jews the justice of Christ, the reaction of the Jews to Paul's preaching is mixed. Commenting on the fearful reaction of the brothers when the cup is discovered in Benjamin's sack, Ambrose sees the Jews "turning back" in fear. The result of their refusal to respond to Paul's

---

53. *De Ioseph* 10.59.

54. *De Ioseph* 11.64.

55. *De Ioseph* 11.64.

preaching is that the Jews are stripped of grace.[56] How Paul's preaching "tore away all their grace" is not clear. Perhaps, by rejecting Paul's gospel, which revealed Christ's forgiveness of even those who rejected Christ and persecuted his followers, the Jews have turned against the Christ and so forfeited their salvation. For, Ambrose goes on to compare the Jews who reject Paul's teaching with those who seized Jesus saying, "Those who lose Christ turn back . . . It is appropriate that they went back, for they fell from heavenly grace to earthly defilement."[57] Yet, there is the figure of Judah who remains with Joseph because he dreads seeing the evil that will come to Jacob. Ambrose interprets this as a prophetic vision of the evils that will befall the Jews. It is not clear how to understand Judah. Although he is the one who sells Joseph to the Ishmaelite,[58] he is also the one who, out of "brotherly bonds," argues that his brothers not kill Joseph.[59] His name Ambrose interprets to mean "confession of sin" and "restored to life" for together with Ruben he makes intercession for Benjamin.[60] Ultimately, Ambrose says that Judah is the forerunner of the Jews who seek forgiveness for sin and are received by Christ.[61] Yet, because the leaders of the Jews do not follow Judah's example, Jesus, like Joseph weeping over his brother, weeps over the Jews.[62]

The Fulfillment of Joseph's Dream

Jesus' lamentation over the unbelief of the Jews will not in the end prove fruitless, for Joseph's prophetic vision of his brothers (the Jews) bowing down to him (Jesus) will come to fulfillment. In his interpretation of Gen 45:2 when Joseph finally reveals his

---

56. "For the free preaching of Paul on behalf of Christ laid bare the people of the Jews and tore away all their grace, and so they who could not see ahead of themselves, went back," *De Ioseph* 11.64–5.

57. *De Ioseph* 11.65.

58. *De Ioseph* 3.14.

59. *De Ioseph* 3.13.

60. *De Ioseph* 9.46.

61. *De Ioseph* 14.84.

62. "*Sed cum adhuc haec ipsa non esset in typo illo pincipum populoi Judaeorum libera praedicatio, flevit Joseph, hoc est, in illo ploravit Jesus*" (But since this very preaching was still not unimpeded in the case of that figure who was symbolic of the chiefs of the Jewish people, Joseph wept, that is, Jesus wept in him), *De Ioseph* 11.66. The referent of "*in typo illo*" is ambiguous. The paragraph begins with a discussion of how Judah desires to avoid the bad things that will befall the Jews and stays with Joseph. Therefore, I take Ambrose to be lamenting that Judah who is the leader of Joseph's brothers and who remains with Joseph is not a type for leaders of the Jews in their response to Jesus. The "*libera praedicatio*" is the same term Ambrose uses for Paul's preaching in 11.64.

identity to his brothers, Ambrose emphasizes Jesus' fraternal affection for the Jews. Christ comes to save the lost sheep of Israel because they are his *brothers*. Joseph's revelatory declaration "I am Joseph. Is my father still alive?" (Gen 45:3) establishes the fraternal bond between Jesus and the Jews; they are brothers because their Father is the same. This is the motive for Christ's mission, "He stretched out his hands to an unbelieving and contradicting people, for he did not seek an envoy or messenger but, as their very Lord, desired to save his own people . . . I do not deny my father, I know my brothers, if you recognize your brother and the Father recognizes his son."[63] Ambrose's emphasis upon Christ's fraternal bond with the Jews is significant because it stresses both Jesus' being Jewish according to flesh and the covenantal bond between God and Israel. Unlike the common hermeneutical move that depicts Jesus as the New Adam and so makes him universal humanity, neither Jew nor Gentile, Ambrose, while holding on to the universal character of Christ's mission to bring salvation to all nations, does not neglect the primacy of Jesus' mission to the lost sheep of Israel who are his brothers. Moreover, he is their Lord who came to save his own people. Although Christ is Lord of all creation, nevertheless the Jews are "his own people" because he singled them out through the Mosaic covenant, ". . . if you will obey my voice and keep my covenant, you shall be my own possession among all the people. . ." (Ex 19:5).

The Jews' handing of Jesus over to be crucified does not permanently cut them off from Christ. Ambrose sees a parallel between Joseph's words of exculpation, "Now be not grieved, and let it not seem to you a hard case, that you sold me here; for God sent me before you for life," (Gen 45:4–5) and Jesus' words from the cross, "Father, forgive them for they know not what they do."[64] Even as Joseph tells his brothers that it was God who in his providence sent Joseph to Egypt to secure the life-giving grain, so too Christ "was not offered up to death by men but was sent by the Lord to life."[65]

Joseph's forgiveness and mercy toward the brothers is not only a figure of Christ's forgiveness and love of his brothers the Jews, but also is a figure of the work of the saints in the church. God's sending of Joseph to give life to his brothers, Ambrose

---

63. *De Ioseph* 12.67.

64. Ambrose affirms the fraternal bond between Jesus and the Jews, "What fraternal devotion! What a good brotherly relation! He would even excuse his brother's crimes and say that it was God's providence and not man's unholiness . . ." *De Ioseph* 12.69. Although these words immediately follow Joseph's words, Ambrose's description refers to Jesus for he proceeds to say "What else is the meaning of that intervention made by our Lord Jesus Christ . . ."

65. *De Ioseph* 12.69.

claims, prefigures Christ's "Great Commission" to the church.[66] Through the lives of the saints, all nations shall be baptized and come to redemption. So too with Israel. Even as Pharaoh orders Joseph's brothers' mounts loaded with grain and invites them to return with Jacob (Gen 45:16–20), God will bless Israel and bring them to himself. Of Pharaoh's invitation, Ambrose says this is a great mystery, "a mystery the Church today does not deny. The Jews will be redeemed; the Christian people rejoice at this union, give aid to the limit of its resources, and send men to preach the good news of the kingdom of God, so that their call may come sooner."[67]

Although the Jews, despite their unbelief, will eventually be reconciled to their brother Christ and enter into the kingdom he proclaimed, nevertheless the church, Ambrose is telling his catechumens, cannot be complacent but must by their preaching and other aid work to bring Jews to the true knowledge of God through faith in Christ. While Ambrose preserves Paul's notion of the mystery of Israel's restoration: "a hardening has come upon part of Israel, until the full number of the Gentiles comes in, and so all Israel will be saved," (Rom 11:25–6), he does not retain the Pauline metaphor of the fig tree. Rather than being restored to the covenant onto which other people have been grafted, the Jews are included in a greater community of all nations united in the church. He interprets God's promise to Jacob, "Go down into Egypt; for there I will make you into a great people," (Gen 46:2–4) to mean that "They are invited from this place to pass over to the Church of God—what could be clearer? Before they were confined within the narrow limits of Judea; they are invited to pass over to the people of God that was gathered together from the whole world, from all tribes and peoples, and was made into a great people. . ."[68] No longer are the Jews to be a provincial people living in segregated isolation, but now they are incorporated into a community consisting of all the people of God, that is Christ's church. Quoting Ps 18:5 (*Vul*) "Their voice has gone out into all the earth"—the psalm Paul cites in Rom 10:18—Ambrose affirms that Israel's praise of God was to extend to all the world in order to draw all the world to the God of Israel. The greatness that God promised Jacob is realized in the inclusion of people from all nations. This is what Jacob's sons who have followed Christ's commission to "make disciples of all nations" recognized. Ambrose expresses the church's mission to the

66. *De Ioseph* 12.71.
67. *De Ioseph* 12.74.
68. *De Ioseph* 14.82.

Jews paradoxically, "Thus Jacob is called by his sons, that is, the people of the Jews are invited to grace by Peter and John and Paul."[69]

The conversion and restoration of Israel, like that of Paul, is a passing from the blindness of unbelief into the vision of faith. Ambrose's operating assumption is Paul's claim in 2 Cor 3:14 that the Jews' minds are hardened and so they read the old covenant through a veil that can be removed only by faith in Christ. So he compares Joseph's placing his hands on the eyes of Jacob (Gen 46:4) to Jesus' placing his hand on the eyes of the blind man to restore his sight (John 9:6–7). Here Jacob is not a type of God the Father, but of the people that bear his name, Israel. When the true Joseph, Christ, places his hands upon Israel the Jews will receive sight and know God. The laying on of hands foreshadows for the catechumens the touch of the bishop's hands in baptism. "Indeed, Christ does not put his hands on those who are going to die but on those who are going to live or, if on those who are going to die, rightly so, because we first die in order that we may live again. For we cannot see God unless we die to sin previously."[70] The death to sin is the sacramental death in baptism, the sacrament of illumination. When the Jews, like Judah, confess their sins, i.e. the hardness of their unbelief and their rejection of Christ, they shall receive faith in Christ and through belief in Christ come to know God the Father whom Christ reveals.[71] Ambrose weds the logic of 2 Cor 3:14 with John 1:18; Christ alone can remove the veil so that Israel may see and know God because he is the only begotten who alone has seen the Father.

Conclusion: The Conversion of the Catechumen and the Conversion of Israel

One long debated question among Augustinian scholars is when was Augustine's conversion? In his reading the books of the Platonists? Or in hearing the conversion stories of St. Antony and Marius Victorinus? Or during his reading Romans in the garden in Milan? For Augustine, and for Ambrose, the conversion from death in sin to new life in God came at baptism. For, although God's grace confers an embryonic form of faith that leads one to seek baptism, it is in the sacrament that the

---

69. *De Ioseph* 14.82.

70. *De Ioseph* 14.83.

71. After interpreting the significance of the seventy-five people from the tribe of Jacob who went down to Egypt as the number of forgiveness, Ambrose comments, "For after such great hardness, after such great sins, they would be considered unworthy unless there were granted them the forgiveness of sins," *De Ioseph* 14.84.

neophyte's soul is bedewed with faith while her body is washed in the water of the font. Then she comes to share in the mystery of God's economy. In faith the baptized receive Christ's forgiveness of sin and citizenship in his heavenly commonwealth. What is interesting is the way Ambrose uses the Joseph saga and the conversion of Israel to prepare his Gentile catechumens for their baptismal conversion. Joseph's magnanimous forgiveness of the very brothers who would have killed him illustrates the extent of Christ's forgiving love toward his brothers, the Jews, who handed him over to be crucified. Although Ambrose repeatedly says the Gentiles who were without the Law were like the unnamed woman in the house of Simon the Pharisee who loved Jesus more because she was forgiven more; nevertheless, following Paul's description of the Jews as hardened in their mind to Christ (Rom 11:25, 2 Cor 3:14), Ambrose presents the Jews as the "other" which defines the Christian identity. They are a stiff-necked people who do not recognize Jesus as the Christ and only Son of the Father. So they do not bow the knee to Christ. Moreover, they are proud and believe that their righteousness before God is not the gift of grace, but by their works according to the Law. Following the modern work of E. P. Sanders and others, we may rightly object that Ambrose's characterization of the "Jews" is inaccurate. This is more a quarrel between Sanders and Paul and only derivatively between Sanders and Ambrose. Nevertheless, Ambrose's stress upon the catechumen's faith in Christ and on his love for the very ones who reject him prepares his catechumens for the life beyond baptism. While the life of the Christian who takes up the demands of the gospel is more demanding than life under the Mosaic law and is the perfection of pagan virtue, there is no room for pride in one's virtue. Indeed, whatever virtue the convert to Christianity attains, this virtue is but the fruit of the gift of faith in Christ's mercy and of the indwelling Spirit who performs works in us that surpass our nature.

Ambrose's catechetical homilies on Joseph would have ended on the eve of Holy Week. Sadly in the history of the church Holy Week has too often seen outbreaks of violence against Jews by Christians whose prejudices were ignited by the gospel narratives of Jesus' arrest and crucifixion. Yet Ambrose's interpretation of Joseph's reconciliation with his brothers addresses head-on the Jewish question. Though they rejected Jesus and were guilty of fratricide, the Jews remain Jesus' brothers whom he continues to love and over whom he weeps, just as Joseph loved and wept over his brothers. Moreover, Ambrose affirms as a point of church doctrine Paul's confidence in Rom 11 that the Jews will in the end be saved. Like Joseph's brothers, the Jews will be reconciled with their brother Jesus. This hope informs the Christian's attitude toward the Jews and the church's mission. Following Paul's insistence that "Faith comes from what is heard and what is heard comes by the preaching of Christ" (Rom 10:21), Ambrose proclaims it the church's duty to preach Christ to Jews, just as Peter, John, and Paul did, in order that the Jews may come to faith in Christ and through faith be incorporated into the new covenant in the body of Christ in whom there is neither Jew nor Gentile.

One question that needs to be answered is whether the eschatological restoration of Israel—the re-grafting of Jacob's children—should be called a "conversion"? The objection to speaking of Israel's restoration as a "conversion" is that Christ in whom Christians have faith is the God of Abraham, Isaac, and Jacob in whom the Jews have faith.[72] Therefore, the Jews simply will come to see that the God of Israel is the Triune God revealed in the Son's incarnation. These Jews are different than Gentiles who converted to Christianity after renouncing their worship of pagan deities. From Ambrose's perspective, however, the Jews who did not receive Jesus as the Christ and Son of the Father willfully rejected God's visitation. Following Jesus' description of the Jews in John's Gospel as having the devil for their father (John 8:44), Ambrose says that the synagogue is no longer the house of God, but of the devil. Within the context of the Joseph typology, the Jews, like Joseph's brothers, have betrayed their Father by not receiving the Son. By their complicity in his death they made themselves enemies of Christ. The restoration of Israel will entail a turning from a state of enmity with Christ to a new state of peace through contrition and confession of Christ. In other words, there is the need for reconciliation between the Jews and Christ whom they rejected and killed. This reconciliation entails the turning (*conversio*) of repentance. Therefore, from Ambrose's perspective the eschatological redemption of Israel is a turning from a state of fault to a state of grace.

As Christians living after the Holocaust we are as uncomfortable with Ambrose's anti-Jewish rhetoric that refers to the synagogue as the house of the devil as we are with the description of the Jews in John's Gospel. Yet, I would argue, Ambrose is in many ways more honest about the profound theological division between those Jews and Gentiles who confess Christ and those Jews who do not. To be sure, Jews who are faithful to Torah and worship the God of Israel are in a different category altogether than converts from paganism. In Rom 11, however, Paul still makes a distinction between two types of Jews. First, there is the faithful remnant of Israel chosen by grace (Rom 11:5) who, like Paul and the other apostles, confessed Christ

---

72. This was a challenging question posed during the discussion of this paper at the North Park Symposium.

and were made righteous by grace apart from the Law. The second group of Jews are those he describes as having stumbled (Rom 11:11), being hardened (Rom 11:7), being rejected (Rom 11:13), and for the present time having been cut off from the covenant on account of their unbelief (Rom 11:20) so that the Gentiles might be grafted on to the promises of the covenant. The unbelief of the second group refers to their failure to believe and receive Jesus as the Christ. The eschatological re-grafting of the Jews will entail their coming to believe in Christ. This is not analogous to the restoration of the Jews after the Babylonian exile who returned to the proper worship of God. For, the eschatological restoration of Israel requires the confession of what was previously deemed blasphemy and anathema: Jesus Christ is Lord and God. In other words, the re-grafting of Israel will require a *turning* to Christ by people whose unbelief, hostility, or indifference to Christ caused their alienation from God. Thus the restoration of the Jews will involve such a drastic change in their worship, piety, and theology that it cannot spoken of as anything other than a conversion. Indeed, if we speak of Paul's undergoing a conversion to Christianity, then the same will also be true for his fellow Jews. Then Paul's lamentation over his brothers' unbelief will be turned to rejoicing.

RESPONSE TO SMITH

George Kalantzis

Warren Smith provides an excellent and insightful look into Ambrose's preaching and theology. To be sure, the fourth century continues to be the most intriguing period in the development of Christian identity. From theology, to homiletics, to ethics, to worship and the sacraments, this post-Constantinian period is imbued with transformative characters and ideas that shape Christianity even to our day. So our author is to be thanked for the careful way in which he opens up for us Ambrose's *De Ioseph* and reveals the bishop's deep love for Scripture and homiletical eloquence that was so appealing even to Augustine. After reading the essay a little voice in my head started saying ever more loudly, *tole, lege, tole, lege et episcopum obsequi!* (Take up and read, take up and read and follow the bishop!).

Ambrose, to be sure, was not the first to approach the Scriptures allegorically, but he was certainly one of the "school's" most eloquent preachers. He stands in the long tradition of Origen (on the Christian side) and Plotinus (on the classical or Hellenic side) who looked for the *pneumatiko* (spiritual) meaning of Scripture, because—on the Christian side—they were fully confident in the power of *the* Spirit to reveal Christ, the Word about whom the whole of God's revelation spoke.[1] Of course, christocentric readings of the whole of Scripture were not limited to the "allegorists," but were a *principium* (first principle) of most early Christian approaches to the Old Testament. As such, the stories—or *the* story—of the Patriarchs as *typoi Christou* (types of Christ) abound in early Christian literature.

For our purposes, we should note that Joseph as a *typos* (type) of Christ was one of the earliest associations in early Christian commentaries and homilies. Origen makes the connection as early as *In Genesim homiliae* II.5, noting that "Joseph was thirty years old when he was led out of prison and received the rule of all Egypt" (Gen 41:46), the same age as Jesus at his baptism (Luke 3:23), which marked the beginning of his ministry. Most commentators on Genesis, from John Chrysostom

---

1. The Antiochenes would use the pejorative term "the allegorists" to describe those guilty of such "fanciful liberties" and would prefer to grant primacy to the *historia* (narrative of events) and *skopos* (goal) of Scripture.

and Cyril of Alexandria to Ephrem the Syrian and many others, received from St. Paul the hermeneutical principle that "Christ is the end (*telos*) of the law" (Rom 10:4), and would, therefore, agree with Cyril that "*every* word of the holy prophets, including Moses, hints to the mystery of Christ," including the story of Joseph.[2] The brothers are types of the Pharisees and the Jews, Jacob of the Father, and the multicolored robe "is a symbol of the multiform glory with which God the Father clothed the Son made similar to us through his human nature."[3]

We are also enlightened by the placing of this treatment of Joseph and the overarching theme of conversion within the liturgical framework of Lenten catechesis. As such, the story of Joseph cannot be isolated either from the homilies on the rest of the Patriarchs, where Ambrose introduces many of the themes he now assumes, nor from the transformative expectations surrounding the baptismal initiation of his primary audience. One could argue that this Lenten environment gives Ambrose freedom to break with the strictly Origenist, or even neo-Platonic, trajectories of his own educational and ecclesial traditions and move away from the prevailing Hellenistic dualism between matter and spirit to a hermeneutic more closely following the Pauline distinction between "flesh" and "body,"[4] expressed in a robust sacramental theology of conversion and baptism. Salvation, then, is not the expected transcendence from the material through *anagōgē* (spiritual or mystical interpretation), but by faith in Christ and participation in the sacraments. As Smith puts it, "faith gains the catechumen access to the *sacramenta* (sacraments) of baptism and Eucharist. It is by faith in Christ's atoning death that the catechumen will gain forgiveness of her sins and have her soul healed of its disorder and divisions between the rational soul and the passions of unholy concupiscence."

What, then, of Joseph's brothers? Again, Smith has shown us clearly Ambrose's logic. It is through faith conferred by the Spirit in baptism that "the Christian is able to receive forgiveness of sin that the Law cannot give and participate in a sanctified humanity of the new creation that is able to resist the impulses of sinful concupiscence and instead burn with a greater love for God." Therefore Joseph's brothers have

---

2. Cyril of Alexandria, *Glaphyra on Genesis*, 5.4, ACCS 2, 228 (emphasis added).

3. Cyril of Alexandria, *Glaphyra on Genesis*, 6.4, ACCS 2, 232.

4. Ambrose did not follow the traditional (Plotinic) dualistic conceptions of the body as a corruptible (and therefore, corrupting) cage of the *pneuma* (spirit). As Colish notes, "for Ambrose the prison of our spirit is our irrational capitulation to sinful passions, whether they arise in the body, the mind, or both, and for which moderation and right reason are the antidotes" (Marcia L. Colish, *Ambrose's Patriarch's: Ethics for the Common Man*, Notre Dame, Ind.: University of Notre Dame Press, 2005, 130).

no means of salvation apart from their own identification with Joseph and his gracious acceptance of them into the new reality of his rule: "I am Joseph your brother!" (Gen 45:4). This, too, Ambrose gets from Paul.

As a result, Ambrose's concept of conversion as a complete identification with Christ becomes the *sine qua non* (essential condition) in his soteriology. As Smith shows us, in describing the washing of baptism, which is the "sacrament of illumination," Ambrose uses the example of Paul to argue that "it is through Paul's faith that the Jews come to know the justice of Christ. Although the Law is impotent to grant forgiveness, its instruction prepared Paul for faith."

A number of questions arise in this discussion of conversion, baptism, faith, and the Law. The obvious one is that of supersession: there is no question in any of the writers from Christian antiquity other than that the cult and its efficaciousness is now obsolete in Christ. Though I will leave the discussion of the merits of this principle to others, I am glad Smith closed his essay with the question of the incipient anti-Judaism that surrounds discussions of conversion. Of course it is anachronistic to speak of "anti-Semitism" in the fourth century, and though Ambrose's language and theology is less inflammatory than most, if it is true that language forms character, then the blatant anti-Jewish sentiment present in most patristic statements on the "Jews" has led to intolerance of the "obstinate" Jews who refuse to accept Christ. Listen to Cyril of Alexandria's language:

> And Joseph was loved by his father a great deal. And he gave him a multicolored garment . . . In fact, the Pharisees were inflamed with anger against the beloved, that is, Christ, because he had been clothed by God the Father with a multiform glory . . . (and Cyril concludes,) therefore for the reasons I have examined, the sons of the concubines were induced to anger and envy and became suspicious after the dream was related . . . and they gnashed their teeth and planned to kill him. And so the Jews were angered too, and not less afflicted, since they understood that the Immanuel would have been superior to the holy patriarchs themselves and would have been necessarily adored by all the world. And being aware of this, they said, 'This is the heir; come, let us kill him, and the inheritance will be ours.' (*Glaphyra on Genesis*, 6.4)

As one reads such comments one cannot but be reminded of Pliny's famous *Letter* 96 to Trajan: "If they persist, I order them to be led away for execution; for, whatever the nature of their admission, I am convinced that their stubbornness and unshakable obstinacy ought not to go unpunished."[5] Only Pliny was referring to Christians. Is obstinacy, then, a cause for intolerance, or does it only become such, and that is my second question, from a position of political and state power? In addition, one has to ask a final question, namely, what is salvation? And by extension, what is the relationship of conversion to salvation? For the pre-Theodosian writers,[6] especially in the Greek East, there is no question that the concepts of *metanoia* (repentance/conversion) and *anagennēsis* (new birth), are inextricably connected with the process of *sōtēria* (salvation), which begins in baptism and finds its fulfilment in the *eschaton* (end times). Yet, following the empire-wide conversion of the Roman State to Christianity in the late fourth-century, one has to question how the relationship between these elements has changed.

This study of Ambrose's theology of conversion provides us an outstanding opportunity to re-evaluate how the transformation of the process of conversion into a punctiliar event and the conflation of these concepts into the cipher of "conversion" has contributed to the individualization of Christian life and ethics.

---

5. Pliny, the Younger. *The Letters of the Younger Pliny* (trans. B. Radice; London: Penguin, 1969), 293.

6. On February 27, 380 Theodosius declared "Catholic Christianity" the only legitimate imperial religion and ended state support for the traditional Roman religion and on November 8, 392 he outlawed even its practices.

I THANK CHRIST JESUS OUR LORD
1 Timothy 1:12–17

Eric James Gréaux Sr.

I thank him who has given me strength for this Christ Jesus our Lord, because he judged me faithful by appointing me to his service, though I formerly blasphemed and persecuted and insulted him; but I received mercy because I had acted ignorantly in unbelief, and the grace of our Lord overflowed for me with the faith and love that are in Christ Jesus. The saying is sure and worthy of full acceptance, that Christ Jesus came into the world to save sinners. And I am the foremost of sinners; but I received mercy for this reason, that in me, as the foremost, Jesus Christ might display his perfect patience for an example to those who were to believe in him for eternal life. To the King of ages, immortal, invisible, the only God, be honor and glory for ever and ever. Amen.[1]

This letter from Paul is the first of three called the Pastoral Epistles. The Pastoral Epistles are 1 Timothy, 2 Timothy, and Titus. Unlike most of Paul's letters that were addressed to entire congregations, these three letters were written to Timothy, a pastor in Ephesus, and to Titus, a pastor in Crete. According to Acts 16:1, Timothy was "the son of a Jewish woman who was a believer" and a Greek father. Second Timothy 1:5 names his mother Eunice and grandmother Lois. After leaving Timothy's home in the city of Lystra, Paul took him on as his protégé. Paul thus became like a spiritual father to the young man, referring to him as "my true son in the faith" (1 Tim 1:2) and "my dear son" (2 Tim 1:2; cf. Phil 2:2). In 1 Corinthians, Paul calls him "my beloved and faithful child in the Lord" (4:17). Paul sent Timothy to that city "to remind [them] of [his, i.e., Paul's] ways in Christ" (1 Cor 4:17). Upon the conclusion of his Second Missionary Journey, Paul probably left him in Ephesus to lead that church. Now Paul writes to Timothy to give him guidance regarding the doctrinal purity and organization of the church, as well as some other personal matters. The instructions that Paul gives to Timothy are certainly applicable to us. We, too, are

---

1. Unless otherwise stated, all biblical quotations are from RSV.

heavily involved in the work of ministry and Paul has words of encouragement for us as well. We need to hear the reasons that Paul offers for giving thanks to Christ.

He Strengthened Me (v. 12a)

First, Paul says that Christ Jesus our Lord *strengthened* him. What a unique term to use—*strengthened* (Aorist tense). It implies a time when Paul was "weak." And that is the exact terminology he uses elsewhere to describe our life apart from Christ. In Romans 5:6, the Apostle declares, "While we were still *weak*, at the right time, Christ died for the ungodly." In other words, apart from Christ, we are weak, powerless, helpless, and impotent to do anything to remedy our sinful condition. Only through Christ can we find right standing before God.

That is what Paul experienced on the Damascus Road. Luke the physician narrates (Acts 9:1–19a), and then records Paul's own testimony (Acts 22:1–16; 26:9–18) of how Christ initially strengthened him by converting him, calling him, and entrusting him with this glorious gospel (Acts 26:11). But not only did the Lord strengthen him in the past by changing him, Christ *continues* to strengthen Paul in the present. You would not expect the mighty Paul to admit to needing strength. But that is exactly what he does:

> And to keep me from being too elated by the abundance of revelations, a thorn was given me in the flesh, a messenger of Satan, to harass me, to keep me from being too elated. Three times I besought the Lord about this, that it should leave me; but he said to me, "My grace is sufficient for you, for my power is made perfect in weakness." I will all the more gladly boast of my weaknesses, that the power of Christ may rest upon me. For the sake of Christ, then, I am content with weaknesses, insults, hardships, persecutions, and calamities; for when I am weak, then I am strong. (2 Cor 12:7–10)

To be honest, there are times when we do not always feel "strong in the Lord and in the power of his might" (Eph 6:10). We all have periods of discouragement. When you find yourself in that predicament, go to Christ because Christ will continue to strengthen you.

- Are you *worn-out* by the constant demands of your job?   Christ will strengthen you.

- Are you *discouraged* by your lack of professional growth?   Christ will strengthen you.

- Are you *frustrated* at trying to make ends meet?   Christ will strengthen you.

- Are you *drained* from the pull in all directions (family, friends, spouse, church, school, office)?   Christ will strengthen you.

- Are you *overwhelmed* by the responsibilities of church work? And homework? And job-work? And deadlines? And more deadlines?   Christ will strengthen you.

- Are you *inundated* with your schedule: attending classes, studying for exams, writing research papers, and the constant reading of books; taking more classes, writing more papers and reading more books?   Christ will strengthen you.

The apostle Paul assures us that we do not need to worry or be anxious. He instructs us to stop wringing our hands and losing sleep. We serve a God who enables us; he strengthens us; he gives us power! He can do this because it is his character. In 1 Sam 15:29, God is called the Strength of Israel. The Psalmist tells us that he is the Lord who is the strength of his people (Ps 28:8). That is why Paul can declare with confidence, "I can do all things through Christ who strengthens me" (Phil 4:13). I can do all things: I can persevere through abundance and lack, I can endure prosperity and poverty, and I can persist when things are going well and not so well. I can do all things through Christ who strengthens me; Christ gives us strength. Paul said, "I thank Christ Jesus our Lord who strengthens me." That same strength that called us into a relationship with Jesus Christ also gives us strength to live a life pleasing to him.

The text says that Christ strengthened Paul because he considered him faithful. What does this mean? It could mean God knew that Paul was a trustworthy person (in the past) and therefore appointed him to ministry. But that's contrary to the thrust of the entire paragraph. Salvation and service are not merited or earned; they are by grace and mercy. On the contrary, I think Paul is saying that God knew he would be trustworthy in the future and therefore appointed him to serve in the present. In other words, God knew that Paul would be faithful and so he appointed Paul to ministry.

God knew that you would be faithful. That is why he placed you here in this ministry. He knew that the gifts and abilities you have would fit where you are placed. To use Paul's body imagery from 1 Cor 12—the Lord knew you would make a good hand, arm, or elbow; leg, foot, or knee; finger, toe, or toenail. He knew that you would thrive as a college professor or employee at the seminary. He knew you would work well with youth. God knew that, given the opportunity, you would share your faith. Paul calls it all service, ministry. And it is one reason that Paul proffers for giving praise to Christ Jesus our Lord.

He Put Me into Ministry (v. 12b)

The second reason why Paul thanks Christ is that he "appointed me to his service." What service? He gives the answer in verse 11, namely, the proclamation of this glorious gospel (cf. 3:16). Whether or not we are ordained ministers, all of us play a role in getting the gospel out to others. This stands in contrast to the error of the false teachers who turned away from the sound instruction that results in love flowing from a pure heart, a good conscience and sincere faith:

> *Certain persons by swerving from these have wandered away into vain discussion, desiring to be teachers of the law, without understanding either what they are saying or the things about which they make assertions. Now we know that the law is good, if any one uses it lawfully, understanding this, that the law is not laid down for the just but for the lawless and disobedient, for the ungodly and sinners, for the unholy and profane, for murderers of fathers and murderers of mothers, for manslayers, immoral persons, sodomites, kidnappers, liars, perjurers, and whatever else is contrary to sound doctrine, in accordance with the glorious gospel of the blessed God with which I have been entrusted.* (1 Tim 1:6–11)

Paul says that any teachings that are opposed to this glorious gospel must be stamped out (1 Tim 1:3). And the primary way to do that is by the faithful exposition of the Scriptures and careful instruction on how to put the word into practice. No wonder Paul said in his final letter to Timothy, "Preach the word..." (cf. 2 Tim 4:1–5). Thank God for pastors that preach the word of God/the truth. Thank God for those professors and scholars who join them in teaching the word of God and sound theology. For it is the anointed preaching and teaching of the word that saves the lost, delivers the bound, and heals the sick.

Paul says Christ gave me this ministry of preaching and teaching because he reckoned me faithful. He gave you a ministry because he knew you would be faithful. He gave you a ministry as a husband, wife, father, mother, teacher, instructor, administrator, youth pastor, and/or worker in the business world. Christ gave you a ministry because he knew you would be faithful. Are you living up to Jesus' expectations? The Bible says, "It is required of stewards that they be found trustworthy" (1 Cor 4:2). Are you being faithful? Are you being trustworthy? Have you demonstrated yourself to be worthy of God's trust? Or are you cutting corners? Are you shirking your responsibilities?

If you are faithful, then great! Keep doing it. Thank God for your faithfulness and service as unto the Lord. Thank God for sticking to the task of this glorious gospel. If not, why not? That is why he saved you. So then:

1. I thank Christ because he strengthened me
2. I thank Christ because he judged me faithful and gave me a ministry

He gave me mercy

The final reason Paul offers for giving Christ thanks is because he received mercy. And here, once again, Paul describes his conversion. Two times Paul says, "I received mercy" (v 13b, 16a). Right standing before God cannot be earned. It is not based upon human merit. Salvation is not deserved; it's by grace. It's something you receive. We cannot earn our way into God's goodness/heaven. God calls all such attempts (i.e., our warped concepts of righteousness) filthy rags (Isa 64:6)! You cannot earn your way into heaven. In Ephesians 2:8, Paul reminds us that it is all by grace: "For by grace you have been saved through faith; and this is not your own doing, it is the gift of God—not because of works, lest any man should boast." According to Romans 10:9–10, the only way to come into a right relationship with God is through repentance from sins, through faith in the finished work of Jesus, and through accepting the gospel.

Paul gives his testimony and describes his conversion. He reviews the first chapter of his autobiography and he says (v. 13), ". . . I was a blasphemer . . . I was a persecutor . . . I was an insolent person" *but*—Chapter Two: I received mercy. Chapter One: I am the foremost of sinners (v. 15b) *but*—Chapter Two: I received mercy. "But" is the adversative conjunction that makes a difference (cf. Eph 2:1–7).

"And the *grace* of God overflowed for me" (v.14). This reminds me of Rom 5:20—"Where sin did abound, grace super-abounded." This grace is unmerited favor that we did not earn, we don't deserve, and we can never repay. Grace is God: God pardoning our sins, blotting out transgressions, snatching us from the gates of a fiery hell, cleansing us from the stain of filthy iniquity, redeeming us from the clutches of Satan's grip, and picking us up from that horrible pit. In the words of hymn writer Julia Johnston:

> *Grace, grace. God's grace. Grace that can pardon and cleanse within.*
>
> *Grace, grace. God's grace. Grace that is greater than all my sin.*[2]

No wonder that John Newton called it *Amazing Grace*!

Paul continues in v. 14: faith overflowed—to counter Paul's lack of faith; love overflowed—so that Paul could love those he formerly persecuted, Christ and Christians. Paul is giving his testimony and, every once in a while, you too should remember those things that are behind you (cf. Phil 3:3–16); go fishing in that Sea of Forgetfulness and recall what you did before you got saved. This is not the time to have a memory lapse. This is not the time to have spiritual Alzheimer's disease. Paul remembered and you ought to remember. You were not always saved. It's all the mercy and the grace and the love of God! This is the motivation for thanks. This is the motivation for service.

When Paul looks back over his life and sees what Jesus Christ did for him, his response is praise (v. 12). When *I* reflect on my life and see what Jesus Christ did for *me*, *my* response is nothing but praise. But what then are the consequences of this? What are the faithful actions that are part of this praise? I have three points to make in closing:

1. Do not *deny* God's grace. Embrace it. Relish it. Bask in it.

2. Do not *de-convert*. Stay at the task. Once again, the apostle Paul exhorts, "... wage the good warfare, holding faith and a good conscience" (1 Tim 1:18b–19a).

3. Do not *distort* the message. The greatest thanks you can give to Christ is your lifestyle.

Do not say one thing and live another. Like it or not, people look to us to display authentic Christianity. So don't mess up your witness with a shoddy lifestyle.

Finally, reflect again on Paul's words:

> *I thank him who has given me strength for this, Christ Jesus our Lord, because he judged me faithful by appointing me to his service, though I for-*

---

2. Julia H. Johnston, *Hymns Tried and True* (Chicago: The Bible Institute Colportage Association, 1911), no. 2.

> *merly blasphemed and persecuted and insulted him; but I received mercy* (1 Tim 1:12–13).

And apply these words again to your own life:

- Christ strengthened me.
- Christ placed me in ministry.
- Christ showed me mercy.

Father, seal your words in our heart and cause us by the work of your Spirit to bear fruit that brings your honor and glory and praise and blessing to you. We ask these things in the name of your son, Jesus. Amen.

ANNOTATED BIBLIOGRAPHY

Apuleius. *Metamorphoses.* Translated by J. A. Hanson. 2 vols. Loeb Classical Library 44 and 453. Cambridge, Mass.: Harvard University Press, 1989. Also known as *The Golden Ass*, this novel from the second century C.E. tells the story of the young man Lucius, whose incautious fascination with sex and magic results in his transformation into an ass. After many adventures, the final Book 11 sees him turned back into a human being through the agency of the goddess Isis and he undergoes ritual initiation into her cult. It is a crucial text for any consideration of conversion in Greco-Roman religion.

Armstrong, Guyda, and Ian Wood, editors. *Christianizing Peoples and Converting Individuals.* International Medieval Research 7. Turnhout: Brepols, 2000. This diverse collection of essays deals with topics in conversion across the wide geographical and chronological expanse of medieval Europe and Central Asia.

Augustine. *Confessions.* Translated by Henry Chadwick. Oxford World's Classics. Oxford: Oxford University Press, 1992. Alongside Paul, Augustine may be the most famous convert in the history of Christianity. In addition to autobiographical accounts of Augustine's many conversions, ultimately resulting in his baptism into the Christian church, his *Confessions* contain a wealth of theological exploration of the nature of humanity and God.

Baillie, John. *Baptism and Conversion.* New York: Charles Scribner's Sons, 1963. Baillie's treatise covers in concise form the history of western Christian thought on conversion. Either baptism (Roman, Lutheran, Calvinist/Reformed) or experience of psychological crisis (Baptist/Free) are seen as the decisive dimension of conversion. Baillie tracks Evangelical Christianity's movement towards the latter and offers a corrective from the perspective of older church traditions.

Beale, Greg K. *The Temple and the Church's Mission: A Biblical Theology of the Dwelling Place of God.* New Studies in Biblical Theology 17. Downers Grove, IL: InterVarsity, 2004. This is a study of the dwelling of God with his people as it unfolds in Scripture, even until the eschaton. It is exegetical in approach and shows in manifold ways how people and institutions are transformed by their encounter with, and response to, God's presence.

Bolsinger, Tod E. *It Takes a Church to Raise a Christian: How the Community of God Transforms Lives.* Grand Rapids: Brazos, 2004. The author argues that personal transformation requires the practices of Christian community, centered upon Word and Sacrament, through which the life of the Triune God is expressed in our everyday world.

Buckser, Andrew, and Stephen D. Glazier, editors. *The Anthropology of Religious Conversion.* Lanham, MD: Rowman and Littlefield, 2003. This is a diverse collection of essays, all employing anthropological methods to study conversion. A critical introduction and overview from Lewis Rambo is included.

Bulkeley, Kelly. *The Wondering Brain: Thinking about Religion with and beyond Cognitive Neuroscience*. New York: Routledge, 2004. This groundbreaking study explores the experience of wonder, integrating insights from religious studies, cognitive neuroscience, and evolutionary psychology. Although not directly about conversion, its relevance to understanding conversion as an experience is clear.

Chesnutt, Randall D. *From Death to Life: Conversion in Joseph and Aseneth*. Journal for the Study of the Pseudepigrapha, Supplemental Series 16. Sheffield: Sheffield Academic Press, 1995. This monograph argues the sober view that *Joseph and Aseneth* is a Diaspora intertestamental Jewish novel that uses Aseneth's conversion to address the impropriety of the patriarch marrying a Gentile woman. In so doing it upholds the status of Gentile converts within Jewish communities. The analysis is thorough and quite technical.

Chester, Stephen J. *Conversion at Corinth: Perspectives on Conversion in Paul's Theology and the Corinthian Church*. Studies of the New Testament and Its World. New York: T. & T. Clark, 2003. Chester provides a study of conversion in Paul's theology, including his use of the vocabulary of calling and his distinct approaches to the conversion of Gentiles and to his own conversion as a Jew. The influence of Greco-Roman social structures and practices upon perspectives of conversion within the Corinthian church is also explored.

Cleveland, Ray. *Embracing The Kingdom: A Bible Study On Conversion*. Emmaus Journey Bible Study. Ijamsville, Md.: Word Among Us Press, 2002. This is a popular but solid work, written from a Roman Catholic perspective, which leads study groups through relevant biblical texts and the process of Christian conversion.

Collins, Kevin J., and John H. Tyson, editors. *Conversion in the Wesleyan Tradition*. Nashville: Abingdon, 2001. Organized into historical, biblical, theological, and pastoral sections, this collection of essays explores various aspects of conversion in the Wesleyan tradition.

Colson, Charles. *Born Again*. Old Tappan, N.J.: Chosen, 1976. New edition with new introduction and epilogue. Grand Rapids: Chosen, 2008. Colson, a former aide of President Nixon, offers an autobiographical account of his conversion in the context of disgrace and imprisonment in the aftermath of Watergate.

Corbin Reuschling, Wyndy. *Reviving Evangelical Ethics: The Promises and Pitfalls of Classic Models of Morality*. Grand Rapids: Brazos, 2008. The author seeks a biblical basis for Christian ethics that respects and learns from classical ethical theories but is not bound by any of them. Important themes in the ethical dimension of conversion arise in the process.

Crook, Zeba A. *Reconceptualising Conversion: Patronage, Loyalty, and Conversion in the Religions of the Ancient Mediterranean*. Beihefte zur Zeitschrift für die neutestamentliche Wissenschaft und die Kunde der älteren Kirche 130. New York: Walter de Gruyter, 2004. Crook challenges what he considers anachronistic psychologized approaches to Paul's conversion and instead interprets Paul's statements about his conversion against the backdrop of ancient practices of patronage and the social dynamic of loyalty.

Davis Patricia M., and Lewis R. Rambo. "Converting: Toward a Cognitive Theory of Religious Change." Pages 159–73 in *Soul, Psyche, Brain: New Directions in the Study of Brain-mind Science*. Edited by Kelly Bulkeley. New York: Palgrave: Macmillan, 2005. This essay attempts to draw out the implications for conversion studies of Bulkeley's work on the relationship between religious experience and cognitive neuroscience.

Diogenes Laertius. *Lives of Eminent Philosophers*. Translated by R. D. Hicks. 2 vols. Loeb Classical Library 184–85. Cambridge, Mass.: Harvard University Press, 1925. Laertius wrote in the third century C.E. and his biographies contain a number of accounts of those skeptical about the life of philosophy who experience what can be termed a conversion to that path.

Donaldson, Terence L. *Judaism and the Gentiles: Jewish Patterns of Universalism (to 135 CE)*. Waco, Tex.: Baylor University Press, 2007. This is a detailed study of ways in which ancient Judaism thought about Gentiles. Judaism had a universal outlook on divine revelation as a result of it monotheism, but no uniform view on how best to relate to Gentiles or on their place in God's future purposes.

Donovan, Vincent J. *Christianity Rediscovered*. 25th Anniversary Edition. Maryknoll, NY: Orbis, 2003. This is an autobiographical account by a Catholic priest of his time in mission among pastoral tribes in East Africa. Donovan argues that effective mission requires respect for indigenous cultures and careful attention to the means by which the gospel may be discovered and contextualized within those cultures.

Dujarier, Michel. *A History of the Catechumenate: The First Six Centuries*. Translated by Edward J. Haasl. New York: Sadlier, 1979. Dujarier argues that the Catechumenate was both vigorous and rigorous while the church existed on the margins of ancient society, but that it underwent decline in the post-Constantinian era as the meaning of conversion changed.

Feldman, Lewis H. *Jew and Gentile in the Ancient World: Attitudes and Interactions from Alexander to Justinian*. Princeton, N.J.: Princeton University Press, 1993. This is a study by a Jewish scholar of all kinds of Jewish/Gentile interactions in the ancient world. It includes the argument that Judaism was a missionary religion and did seek to make converts.

Ferguson, Everett. *Baptism in the Early Church: History, Theology, and Liturgy in the First Five Centuries*. Grand Rapids: Eerdmans, 2009. Ferguson provides a comprehensive critical discussion (over 950 pages) of almost everything known about baptism in the early centuries of church history.

Fletcher, Richard. *The Barbarian Conversion: From Paganism to Christianity*. Berkeley, Calif.: University of California Press, 1999. This book is a magisterial narrative history of the conversion of Europe to Christianity covering a thousand years and a comprehensive range of contexts.

Fowler, James W. *Stages of Faith: the Psychology of Human Development and the Quest for Meaning*. San Francisco: Harper & Row, 1981. Fowler's work weds personal experience with sophisticated sociological and psychological theory. The focus of Part V is specifically on conversion and is not limited to the Christian faith. Theoretical discussion is preceded by a case study, giving concrete form to the discussion of stages and processes of conversion.

Fredriksen, Paula. "Paul and Augustine: Conversion Narratives, Orthodox Traditions and the Retrospective Self." *Journal of Theological Studies* 37 (1986) 3–34. Conversion narratives are approached as exercises in legitimating a convert's present. They are apologetic and anachronistic accounts through which a past and a self are created to support that present.

Frisk, Donald C. *The New Life in Christ*. Chicago: Covenant, 1969. The opening chapter contains an extended discussion of conversion from the perspective of the Evangelical Covenant Church. Frisk characteristically moves from treatments of scripture to practical ecclesiological concerns. The roots of the Evangelical Covenant Church are highlighted in Lutheranism, in believer's church traditions, and in Pietism.

Gaventa, Beverly. *From Darkness to Light: Aspects of Conversion in the New Testament*. Overtures to Biblical Theology 20. Philadelphia: Fortress, 1986. This is an early attempt to apply social-scientific resources to the study of conversion in the NT. Although a little dated in its theoretical aspects, the book remains exegetically insightful.

Gelston, Anthony. "Universalism in Second Isaiah." *Journal of Theological Studies* 43 (1992) 377–98. Gelston explores the theme in Isaiah of the place in the divine plan of Israel's call to be a witness to all nations.

Goldenberg, Robert. *The Nations That Know Thee Not: Ancient Jewish Attitudes toward Other Religions*. Reappraisals in Jewish Social and Intellectual History. New York: New York University Press, 1998. This detailed volume explores the variety of Jewish perspectives on other religious beliefs and practices. Goldenberg suggests that there was no consensus on whether and how Judaism should reach out to other religious traditions.

Goodman, M. *Mission and Conversion: Proselytizing in the History of the Roman Empire*. Oxford: Clarendon, 1994. Contra Feldman (*Jew and Gentile in the Ancient World*), this historical study, also by a Jewish scholar, argues that ancient Judaism was not a missionary religion and did not characteristically seek converts.

Gooren, Henri Paul Pierre. "Reassessing Conventional Approaches to Conversion: Towards a New Synthesis." *Journal for the Scientific Study of Religion* 46.3 (2007) 337–53. This is the most recent of several articles in which Gooren is developing a new approach to the study of conversion careers. He distinguishes five levels of religious participation which are influenced by a range of different factors: personality factors, social factors, institutional factors, cultural factors, and contingency factors. The only major new social scientific approach to studying conversion since Rambo's *Understanding Religious Conversion*, Gooren's approach is stated fully in his *Religious Conversion and Disaffiliation: Tracing Patterns of Change in Faith Practices* (Palgrave MacMillan, 2010).

Green, Joel B. *Body, Soul, and Human Life: The Nature of Humanity in the Bible.* Studies in Theological Interpretation. Grand Rapids: Baker, 2008. Green presents a multi-disciplinary approach helpful for understanding the dynamics of human formation. Of particular note is chapter 4, which has a focus on conversion.

Green, Michael. *Evangelism in the Early Church.* Grand Rapids: Eerdmans, 1970. This study traces the evangelistic activity of the early church from its beginnings to the middle of the third century C.E. Green is interested in what can be known historically about evangelism and particularly what this reveals of missionary strategy.

Greenlee, David H. *One Cross, One Way, Many Journeys: Thinking Again about Conversion.* London: Authentic, 2007. Blending anthropological, missiological, and theological perspectives, Greenlee considers whether the term conversion remains helpful in the contemporary world and whether it is best understood as an event or a process.

Guder, Darrell L. *The Continuing Conversion of the Church.* The Gospel and Our Culture Series. Grand Rapids: Eerdmans, 2000. Guder argues that the church has lost its proper sense of being sent by God and calls for a return to intentional mission.

Hayes, Christine Elizabeth. *Gentile Impurities and Jewish Identities: Intermarriage and Conversion from the Bible to the Talmud.* Oxford: Oxford University Press, 2002. A detailed and technical discussion of conversion to Judaism through marriage as discussed in Scripture and in the rabbinic sources.

Hefner, Robert W. *Conversion to Christianity: Historical and Anthropological Perspectives on a Great Transformation.* Berkeley, Calif.: University of California Press, 1993. Largely written by anthropologists, these essays focus on interactions between Christianity and 'traditional' religions, especially issues surrounding the perceived rationality (or otherwise) of the conversion process.

Hempton, David. *Evangelical Disenchantment: Nine Portraits of Faith and Doubt.* New Haven, Conn.: Yale University Press, 2008. Nine case studies are presented of well-known figures like George Eliot (Mary Ann Evans) who embraced evangelical faith only subsequently to turn away from it, especially for moral reasons. Hempton challenges Evangelicals' understanding of conversion and probes the implications of their actions and attitudes.

Hengel, Martin, and Anna Maria Schwemer. *Paul Between Damascus and Antioch: the Unknown Years.* Translated by John Bowden. Louisville: Westminster John Knox, 1997. This volume is the successor to Hengel's *The Pre-Christian Paul* and begins from the point of Paul's conversion. Exegesis is combined with archaeological and literary study to present a portrait of Paul in the early years after his conversion.

Hiebert, Paul G. *Transforming Worldviews: An Anthropological Understanding of How People Change.* Grand Rapids: Baker, 2008. Missiologists have often concentrated on changes in belief and behavior as evidence of conversion. Hiebert argues that a change in worldview is also necessary for effective biblical mission.

Hindmarsh, D. Bruce. *The Evangelical Conversion Narrative: Spiritual Autobiography in Early Modern England*. Oxford: Oxford University Press, 2005. This is a study of the emergence of the conversion narrative as a recognizable genre in early modern England. The complex relationships are examined between the conversion experiences described and their social and historical contexts.

Holladay, William L. *The Root Šûbh in the Old Testament: With Particular Reference to Its Usages in Covenantal Contexts*. Leiden: Brill, 1958. This monograph explores key Hebrew vocabulary expressing the idea of change of loyalty. It is used in the OT, especially by Jeremiah, to express the idea of Israel either returning to evil or returning from evil to covenant loyalty to Yahweh.

James, W. *The Varieties of Religious Experience: A Study in Human Nature*. New York: Penguin, 1982; original 1902. James provides *the* classic text in the scientific study of conversion which has influenced all subsequent work. He considers conversion critically but sympathetically from a psychological perspective.

Jones, E. Stanley. *The Christ of the Indian Road*. New York: Abingdon, 1925. Written during the early years of the Indian Independence Movement, this study provides important background for the work of the Church Growth movement a few decades later. It also provides a scathing critique for western Christians of their concepts of conversion and considers how these hinder the conversion of non-westerners.

Joseph and Aseneth. Translated with introduction by C. Burchard. Pages 177–248 in *The Old Testament Pseudepigrapha*, vol. 2. Edited by James H. Charlesworth. New York: Doubleday, 1983–85. This primary source, probably intertestamental in date, fills in gaps in the Genesis narrative by telling the story of the conversion to Judaism of the daughter of the Egyptian Pharaoh and her marriage to Joseph. Scholarly theories about the origins and purpose of the text range widely.

Kim, Seyoon, *The Origin of Paul's Gospel*. Tübingen: Mohr (Siebeck), 1981. In this detailed exegetical study Kim argues that the major themes of Paul's theology, especially his doctrine of justification, derive from his conversion experience of Christ as the image (*eikon*) of God.

Kreider, Alan. *The Change of Conversion and the Origin of Christendom*. Christian Mission and Modern Culture. Harrisburg, Pa.: Trinity, 1999. Kreider argues that between the second and sixth centuries C.E. what it meant to become a convert to Christianity changed and developed. Conversion itself has an evolving history.

Lamb, Christopher, and M. Darrol Bryant, editors. *Religious Conversion: Contemporary Practices and Controversies*. Issues in Contemporary Religion. London: Cassell, 1999. This volume includes essays on theoretical perspectives on conversion, conversion in world religions, conversion to Christianity, and various specific cases of conversion.

Lewis, C. S. *Surprised by Joy: The Shape of My Early Life*. Harvest Book. New York: Harcourt, Brace, 1955. From its publication this has been an influential autobiographical description of the spiritual journey of the Oxford English professor who became a reluctant convert and later a theologian and Christian apologist.

Lofland, John and N. Skonovd, "Conversion Motifs." *Journal for the Scientific Study of Religion* 20 (1981) 373–85. As the title indicates, this article provides a suggestive classification of conversion experiences into different categories or motifs.

Lofland, John, and Rodney Stark, "Becoming a World-Saver: A Theory of Conversion to a Deviant Perspective." *American Sociological Review* 30 (1965) 862–75. This is a very influential sociological article on the early career of the "Moonies" in North America. Unlike earlier work it emphasized not only the psychological predispositions of converts, but also the part played in conversion by social processes such as the formation of affective ties.

Longenecker, Richard N., editor. *The Road from Damascus: The Impact of Paul's Conversion on his Life, Thought, and Ministry*. McMaster New Testament Studies. Grand Rapids: Eerdmans, 1997. Essays in this volume explore the impact of Paul's conversion experience on his theology and ethics. Contributors consider the ways in which Paul's experience serves as a paradigm for Christian thought and action today, and a chapter on the history of interpretation of Paul's conversion is also included.

MacMullen, Ramsay. *Christianizing the Roman Empire (A.D. 100–400)*. New Haven, Conn.: Yale University Press, 1984. This study by a leading historian examines the means by which the Roman Empire became Christian. The persuasive power of the miracles believed to have been wrought by the Christian God is emphasized.

McKnight, Scott. *A Light among the Gentiles: Jewish Missionary Activity in the Second Temple Period*. Minneapolis: Fortress, 1991. McKnight argues that while Judaism was not a missionary religion with a clear goal of the conversion of the world or an organized missionary effort, Jewish communities were open to receiving Gentile converts. Included is discussion of "God-fearers," Gentiles who became attached to Judaism and participated in synagogue worship.

———. *Turning to Jesus: The Sociology of Conversion in the Gospels*. Louisville: Westminster John Knox, 2002. Contemporary social-scientific studies of conversion are applied to the experience of the disciples in the Gospels in order to suggest that their gradual emergence into full faith is more typical of conversion than sudden transformation.

McKnight, Scott, and Hauna Ondrey. *Finding Faith, Losing Faith: Stories of Conversion and Apostasy*. Waco, Tex.: Baylor University Press, 2008. This study seeks to identify the common threads, and their pastoral implications, in contemporary accounts of conversion from Christianity to secularity, Judaism to Christianity, Evangelicalism to Catholicism and vice versa.

Meilaender, Gilbert. *The Freedom of a Christian: Grace, Vocation, and the Meaning of Our Humanity.* Grand Rapids: Brazos, 2006. A Lutheran theological ethicist here offers a series of essays reflecting on the relationships between freedom, vocation, and ways of living in the world consonant with Christian faith.

Méndez-Moratalla, Fernando. *The Paradigm of Conversion in Luke.* Journal for the Study of the New Testament, Supplemental Series 252. New York: T. & T. Clark, 2004. This monograph explores the Gospel of Luke, suggesting that Luke contains a consistent, although not invariable, paradigm of conversion to which repentance is central.

Mills, Kenneth, and Grafton, Anthony, editors. *Conversion in Late Antiquity and the Early Middle Ages: Seeing and Believing.* Studies in Comparative History. Rochester, N.Y.: University of Rochester Press, 2003. This is a diverse collection of essays by historians considering the interplay between social processes and the singular conversion events described by ancient and medieval writers.

———. *Conversion: Old Worlds and New.* Studies in Comparative History. Rochester, N.Y.: University of Rochester Press, 2003. This is another diverse collection of essays by historians considering conversion to Christianity over a broad expanse of time and space. Cases are discussed from the thirteenth to the twentieth century and from settings across the world.

Morrison, Karl Frederick. *Conversion and Text: The Cases of Augustine of Hippo, Herman-Judah, and Constantine Tsatsos.* Charlottesville: University of Virginia Press, 1992. Morrison argues that there is nothing to distinguish autobiographical conversion accounts from fictional ones. Text and experience can only be related to each other in fictive ways.

———. *Understanding Conversion.* Charlottesville: University of Virginia Press, 1992. Regarding conversion as a specifically western concept, Morrison disputes that any universal definition of conversion is possible. An account of conversion in twelfth century monasticism is provided that highlights its continuous life-long nature in contrast to the abrupt nature of conversion in other contexts.

Muldoon, James, editor. *Varieties of Religious Conversion in the Middle Ages.* Gainesville: University of Florida Press, 1997. As the title suggests, this volume explores the diversity of experiences and events to which the label conversion was applied in Christianity during the medieval period.

Nock, Arthur Darby. *Conversion: The Old and the New in Religion from Alexander the Great to Augustine of Hippo.* Oxford: Oxford University Press, 1933; reprinted by John Hopkins University Press, 1998. Nock's classic study of religious change in the ancient world defines conversion as characteristic of Judaism and Christianity but alien to Greco-Roman religion. Nock's vast knowledge of historical detail and ability to synthesize continue to command respect, but his definition of conversion is now widely challenged.

Partridge, Christopher H., and Helen Reid, editors. *Finding and Losing Faith: Studies in Conversion.* Studies in Religion and Culture. Milton Keynes, UK: Paternoster: 2006. As part of a series exploring diverse aspects of religion and culture, this volume includes essays on conversion to Christianity and on conversion in post-Christian and multi-faith (Buddhist, Hindu, Muslim, Jewish, Sikh) contexts.

Peace, Richard. *Conversion in the New Testament: Paul and the Twelve.* Grand Rapids: Eerdmans, 1999. Peace argues that the conversion experiences of Paul and the twelve disciples offer a contrast between sudden transformation and more gradual change, and that it is an error to regard sudden transformation as normative.

Percy, Martyn. *Previous Convictions: Conversion in the Present Day.* London: SPCK, 2000. A lecture series entitled "Why Do People Change?" gave rise to this miscellaneous collection of essays on various aspects of conversion.

Pettit, Norman. *The Heart Prepared: Grace and Conversion in Puritan Spiritual Life.* 2nd edition. Middletown, Conn.: Wesleyan University Press, 1989. Pettit's historical study of Puritanism explores the tension between concepts of sudden grace and belief in the necessity of careful preparation for conversion through self-examination.

Pickett, J. W., A. L. Warnshuis, G. H. Singh, and D.A. McGavran. *Church Growth and Group Conversion.* Foreword by John R. Mott. 4th edition. Lucknow, India: Lucknow, 1962. A classic study originating from the mission field, this book eventually became significant for the development of the Church Growth Movement.

Popp-Baier, U., "Conversion as a Social Construction: A Narrative Approach to Conversion Research." Pages 41–61 in *Social Constructionism and Theology.* Edited by C. A. M. Hermans, Gerrit Immink, Aad de Jong, and Johannes A. van der Lans. Empirical Studies in Theology 7. Leiden: Brill, 2002. This article explores the way in which social context shapes the language used in conversion accounts and enables converts to construct new identities.

Rambo, Lewis R. *Understanding Religious Conversion.* New Haven, CT: Yale University Press, 1993. In what is undoubtedly the most influential work on conversion of recent decades, Rambo proposes a seven stage process model of conversion applicable to experiences of conversion in a wide range of religious traditions and social contexts.

Rambo, Lewis R., and Farhadian, C. E. "Conversion." Pages 1969–74 in *Encyclopedia of Religion.* Vol. 3. Edited by L. Jones. 2nd Edition. Detroit: Thompson & Gale, 2005. This short entry provides a helpful introduction to major currents within the academic study of conversion.

———, editors. *The Oxford Handbook of Religious Conversion.* New York: Oxford University Press, forthcoming. This volume will provide a significant reference resource for those exploring different approaches to the study of conversion.

Rambo, Lewis R., and Reh, L. A. "The Phenomenology of Conversion." Pages 229–58 in *Handbook of Religious Conversion.* Edited by H. N. Malony and S. Southard. Birmingham, Ala.: Religious Education Press, 1992. Rambo and Reh provide an exploration of the difficulties involved in using words to describe experiences. Their method provides some standard vocabulary for describing the conversion experiences of individuals.

Reuschling, Wyndy Corbin. *Reviving Evangelical Ethics: The Promises and Pitfalls of Classic Models of Morality.* Grand Rapids: Brazos, 2008. The author seeks a biblical basis for Christian ethics that respects and learns from classical ethical theories but is not bound by any of them. Important themes in the ethical dimension of conversion arise in the process.

Richardson, J. "The Active vs. Passive Convert: Paradigm Conflict in Conversion/Recruitment Research." *Journal for the Scientific Study of Religion* 24 (1985) 163–79. In the 1970s and 1980s cults in North America were often accused of employing duress or brainwashing techniques in order to secure converts. This is one of a number of studies that emphasize instead the active part played by converts in their own transformation.

Rink, Tobias. "An Inter-disciplinary Perspective on Conversion." *Missionalia* 53 (2007) 18–43. This short article provides a straightforward introduction to some of the major approaches (religious, sociological, psychological) to studying conversion.

Sanders, Jack T. *Charisma, Converts, Competitors: Societal Factors in the Success of Early Christianity.* London: SCM, 2000. Sanders argues that conversion to early Christianity should be studied in the context of its competitors. Christianity offered similar social benefits to other cults but ultimately succeeded over them because of its cohesiveness, adaptability, and greater attention to the sick and to women.

Schnabel, Eckhard J. *Early Christian Mission.* 2 Vols. Vol. 1: *Jesus and the Twelve.* Vol. 2: *Paul and the Early Church.* Downers Grove, Ill.: InterVarsity, 2004. In two volumes and nearly 2000 pages, Schnabel provides a comprehensive critical study of the historical and theological foundations of Christian mission.

Segal, Alan F. *Paul the Convert: The Apostolate and Apostasy of Saul the Pharisee.* New Haven, Conn.: Yale University Press, 1990. Segal employs contemporary social-scientific studies of conversion to argue that although Paul remained Jewish after his Damascus road experience, the radical change he experienced nevertheless justifies the label 'convert'.

Shumate, Nancy. *Crisis and Conversion in Apuleius' Metamorphoses.* Ann Arbor: University of Michigan Press, 1996. Shumate argues that Lucius experiences the collapse of one cognitive paradigm through which he makes sense of the world and its replacement by another. He is a convert in a sense that Nock (*Conversion: The Old and the New in Religion from Alexander the Great to Augustine of Hippo*) denied was possible within Greco-Roman religion.

Smith, Gordon T. *Beginning Well: Christian Conversion and Authentic Transformation.* Downers Grove, Ill.: InterVarsity, 2001. Smith examines the many dimensions of conversion with the intention of recovering its centrality for Christian faith and practice.

———. *Transforming Conversion: Rethinking the Language and Contours of Christian Initiation.* Grand Rapids: Baker, 2010.

Smith, Rob. *Leading Christians to Christ: Evangelizing the Church.* Harrisburg, Pa.: Morehouse, 1990. Smith explores the reality of nominal Christianity from an Episcopalian perspective and considers ways in which the liturgical practices of the church may be effective in promoting conversion. Some sections focus exclusively on the Book of Common Prayer, but others are applicable to all denominational backgrounds.

Snow, D. A. and Machalek, R. "The Convert as a Social Type." Pages 259–89 in *Sociological Theory 1983*. Edited by Randall Collins. Jossey-Bass Social and Behavioral Science Series. San Francisco: Jossey-Bass, 1983. This article attempts to define the convert as a distinct social type on the basis of the different changes made by individuals in order actively to embrace the role of convert.

Spohn, William. *Go and Do Likewise: Jesus and Ethics*. New York: Continuum, 1999. Spohn grounds an ethics of character and virtue in the story of Jesus and the practices of Christian spirituality. The importance of the Christian community for continual conversion and growth is emphasized.

Stark, Rodney. *The Rise of Christianity: A Sociologist Reconsiders History*. Princeton, N.J.: Princeton University Press, 1996. A veteran social scientist, Stark argues that the conversion of the Roman Empire is explicable entirely in rational terms, largely as a consequence of the social virtues inculcated by the Christian message.

Stendahl, Krister. *Paul among Jews and Gentiles, and Other Essays*. Philadelphia: Fortress, 1976. In the section "Call not Conversion" Stendahl famously argues that Paul, whose Damascus Road experience is the archetypal image of conversion for many, was not a convert. He did not change religions and abandon Judaism but rather was called to be apostle to the Gentiles.

Stromberg, Peter G. *Language and Self-transformation: A Study of the Christian Conversion Narrative*. Publications of the Society for Psychological Anthropology 5. Cambridge: Cambridge University Press, 1993. Stromberg contends that the language used in autobiographical conversion accounts does not refer to the experiences described. Instead it is the very use of the language employed in conversion narratives that constitutes the transformation of the individuals concerned.

Taylor, John Vernon. *The Primal Vision: Christian Presence amid African Religion*. Philadelphia: Fortress, 1963. Western culture's perceived ownership of Christianity has often made conversion for non-westerners difficult. Taylor explores from a missiological perspective the contextualization of Christianity in Africa.

Taylor, Nicholas. "The Social Nature of Conversion in the Early Christian World." Pages 128–36 in *Modeling Early Christianity: Social-Scientific Studies of the New Testament in Its Context*. Edited by Philip F. Esler. London: Routledge, 1995. Drawing attention to the non-individualistic nature of ancient society, Taylor argues that conversion in the Greco-Roman world was always shaped by and impacted social allegiances and identity.

Volf, Miroslav. *Exclusion and Embrace: A Theological Exploration of Identity, Otherness, and Reconciliation*. Nashville: Abingdon, 1996. Volf's work on Christian reconciliation offers insights into the nature of God's judgment, love, and forgiveness that impact the understanding of conversion.

———. *Work in the Spirit: Toward a Theology of Work.* Oxford: Oxford University Press, 1991. Reprint, Eugene, Ore.: Wipf and Stock, 2001. This detailed study explores the complexity of work in industrial societies and how it may (or may not) contribute to God's intentions for the world.

Van Dam, Raymond. *Becoming Christian: The Conversion of Roman Cappadocia.* Philadelphia: University of Pennsylvania Press, 2003. This study explores in detail the impact of Christianity upon traditional Greek and Roman society in fourth century Cappadocia.

Wallis, Jim. *The Call to Conversion: Why Faith is Always Personal but Never Private.* Revised and updated edition. New York: Harper San Francisco, 2005. Wallis provides a classic attack from within evangelicalism on narrowly individualistic concepts of conversion and their ethical consequences.

Wells, David F. *Turning to God: Biblical Conversion in the Modern World.* Grand Rapids: Baker, 1989. Emerging from a symposium on conversion, this book explores conversion for both the churched and the un-churched from a Reformed perspective. Both theoretical and practical dimensions of conversion are considered.

Willard, Dallas. *The Great Omission: Reclaiming Jesus' Essential Teachings on Discipleship.* San Francisco: HarperSanFrancisco, 2006. Emphasizing the claim of Christ's lordship, Willard reminds readers of the intricate relationships between salvation, conversion, discipleship, and on-going spiritual formation.

Winner, Lauren F. *Girl Meets God: On the Path to a Spiritual Life.* Chapel Hill, N.C.: Algonquin, 2002. An autobiographical account of the conversion to Christianity of a young Jewish woman, this book is remarkable for combining conventional Christian doctrinal commitments with a post-modern absence of narrative structure or single conversion event.

Wright, Christopher J. H. "Implications of Conversion in the Old Testament and the New." *International Bulletin of Missionary Research* 28 (2004) 14–19. This brief essay considers a number of ways in which Christian theology may find resources regarding conversion in the OT.

NORTH PARK THEOLOGICAL SEMINARY
SYMPOSIUM ON THE THEOLOGICAL INTERPRETATION OF SCRIPTURE

SEPTEMBER 24–26, 2009

CONVERSION

PRESENTERS

MARKUS BOCKMUEHL
University of Oxford, Professor of Biblical & Early Christian Studies

STEPHEN CHESTER
North Park Theological Seminary, Professor of New Testament

WYNDY CORBIN REUSCHLING
Ashland Theological Seminary, Professor of Ethics and Theology

ANDREW DEARMAN
Fuller Theological Seminary, Professor of Old Testament

ERIC JAMES GRÉAUX SR.
Winston-Salem State University, Assistant Professor of Religion

FRANK MACCHIA
Vanguard University, Professor of Theology

SCOT MCKNIGHT
North Park University, Karl A. Olsson Professor in Religious Studies

LEWIS RAMBO
San Francisco Theological Seminary, Benton & Faye French Tulley Professor of Pastoral Psychology

J. WARREN SMITH
Duke University Divinity School, Associate Professor of Historical Theology

RESPONDENTS

MICHAEL J. GORMAN
 St Mary's Seminary and University, Baltimore, Professor of Sacred Scripture

RAJKUMAR BOAZ JOHNSON
 North Park University, Professor of Biblical and Theological Studies

ERIC JAMES GRÉAUX SR.
 Winston-Salem State University, Assistant Professor of Religion

GEORGE KALANTZIS
 Wheaton College, Associate Professor of Theology

ELIZABETH MUSSELMAN PALMER
 University of Chicago, PhD Candidate, Theology

PHILLIS SHEPPARD
 North Park Theological Seminary, Associate Professor of Pastoral Care

D. CHRISTOPHER SPINKS
 Wipf and Stock Publishers, Editor of New Testament
 and Theological Interpretation

MARY VEENEMAN
 North Park University, Assistant Professor of Biblical and Theological Studies

EX AUDITU

Volumes Available

Vol. 1 (1985) consists of selected articles presenting the issues inherent in the theological interpretation of Scripture.

Vol. 2 (1986) discusses the theme: "Church and State Relationship." In addition, there are two lead articles: one by Peter Stuhlmacher on "EX AUDITU and the Theological Interpretation of Holy Scripture," and the second by Ben F. Meyer on "The Primacy of Consent and the Uses of Suspicion."

Vol. 3 (1987) "Creation."
Vol. 4 (1988) "The Church and Israel (Romans 9-11)."
Vol. 5 (1989) "What is Salvation?"
Vol. 6 (1990) "Prophetic and/or Apocalyptic Eschatology."
Vol. 7 (1991) "Christology and Incarnation"
Vol. 8 (1992) "Worship."
Vol. 9 (1993) "Resurrection."
Vol. 10 (1994) "The Church."
Vol. 11 (1995) "Biblical Law and Liberty."
Vol. 12 (1996) "Holy Spirit."
Vol. 13 (1997) "What is a Human?"
Vol. 14 (1998) "The Theological Significance of the Earthly Jesus."
Vol. 15 (1999) "Idolatry and the Understanding of God."
Vol. 16 (2000) "The Task of Interpreting Scripture Theologically."
Vol. 17 (2001) "Biblical Ethics."
Vol. 18 (2002) "Spiritual Formation."
Vol. 19 (2003) "The Authority and Function of Scripture."
Vol. 20 (2004) "Judgment."
Vol. 21 (2005) "Health and Healing."
Vol. 22 (2006) "Justice."
Vol. 23 (2007) "Christianity's Engagement with Culture."
Vol. 24 (2008) "The Idolatry of Security."
Vol. 25 (2009) "Conversion."

Pickwick Publications
An imprint of Wipf and Stock Publishers
199 West 8th Avenue, Ste. 3
Eugene OR 97401

www.ingramcontent.com/pod-product-compliance
Lightning Source LLC
Chambersburg PA
CBHW081350230426
43667CB00017B/2782